ISBN 978-0-265-87685-5
PIBN 10903156

'NG PEOPLE'S USE AND APPRAISAL OF
ATURAL AND COMPETING FIBERS IN
WEARING APPAREL

by

Special Surveys Branch
Standards and Research Division
Statistical Reporting Service

INTRODUCTION

expansion in recent years in the use of manmade fibers necessitates up-
ions of markets for natural fibers as compared with synthetic fibers.
sted in improving natural fibers and in increasing their use need informa-
g consumer attitudes. The major purpose of this study is to provide the
industries with information on the beliefs and attitudes of teenage boys
cotton, wool, and manmade fibers in the clothing they wear, and on their
h these fibers. Armed with such information, the natural-fiber industries
r laboratory research and public information efforts more sharply toward
heir position with the teenage population, which constitutes a large mar-
ural products. The members of this group--many of them just starting to
opping--are developing opinions and loyalties toward fibers which may
t, for good or ill, the future of natural fibers.

ey is an extension of research conducted in 1955 on teenage girls' opinions
rs.[1] The subject areas covered were revised somewhat to reflect current
. The survey was also broadened to include teenage boys' opinions of
.

gs reported here are based on a multistage area probability sample of
. 1,648 boys. The sample was designed to represent all persons between
and 17 in the contiguous United States. Interviews were made in person at
ie teenagers in June and early July 1963.[2]

CAUTION IN INTERPRETING THE DATA

vey in which interviews are conducted with less than 100 percent of the
e group being studied is subject to some possible sampling variation. For
his study, approximate confidence limits for various percentages have
l and are shown in the appendix.

gs are presented as summaries of the statements made by the teenagers
t to any errors they made in reporting their beliefs and attitudes. It is
ortant to keep this in mind when analyzing data on fiber experience, since
h fiber identification have some influence on the validity of teenagers'
ut what materials they have used. Inadvertent misstatements by respond-
: because of oversights, lack of information, or confusion about fiber con-
e many kinds of fibers and fiber combinations on the market, and problems
n may arise from the use of descriptive or brand names for a product.

sther S. Teenage Girls Discuss Their Wardrobes and Their Attitudes Toward Cotton and
S. Dept. Agr. Mktg. Res. Rpt. 155, April 1957.
idix for a more detailed discussion of interviewing procedures and sampling.

Furthermore, clothing items made of sucn mixtures as polyester and cotton, for example, may have been identified as polyester or cotton, and there may have been confusion among such fibers as rayon, acetate, polyester, and silk. However, since this study was not intended to provide estimates of fiber consumption, but to gather attitudes and impressions teenagers hold toward the various materials, the statements made were accepted as given. No closet inventories of garments nor analyses of fiber content were conducted.

Other persons were present during about two-fifths of the interviews (tables 106 and 209).[3] The interviewers indicated that, in about one-tenth of the interviews, it was their opinion that the other persons may have had some influence on the responses given by the teenagers (tables 107 and 210).

If a trademark was reported it was converted into the generic name when the data were tabulated. Trademarks for polyester fibers include Dacron, Fortrel, Kodel, and others; trademarks for acrylic fibers include Orlon, Acrilan, and others. Rayon and acetate were combined because previous studies indicate many consumers do not distinguish between the two; the "rayon/acetate" category also includes registered trademarks, such as Arnel.[4]

Throughout the text of this report, the words "material," "fiber," and "fabric" are used interchangeably. During the actual interviewing, however, the questions were phrased in terms of "materials," a term found to be more familiar to teenagers when the questionnaires were pretested. When a teenager answered a question in terms of a material whose fiber content was not readily identifiable because of the growing use of manmade or blended fibers (corduroy, for example), an attempt was made to have the respondent identify the specific fiber content.

AREAS OF QUESTIONING

For selected readymade items of clothing, the teenagers were asked which ones they possessed, the fiber content of those items, what fiber they preferred, their reasons for preferring the fiber for that article of clothing, and what criticisms they had, if any, of the preferred fiber. The selected readymade items of clothing were girls' winter and summer skirts, blouses, and everyday dresses; girls' regular-length and half slips; girls' and boys' sweaters, winter outer jackets or short coats, and rainwear; and boys' winter and summer sport shirts, sport jackets, and everyday and dress slacks. Information was obtained on the care and laundering of these items, with the exception of winter outer jackets or short coats, and rainwear.

Teenagers were also asked about their role in shopping for and selecting their clothing, their opinions of permanent pleating and creasing of wool garments, and their opinions about machine washability of wool sweaters.

A listing of the questions asked is in the appendix.

TEENAGE GIRLS DISCUSS THEIR WARDROBES

The percentage of girls owning most of the clothing items studied was very high. The following list indicates the percentage of girls who said they owned at least one item in each clothing category:

Item	Percent
Winter skirts	99
Winter blouses	99
Sweaters	97

[3] See appendix for tables 5-211.

[4] The use of trademark names does not imply endorsement of the products by the U.S. Department of Agriculture.

Item	Percent
Summer blouses	97
Summer skirts	95
Half slips	89
Full-length slips	84
Winter outer jackets or short coats	84
Summer everyday dresses	80
Winter everyday dresses	65
Multipurpose coats (for both dry and rainy weather)	64
Raincoats	24

ls' winter wardrobes consisted mainly of skirts worn with blouses or
lmost every girl had a winter skirt and a blouse or sweater combination, as
adymade winter dress. About one-fourth of the girls reported that they
winter skirts worn with blouses or sweaters; just 1 percent said that they
dymade winter dresses (table 5).

vith blouses also predominated in the summer wardrobes; however, only 1
ported not owning a summer dress. The percentage of girls who owned
ses was higher for summer clothes (25 percent) than for winter clothes (7
bles 5 and 34).

girls who owned winter or summer dresses, about one-fourth of them used
esses for everyday and dress-up wear. About 6 out of 10 had different
everyday and dress-up occasions, and slightly more than 1 out of 10 said
ned only dress-up dresses (table 23).

was the most widely owned and preferred fiber reported by the teenage girls
iing items selected for this study. Tables 1 and 2 give this information for
s studied.

lowing is a detailed report of the interviews held with teenage girls, ages 14
concerning their wardrobes and the factors affecting the purchasing of these

WINTER SKIRTS

ally all of the teenage girls owned readymade winter skirts.

wned and preferred

as the most popular material for winter skirts among girls who owned them--
said they had at least one wool skirt, 85 percent reported that all or most of
skirts were wool, and 75 percent said they preferred wool. Cotton winter
owned by 43 percent, but, only 11 percent preferred them. A less frequently
kirt material was wool-polyester, owned by 9 percent of the skirt owners and
y 4 percent (table 6).

ence for wool in winter skirts was highest among girls from the large metro-
s, the Northeast, and from families in the upper income group (table 8).

preferences

t was the primary consideration in preferences for a specific material for
s. Three-fourths of the girls who preferred wool specified its comfort,
rmth. For the girls who preferred cotton, comfort meant mainly that cotton
itate, itch, or scratch; and for those who chose wool-polyester, comfort

Table 1.--Teenage girls who owned certain items of clothing: Materials owned by 10 percent or more

Items of clothing	Wool	Cotton	Wool-acrylic	Cotton-polyester	Polyester	Silk	Rayon/acetate	Nylon	Acrylic	Suede, leather	Plastic	Cases
	Percent	Percent	Percent	Percent	Percent	Percent	Percent	Percent	Percent	Percent	Percent	Number
Winter:												
Skirts	93	43	--	--	--	--	--	--	--	--	--	1,671
Blouses	--	95	--	24	13	10	--	--	--	--	--	1,666
Everyday dresses. . .	56	71	--	--	--	--	--	--	--	--	--	1,101
Outer jackets or short coats	46	33	--	--	--	--	--	--	--	16	--	1,416
Summer:												
Skirts	--	95	--	17	--	--	17	--	--	--	--	1,605
Blouses	--	95	--	24	12	11	--	14	--	--	--	1,645
Everyday dresses. . .	--	95	--	17	--	--	11	--	--	--	--	1,357
Sweaters.	69	--	17	--	--	--	--	20	46	--	--	1,641
Half slips	--	44	--	--	--	15	11	68	--	--	--	1,500
Full-length slips	--	40	--	--	--	10	--	66	--	--	--	1,424
Raincoats	--	17	--	--	--	--	--	--	--	--	58	414
Multipurpose coats.	--	51	--	11	--	--	--	--	--	--	--	1,086

Table 2.--Teenage girls who owned certain items of clothing: Material liked best by 10 percent or more

Items of clothing	Wool	Cotton	Cotton-polyester	Suede, leather	Acrylic	Nylon	Plastic	Cases
	Percent	Percent	Percent	Percent	Percent	Percent	Percent	Number
Winter:								
Skirts	75	11	--	--	--	--	--	1,671
Blouses	--	74	11	--	--	--	--	1,666
Everyday dresses	31	46	--	--	--	--	--	1,101
Outer jackets or short coats.	37	19	--	13	--	--	--	1,416
Summer:								
Skirts.	--	74	--	--	--	--	--	1,605
Blouses	--	68	13	--	--	--	--	1,645
Everyday dresses.	--	71	--	--	--	--	--	1,357
Sweaters	35	--	--	--	22	--	--	1,641
Slips.	--	18	--	--	--	51	--	1,685
Rainwear.	--	37	--	--	--	--	13	1,289

4

ncluded warmth as well as lack of irritation to the skin from the material. Both wool
and wool-polyester were further cited for their performance and durability, with em-
phasis on not wrinkling or soiling and on holding shape. Cotton scored well on its launderability (table 9).

Disadvantages of preferred material

Sixty percent of the girls who preferred wool for winter skirts mentioned a disadvantage, whereas only about 30 percent of the girls who preferred either cotton or wool-
polyester mentioned a disadvantage. The leading criticism of wool was that it itches and
scratches. Less frequent were complaints that it is not washable and has to be drycleaned. Cotton drew criticism from some of its adherents as not being warm enough for
winter wear. Wool-polyester was criticized because it irritates the skin (table 10).

Methods of care

Among girls with predominantly wool winter-skirt wardrobes, 83 percent reported
that most of their winter skirts were commercially cleaned, 5 percent said they sent
their skirts to a coin-operated cleaner, and 12 percent said that most of their skirts were
washed by machine or hand.

For girls with wardrobes in which cotton was the main fiber in winter skirts, home
cleaning was the usual method of care reported: 43 percent said that most of their cotton skirts were machine washed, and 24 percent said that most were hand washed. Only
31 percent usually sent their cotton winter skirts to commercial cleaners (table 76).

Almost all of the winter skirts not commercially cleaned were ironed before wearing (table 79).

Ownership of pleated winter skirts

Pleated winter skirts were owned by 87 percent of the girls. About two-thirds of the
girls reported that they owned pleated skirts in which the pleats were not specially
processed to stay in. Of these, 68 percent owned a wool pleated skirt, 25 percent owned
at least one of cotton, and 5 percent owned a wool-polyester pleated skirt. Over half of
the girls (56 percent) had a pleated skirt which had been specially processed ("permanently" pleated). Wool was by far the leading fiber. Eighty-one percent of these girls had
at least one skirt made of wool, 9 percent had wool-polyester, and 6 percent had cotton
(table 11).

Reaction to idea of permanently pleated wool skirts

All owners of winter skirts were asked what they thought of the idea of permanently
pleated wool skirts--that is, wool skirts which have been processed or treated so that
the pleats stay in without pressing, even when the skirt is washed or cleaned. Quite a
large majority (93 percent) regarded this as a good idea. The percentage of those who
thought that it was a good idea was slightly higher among the girls who reported they
already owned one (table 12). The reasons for the favorable attitudes were basically the
same whether or not the girls reported owning a "permanently" pleated wool skirt--
girls liked the idea of having a pleated wool skirt stay pleated or of having one that
would require little or no pressing (table 13).

The few skirt owners (7 percent) who were not in favor of permanently pleated wool
skirts were most likely to say they did not think the pleats would stay in regardless of
how the skirts were processed or treated. Other reasons mentioned less frequently
were that the skirts would have to be pressed anyway, and that the styles in permanently pleated skirts are unattractive. Some girls stated that they did not like any
pleated skirt (table 14).

The girls were then asked if permanent pleating would be an important factor in their decision to buy a particular pleated wool skirt. They were shown a rating scale (see 8a of questionnaire) and asked to give a rating from 1 to 5. The highest rating possible was 5 (next to it was written "most important"), and 1 was the lowest (next to it was written "not important at all"). About two-thirds of the girls gave the process a rating of either 5 or 4 (table 15).

The ratings varied little between the girls who had already owned a "permanently" pleated wool skirt and those who were just speculating about the importance of the process in their decision to buy a pleated skirt (tables 15 and 16).

The girls who gave the high ratings said that permanent pleating was important to them primarily because they liked having the pleats stay in and liked not having to iron the skirt to keep it neat (table 17).

One-third of the girls who thought this process was not important at all or not very important (rating 1, 2, or 3) generally felt that other features such as the style or color of the skirt would be more important. Some girls' dislike of pleated skirts or wool skirts in general also contributed to the low ratings (table 17).

WINTER BLOUSES

Almost all teenage girls reported owning readymade winter blouses.

Materials owned and preferred

Cotton's popularity in winter blouses was undisputed. All but 5 percent of the girls had a cotton blouse, and almost 9 in 10 had mainly or only cotton blouses for winter wear. About three-fourths of the girls preferred cotton over all other materials. Cotton-polyester was the only other frequently mentioned material--slightly less than one-fourth of the girls owned a blouse of that material. Only about 1 in 10 expressed a preference for cotton-polyester. Other less frequently mentioned materials in winter blouses were polyester (13 percent), silk (10 percent), rayon/acetate (9 percent), and nylon (8 percent). None of these materials was preferred for blouses by as many as 5 percent of the girls (table 18).

The widespread ownership of and preference for cotton winter blouses was about the same regardless of the girls' ages or family income, or the location or size of their community. However, the cotton-polyester blouses were more frequently owned and preferred by girls whose families were in the middle or upper income bracket (tables 19 and 20).

Reasons for preferences

The care and laundering features were the most frequently mentioned determinants in material preferences for winter blouses. Cotton scored about twice as well on washability as did cotton-polyester. However, only 4 girls in 10 who chose cotton, compared with 7 in 10 who chose cotton-polyester, cited ironing reasons. While both materials were considered easy to iron by a sizable proportion of the girls, cotton-polyester was further referred to as a material that requires little or no ironing. Performance, stressing not wrinkling, was another strong point for the cotton-polyester blouse (table 21).

Disadvantages of preferred material

Less than one-third of the girls who preferred either cotton or cotton-polyester blouses reported any disadvantages. The only important criticism, mentioned by slightly more than 10 percent of the cotton advocates, was that cotton blouses wrinkle (table 22).

Methods of care

The girls were questioned concerning the usual method used to clean most of their winter blouses: 77 percent said most were machine washed, 20 percent said hand washed, and 3 percent said commercially cleaned. Among the girls who had mainly cotton blouses in their wardrobes, only 18 percent said most of them were usually hand washed; of the girls who had mostly cotton-polyester, 27 percent reported that most of their blouses were usually hand washed (table 76). Almost all (99 percent) of the girls reported that most blouses washed at home were usually ironed after washing (table 79).

EVERYDAY WINTER DRESSES

About three-fourths of the teenage girls owned readymade winter dresses. These girls were asked if they bought some of their winter dresses for everyday wear and others for Sunday or special occasions, or if they bought the same kind for both everyday and dress-up. The majority of these girls reported that they had different dresses for each; some said they had only dresses for dress-up (table 23).

Altogether, about two-thirds (65 percent) of the teenage girls owned readymade dresses for everyday winter wear.

Materials owned and preferred

The most frequently reported everyday winter dresses were those of cotton, owned by 71 percent of these dress owners, and those of wool, owned by 56 percent. About half of the girls reported a predominance of and a preference for cotton everyday winter dresses; wool was the fiber owned most often and liked best by about one-third of the girls. No other fibers were preferred by as many as 5 percent. Ten percent of the girls indicated no choice in fibers for winter everyday dresses (table 24).

The highest incidence of cotton winter dresses from the standpoint of both ownership and preference was among the southern girls and those living in towns or on farms; the highest incidence of wool dresses was among the girls who lived in the Northeast and large cities (tables 25 and 26).

Reasons for preferences

In evaluating cotton for winter dresses, about 6 out of 10 of their adherents spoke of good laundering qualities; about 5 out of 10 found them comfortable to wear, mainly because they do not itch or scratch and are not too warm. Wool, on the other hand, was preferred primarily for its warmth (reported by 7 out of 10 of the girls who selected wool), and less frequently because it does not wrinkle (table 27).

Disadvantages of preferred material

One-third of those preferring cotton winter dresses and one-half of those preferring wool reported disadvantages of their preferred fibers. Cotton drew some criticism for wrinkling easily and for not being warm enough for winter wear. Wool was criticized by some of its adherents because it irritates the skin and because it has to be drycleaned (table 28).

Methods of care

Girls were asked how their winter everyday dresses were usually cared for. In wardrobes where cotton was the predominant dress material, 66 percent of the girls said most of their dresses were usually machine washed, 19 percent said most of their dresses were hand washed, and 14 percent reported sending most of their dresses to the commercial cleaners. However, in wardrobes where wool dresses predominated, only 10 percent of the girls reported that most of their dresses were machine washed, 6 percent said most dresses were hand washed, and 81 percent sent most of their winter everyday wool dresses to the commercial cleaners (table 76). Almost all of the girls owning winter everyday dresses not commercially cleaned said that these dresses were pressed before wearing (table 79).

RESPONSIBILITY FOR HAND WASHING AND IRONING

Those girls who said that any of their winter skirts, blouses, or dresses were hand washed were then asked who generally did that hand washing. About half of the girls reported that they usually did the hand washing and half reported that their mothers usually did the hand washing. More of the older than of the younger girls reported hand washing their own winter clothes (table 77).

Girls who owned winter skirts, blouses, or dresses that were pressed by other than a commercial cleaner were asked who usually did most of the pressing. About as many girls reported that they did the pressing as that their mothers did the pressing. The older the girls, however, the more frequently they said that they themselves generally pressed their winter clothes (table 80).

WINTER OUTER JACKETS AND SHORT COATS

Winter outer jackets or short coats were owned by 84 percent of the teenage girls.

Materials owned and preferred

Wool had a slight lead over cotton among the girls who owned outer jackets and short coats--46 percent had wool and 33 percent had cotton. Suede and leather outer jackets and short coats placed third, owned by 16 percent, followed by nylon, owned by 6 percent (table 29).

Twice as many girls living in the Northeast and the large metropolitan areas owned wool outer jackets or short coats as owned cotton. Cotton and wool about equally shared the market among southern girls--40 percent had at least one cotton outer jacket or short coat and 37 percent had wool. Suede and leather jackets were also popular among southern girls, 23 percent of whom owned one. Cotton held its own among girls from the small towns or farms, where 40 percent had cotton and 41 percent had wool (table 30). Among girls who had winter outer jackets and short coats, wool was preferred by 37 percent, 19 percent preferred cotton, and 13 percent preferred suede or leather. Any preference for another fiber ran less than 5 percent; 11 percent indicated that they had no preference (table 29).

Reasons for preferences

Wool's popularity in winter outer jackets or short coats was based primarily on its warmth, according to more than 8 out of 10 of the girls who preferred this material. Durability, and wrinkle and stain resistance were less frequently cited. Cotton advocates stressed its warmth, its not being too warm, and its being lightweight but warm as main reasons for their preference. Suede and leather were frequently preferred because of warmth and resistance to stain, and because the girls who liked them considered them fashionable (table 32).

Disadvantages of preferred material

Although 64 percent of the girls who preferred wool had no criticism of it, 9 percent mentioned its irritation to the skin, and 7 percent objected to its having to be drycleaned. Of those who preferred cotton, 60 percent had no criticism, but 10 percent objected to its lack of soil resistance and 8 percent considered it not warm enough to be worn for winter jackets or short coats. Only 46 percent of the suede and leather advocates had no criticisms. The chief disadvantages cited were soiling and staining easily (18 percent), having to be drycleaned (7 percent), and tearing and snagging easily (5 percent) (table 33).

8

SUMMER SKIRTS

ιst one readymade summer skirt was in the wardrobe of 95 percent of the

owned and preferred

n was by far the leading fiber owned and preferred in summer skirts. Ninety-
ιnt of the skirt owners reported at least one cotton skirt in their summer
s, 88 percent had mostly or only cotton skirts, and 74 percent reported that
s their favorite summer skirt fiber. Cotton-polyester and rayon/acetate each
in 17 percent of the summer skirt collections, but were preferred only by 9
ιd 5 percent respectively (table 35).

)f the girls, family income, and community size and locality made only a minor
ς in the proportion who owned cotton skirts. However, rayon/acetate skirts
e frequently owned by girls who lived in the Northeast and in large cities. A
ιily income was related to cotton-polyester ownership--more girls from
ιome families owned cotton-polyester than did those from the lower income
ιle 36).

or preferences

ιain advantages of wearing cotton summer skirts, according to the girls who
l them, were that cotton is comfortable--cool, lightweight, and airy--and easily
l. Advocates of cotton-polyester and rayon/acetate were similarly impressed
e materials, although in varying proportions. Cotton-polyester and rayon/
ere also frequently preferred because of the advantages of not wrinkling and
ittle or no ironing (table 38).

tages of preferred material

ɔn as a skirt material was a little more likely to be criticized than either
ɔlyester or rayon/acetate. Wrinkling is cotton's main disadvantage, according
one-fourth of the girls who preferred it for summer skirts. Only 9 percent of
:ates of rayon/acetate and 8 percent of the girls who liked cotton-polyester
d a wrinkling problem (table 39).

of care

e than three-fourths (79 percent) of the girls reported that most summer skirts
ally machine washed, 17 percent said hand washed, and 4 percent said commer-
:aned (table 76). Almost all (99 percent) reported that most skirts washed at
re ironed before being worn (table 79).

SUMMER BLOUSES

ɔst all (97 percent) of the teenage girls owned summer readymade blouses.

s owned and preferred

on was the leading material among the blouse owners--95 percent of these girls
tton blouses, 85 percent had mostly or only cotton blouses in their wardrobes,
:rcent preferred cotton over all other fibers for summer wear. Its closest com-
:otton-polyester, was owned by 24 percent and preferred by 13 percent. The
s frequently owned materials were nylon (14 percent), polyester (12 percent),
(11 percent). None of these fibers was preferred by more than 5 percent of the
ɔle 40).

9

The percentage of girls both owning and preferring cotton summer blouses was about the same regardless of socioeconomic background. However, relatively more girls whose families were in the higher income group owned and preferred cotton-polyester blouses (tables 41 and 42).

Reasons for preferences

Cotton scored well in summer blouses because the girls who liked it found it cool, lightweight, and airy, and easy to wash and iron. The girls who preferred cotton-polyester also found it comfortably cool and easily laundered. They frequently reported that cotton-polyester requires little or no ironing and is wrinkle resistant (table 43).

Disadvantages of preferred material

Only about 30 percent of the girls who preferred cotton and about 25 percent of those who preferred cotton-polyester reported any disadvantages for these materials in summer blouses. The main comments were that cotton wrinkles (14 percent) and cotton-polyester discolors (6 percent) and is hard to iron (5 percent). Other criticisms were widely scattered (table 44).

Methods of care

The overwhelming majority of the girls reported that their summer blouses were washed at home. Eighty-four percent of the girls reported machine washing most of their blouses, and 15 percent said most of their blouses were washed by hand (table 76). Practically all (99 percent) of the girls whose summer blouses were washed at home said that their blouses were ironed after washing (table 79).

EVERYDAY SUMMER DRESSES

Almost 90 percent of the teenage girls owned readymade summer dresses. These girls were asked if they bought some of their summer dresses for everyday wear and others for Sunday or special occasions, or if they got the same kind for both everyday and dress-up wear. The majority reported having different dresses for each use; some had only dress-up dresses (table 45).

Altogether, four out of five girls reported owning a readymade summer dress for everyday wear.

Materials owned and preferred

Cotton was by far the leading fiber owned in everyday summer dresses. Of all the girls who owned summer everyday dresses, 95 percent had at least one made of cotton. In almost 9 out of 10 of the dress wardrobes, cotton was the prevailing fiber. Only two other fibers rated over a 10-percent ownership; they were cotton-polyester (17 percent) and rayon/acetate (11 percent). Overall, cotton was best liked by 71 percent of these dress owners (table 46).

Cotton was especially popular among the girls living in the small towns and farm areas--8 out of 10 of these girls preferred cotton. Cotton-polyester, the second ranked fiber, lagged far behind with only 8 percent of the girls preferring it over other fibers (table 48).

Reasons for preferences

Teenage girls liked cotton best mainly because it is cool and easy to iron or press. The two main reasons given for the cotton-polyester preference were its coolness and its wrinkle resistance (table 49).

Disadvantages of preferred material

Again, wrinkling was the main criticism of cotton, mentioned by 18 percent of the girls who preferred it for their everyday dresses. None of the disadvantages cited for cotton-polyester were dominant (table 50).

Methods of care

Three-fourths of the owners of everyday summer dresses indicated that most of these dresses were machine washed, 17 percent said that most of their summer dresses were hand washed, and 7 percent sent most of their summer dresses to the cleaners. Practically all of the girls whose dresses were cleaned at home said they were ironed after washing (table 79).

RESPONSIBILITY FOR HAND WASHING AND IRONING

Those girls who said that any of their summer skirts, blouses, or dresses were hand washed were asked who generally did that hand washing. About half of the girls reported that their mothers did the hand washing; most of the rest did their own hand washing. A larger proportion of the younger girls reported that their mothers did the hand washing (table 77).

Girls who owned summer skirts, blouses, or dresses that were pressed by other than a commercial cleaner were asked who usually did most of the pressing. Twice as many of the girls reported that they usually did the pressing as reported that their mothers usually did the pressing. In general, the younger girls more frequently reported that their mothers did the pressing, and the older girls more frequently reported that they did their own pressing (table 80).

SWEATERS

Almost all (97 percent) of the girls reported owning readymade sweaters.

Materials owned and preferred

Wool topped the long list of fibers in girls' sweaters--69 percent of the owners had wool sweaters, 46 percent, acrylic; 20 percent, nylon; and 17 percent, wool-acrylic. Less than one-tenth of the girls owned cashmere, cotton, or polyester sweaters (table 51).

Wool appeared in a higher proportion of the wardrobes of girls from higher income families, of those living in and around metropolitan areas, and of those living in the Northeast. Ownership of acrylic sweaters was only slightly related to background characteristics of the girls. The proportion of girls with nylon sweaters was greater in the lower income households and in towns and farm areas. Nylon sweaters were owned less frequently by girls living in the West (table 52). About one-half of the girls (46 percent) said they had only or mostly wool sweaters, and about one-fourth (24 percent) said acrylic. Wool was preferred by 35 percent of the sweater owners, and 22 percent liked acrylic best. These were followed by wool-acrylic (8 percent), nylon (7 percent), and cashmere (6 percent) (table 51).

Reasons for preferences

Among the girls who preferred wool for their sweaters, warmth (mentioned by 65 percent) was the chief reason, followed by wool's ability to hold its shape and not shrink or stretch (22 percent). Among the girls who preferred acrylic sweaters, lack of skin irritation (51 percent) and retention of shape (35 percent) were cited as the important reasons for their choice. However, half of the acrylic advocates also mentioned acrylic's good laundering features. Among the girls who liked wool-acrylic sweaters best, shape retention and lack of irritation to the skin were most frequently mentioned. Nylon advocates stressed launderability, retention of shape, and lack of irritation to the skin as

11

not irritate the skin (table 54).

Disadvantages of preferred material

About 6 in 10 of the girls who preferred wool, nylon, or cashmere sweaters mentioned a disadvantage; only about 4 in 10 of the girls who preferred acrylic or wool-acrylic sweaters mentioned a disadvantage. The girls criticized wool sweaters mainly because they irritate, scratch, and itch. Loss of shape and fuzzing, balling up, or shedding were criticisms against all of the fibers. Nylon advocates were critical of nylon mainly because it tears, rips, and snags easily (table 55).

Methods of care

Most sweaters were hand washed, especially sweaters made of synthetic fibers. Among girls who had predominantly wool sweaters, 56 percent said the sweaters were usually hand washed; 37 percent, that they were commercially cleaned; and only 5 percent, that they were usually machine washed. Among girls who had predominantly acrylic sweaters, on the other hand, hand washing was reported by 68 percent; 11 percent said their sweaters were sent to the cleaners; and 19 percent said their sweaters were machine washed (table 76). The hand washing of sweaters was split almost evenly between the mothers and daughters. But the responses showed that the older the girl, the more apt she was to do most of the hand washing herself (table 78).

Almost two-thirds of the girls whose sweaters were not commercially cleaned said their sweaters were usually pressed. Type of fiber made little difference in regard to whether a sweater was pressed or not (table 79). Fifty-six percent of these girls said that they pressed their own sweaters and 40 percent said that their mothers pressed their sweaters for them (table 81).

Reaction to idea of machine-washable wool sweaters

Teenage girls owning sweaters were asked their opinions concerning a new kind of wool sweater, treated so that it is safe to wash in a machine without special care.

An overwhelming majority (89 percent) of the sweater owners thought machine-washable wool sweaters would be a good idea. There were only slight differences between the answers from the girls who owned wool sweaters and those who owned only sweaters of other fibers (table 56). The girls thought machine-washable wool sweaters a good idea because they would save time and money, and it would be nice to have a wool sweater that retained its shape after machine washing (table 57).

Only 11 percent of the sweater owners said they thought it not such a good idea; the major reasons were that they did not believe that a wool sweater would hold its shape and that machine washing would not be safe (table 58).

The girls were then asked to rate the importance of machine washability in the decision to buy a new wool sweater. On the rating scale, 5 was the highest rating possible and 1 was the lowest. About 6 in 10 girls owning sweaters rated this new development either 5 or 4. These higher ratings were more frequently given by the younger girls, the girls living in lower income families, and the girls living in town and farm areas (table 58). The major reasons for the higher ratings were that girls liked the idea of saving time and money by being able to wash wool sweaters by machine, and they liked the idea of having a guarantee that the sweaters would retain their shape if machine washed (table 60).

The girls (41 percent) who thought this development was not important at all or not very important frequently said that they considered style and color more important. Others believed that machine washing of wool sweaters could not possibly be safe, and some did not like wool sweaters at all (table 60).

12

SLIPS

hree-fourths of the girls owned both half slips and regular (full-length)
jority of these girls who owned both (59 percent) said they wore a half slip
an a regular slip. This was especially common among the girls living in
in the Northeast.

aining one-fourth of the girls were split almost evenly between those who
alf slips and those who owned only regular slips (table 61).

ned and preferred

s the most frequently owned material in both half and regular slips, being
thirds of the girls' wardrobes for either style slip. However, cotton was
bout two-fifths of these slip wardrobes. Other less frequently owned mate-
lk, rayon/acetate, and cotton-polyester.

more than half of the slip owners mentioned that all or most of their slips
and about one-fifth reported a predominance of cotton half or regular slips
d 63). The type of slip generally worn did not seem to influence preferences
Just over half (51 percent) preferred slips made of nylon, 18 percent pre-
, and 7 percent preferred silk (table 67).

preferences

lected the material liked best for their slips primarily on the basis of its
table to wear. About 9 out of 10 of those choosing cotton mentioned com-
ressed that cotton does not cling, stick, or bind, and that it is cool.

was mentioned by 6 out of 10 of the nylon advocates. Silk also was pre-
s comfort--coolness and softness were most often mentioned. About one-
ylon advocates and about one-fourth of the cotton or silk advocates men-
ering features. Little or no ironing, ease in washing, and quick drying were
haracteristics attributed most often to nylon (table 68).

es of preferred material

out one-fourth of the girls who preferred cotton slips mentioned any disad-
npared with almost half of the nylon and silk advocates, who gave sticking
and static electricity as drawbacks (table 69).

are

ly, the method of care did not vary greatly by the fiber. Overall, 70 percent
s of slips said that their slips were washed by machine, and 30 percent said
le 76). While 60 percent of the teenage girls did the hand washing them-
ounger girls were more likely to have their mothers do it for them (table
ade of a synthetic fiber were less likely to be pressed than those made of
s. Only 31 percent of the girls who generally wore nylon slips had them
reas 56 percent of those owning mainly cotton and 45 percent of those
ad theirs pressed (table 79).

ial pressing of the slips was more frequently done by the teenage girls than
hers--52 percent of the girls did the pressing themselves, 42 percent of
did it, and 6 percent was done by someone else.

RAINWEAR

ree-fourths of all teenage girls owned either raincoats or multipurpose
2 percent owned both. Rainwear ownership ranged from 65 percent of the

Multipurpose coats

Multipurpose coats (coats meant for both dry and wet weather), were owned by 64 percent of the girls. Just over half of the girls who owned one of these coats, owned cotton; 11 percent owned cotton-polyester; and 7 percent owned cotton-rayon/acetate. Twelve percent of the owners were unable to identify the fiber of their multipurpose coat (table 71).

Raincoats

Raincoats (coats meant only for rainy weather) were owned by 24 percent of the girls. Plastic raincoats were the most popular--58 percent of the owners had one. Cotton raincoats were owned by 17 percent. No other fiber was owned by more than 3 percent of the girls; however, 8 percent did not know of what material their raincoat was made (table 71).

Materials preferred for rainwear

All the girls who owned either raincoats or multipurpose coats were asked which fiber they liked best for rainwear. Cotton was the most popular fiber; it was the choice of 37 percent of the rainwear owners. Plastic was preferred by 13 percent, and cotton-polyester was liked best by 9 percent. Among the garments studied, rainwear was the only item for which a substantial number of the girls did not name a preferred fiber-- almost one-fourth of the girls indicated no fiber preference (table 71).

Reasons for preferences

Cotton rainwear was liked not only because it is water repellent, but because it can be worn in good weather too, and because it is not too warm. The main reason given for preferring plastic rainwear was its waterproof quality. Less frequently mentioned was that plastic can be rolled or folded, making it easy to carry, and that is is lightweight. Cotton-polyester was liked best for its water repellency, its versatility, and its characteristic of not wrinkling when wet (table 74).

Disadvantages of preferred material

About one-fourth of the girls who liked plastic rainwear thought that it tears easily, and one-tenth complained that it is too hot. About one-tenth of the cotton and cotton-polyester advocates said that these materials wrinkle easily when wet (table 75).

OVERALL OPINIONS OF SELECTED FIBERS

The girls were asked to indicate which of six fibers used in clothing they thought was best for each of a number of characteristics. The fibers included cotton, rayon, nylon, Orlon, Dacron, and wool. As in the 1955 study (see footnote 1, p. 1), the trademark names of Orlon and Dacron were used rather than generic names of acrylic and polyester because during the pretesting of the questionnaire many girls were unfamiliar with the generic names and recognized these fibers only by various trademark names. Consequently, the only acrylic fiber included in the list was Orlon and the only polyester was Dacron; no information was gathered on other popular acrylic or polyester fibers.

14

d by far the best fiber for hot weather--78 percent of the girls
named by 13 percent of the girls, and 5 percent said nylon

ly the fiber considered best for cold weather--over 9 out of 10
ide a slight dent in wool's lead in the South, where 8 percent of
the best for cold weather (table 84).

ht) of the girls said they thought wool lasts the longest of these
d cotton, 7 percent said Dacron, and 5 percent said nylon.
vas lowest among the 14-year-old girls, the girls from the lower
s from small towns or farm areas, and among southern girls

41 percent of the girls as the best fiber for keeping its shape.
percent, followed by Dacron, 13 percent, and nylon, 7 percent.
ame from the town and farm areas where almost one-half (49
cotton kept its shape best; about one-fourth (23 percent) said
the large cities rated wool and cotton about evenly--wool was
and cotton, by 33 percent. Polyester was strongest among the
families--18 percent of them said Dacron kept its shape best

is the easiest to care for by 61 percent of the girls, followed by
on (11 percent), and wool (7 percent). Although cotton was strong
fewer responses from the older girls, girls from upper income
ze cities, and girls from the Northeast (table 87).

named as least likely to wrinkle were wool, Dacron, and nylon.
st likely to wrinkle by 38 percent of the girls, 21 percent thought
ind 19 percent said nylon (table 88).

y

ton somewhat more often than wool as the fiber they considered
oney--43 percent of the girls thought cotton was the best value,
. Dacron was regarded as the best value for the money by only
Again, cotton was stronger among the town and farm girls. Wool
out evenly by the girls from middle income families, girls from
from large cities (table 89).

THE TEENAGER'S ROLE IN CLOTHING SELECTION

PLANNING THE SHOPPING

Interest in Clothes

All the girls were asked whether they considered themselves very interested, fairly interested, or not very interested in their clothes. A large majority (81 percent) described themselves as being very interested in their clothes; 17 percent said they were only fairly interested, and 2 percent said they were not very interested (table 90).

The girls were also asked how interested they were in actually choosing their clothes. An even larger majority (89 percent) said they were very interested; 9 percent said fairly interested, and 2 percent were not very interested (table 91).

Those girls who were very interested in selecting their own clothes said it was primarily because they thought their appearance, being stylish, and getting the right size and color clothes were very important for a teenager, or because they preferred their own tastes and wanted to select styles themselves (table 92). Some of the girls who described themselves as being fairly interested in selecting their own clothes agreed that appearance, size, fit, and stylishness were fairly important. However, more of the girls who were only fairly interested said they were satisfied that their mothers did a good job (table 92). The few girls who said that they were not very interested in choosing their own clothes were most likely to say that their mothers did a good job in selecting their clothes.

Sources of Ideas

Teenage girls got their ideas about clothing from many sources. The two most frequently mentioned sources (reported about equally) were formal media--magazines, catalogs, newspapers, television, and movies--and friends or relatives. Another important source of ideas came from shopping, either inside the stores or window shopping (table 93). When the girls were asked which one source was most helpful, 29 percent of the girls said their friends gave them the most helpful ideas, 20 percent said they got their best ideas from looking in stores, and 17 percent said fashion magazines were the most helpful source (table 94).

Decision to Buy

The conclusions which follow concerning buying practices are based on the information provided by the girls themselves, and were not checked with their families.

The teenage girls said they were usually the ones who suggested a need for buying clothing items such as dresses or coats, and skirts or blouses, but that it was their mothers who actually had the most to say about whether there was to be a purchase. Older girls were more likely to say that they were responsible for suggesting the purchase of clothes, and had more to say in the final decision on whether to buy.

About three-fourths of the girls said they usually suggested the purchase of a dress or coat, but only one-tenth of the girls actually had the most to say about whether it was to be bought. Mothers made the final decision to buy a dress or coat 74 percent of the time, and fathers, 13 percent of the time. A larger proportion (85 percent) of the girls suggested that they needed new blouses or skirts, and twice as many girls (20 percent) had the most to say about whether there would be a purchase. Mothers, nevertheless, still made the final decision to buy a skirt or blouse in 71 percent of the homes, and fathers decided in 8 percent of the homes (tables 95 and 96).

16

e selection? ·

were asked who usually shopped for and who usually made the final selec-
f their articles of clothing. The majority of the girls said they shopped
made the final selection on skirts, blouses, everyday dresses, and
ever, the mothers' influence was very apparent in shopping for and select-
rls' clothing, particularly outer jackets or short coats (tables 97 and 98).

rity (55 percent) of the girls said they shopped alone for their skirts, 31
hey shopped with their mothers, and 10 percent said their mothers shopped
wo-thirds of the girls actually made the final selection.

ut of 10 of the 14-year-olds and over 7 out of 10 of the 17-year-olds shopped
r skirts. Only 59 percent of the youngest girls, compared with 79 percent of
ls, said they themselves made the final selection of their skirts (tables 97

ority of the girls (60 percent) maintained that they shopped alone for blouses,
ported they shopped with their mothers, and 11 percent said their mothers
e. Three-fourths of the teenagers had the final say in the selection of

centage of girls who shopped alone for blouses ranged from 43 percent of the
to 77 percent of the 17-year-olds. The proportion who made the final selec-
es varied from 67 percent of the youngest girls to 86 percent of the oldest
97 and 98).

·esses

.e-half (54 percent) of the teenage girls shopped alone for their everday
renty percent of the girls were responsible for the final selection and 28 per-
mothers made the final selection. Mothers shopped alone for their daughters'
l percent of the cases, and shopped with them in 31 percent of the cases.

out of 10 of the 14-year-old girls, compared with less than 2 out of 10 of the
girls, shopped with their mothers for everyday dresses. The final   selection
r 58 percent of the 14-year-old girls and by 82 percent of the 17-year-old
97 and 98).

.an one-half of the teenagers shopped alone for sweaters, and over two-thirds
.al selection. Less than one-third of the mothers and daughters shopped
sweaters.

percent of the youngest girls, compared with 70 percent of the oldest girls,
ie for sweaters. Fifty-eight percent of the 14-year-olds made the final selec-
weater; 78 percent of the 17-year-olds made the final selection (tables 97

:s or short coats

percent of the girls shopped alone for outer jackets or short coats, 20 per-
· mothers shopped alone, and 38 percent of the mothers and daughters shopped

17

together. The majority (56 percent) of the teenage girls made the final selection, and 41 percent of the mothers had most to say about the selection.

About one-fifth of the 14-year-old girls and over one-half of the 17-year-old girls shopped alone for outer jackets or short coats. Those making the final selection ranged from 44 percent of the youngest girls to 69 percent of the oldest girls (tables 97 and 98).

Age of Shopping Independence

The teenage girls on the average felt that at about 15 years of age a girl is old enough to do her own shopping and to select her clothing by herself.

The younger girls suggested a slightly lower age than the older girls. The median age suggested by 14-year-old girls was 15.0; by 15-year-old girls, 15.2 years; by 16-year-old girls, 15.4 years; and by 17-year-old girls, 15.7 years (table 99).

BACKGROUND INFORMATION ABOUT THE GIRLS
SCHOOL ENROLLMENT

Practically all (96 percent) of the girls were schoolgirls during the term between January and June, 1963. Of these only 7 percent went to all-girl schools. About three-fourths of the girls were in high school, 19 percent had not begun high school, and 1 percent were in college. As would be expected, there was a high correlation between the girls' ages and their school grade. For example, the majority of the 14-year-old girls had not begun high school; only 2 percent of the 17-year-old girls were completing their freshman year in college (table 100).

WORKING STATUS

The girls were asked if they had done any work at all for pay in the past 12 months. About two-thirds reported that they had held some kind of job: 16 percent had held a regular weekly job, 41 percent had worked occasionally, and 7 percent had held a regular job and also had done other work occasionally. About twice as many 17-year-old girls had held regular weekly jobs as 14-year-old girls (table 101).

Babysitting was the most popular form of work done by both the girls with regular jobs and the girls with nonregular jobs. Almost half of the girls with regular jobs reported that they worked 10 hours or less a week. Although the majority (63 percent) of the girls who worked on a nonregular basis said there was no particular time or season when they worked, 23 percent of them worked mostly in the summer when school was over.

AMOUNT OF MONEY EARNED

Most girls who had worked at some kind of job had earned over $25 during the past year. Only 13 percent of the 14-year-old girls said that they had made $100 or more. Almost half (49 percent) of the 17-year-old girls reported having made $100 or more, and 11 percent of the 17-year-olds had made $500 or more (table 102).

USES OF MONEY EARNED

Girls who had earned $25 or more were asked, "What did you do with most of the money you earned?" and "What did you do with the rest of the money?" If the girls answered they "saved it" to either question they were then asked "What are (were) you saving for?"

About two-thirds (68 percent) of the girls said that most of their money was spent on clothing, and 18 percent said they saved most of the money they earned, mainly for educational expenses and less frequently to buy clothing. Other uses girls mentioned for

18

ation and amusement, gifts, and school supplies, and

most of their money was spent for clothing. As the
they were more apt to name education as the purpose
104, and 105).

DISCUSS THEIR WARDROBES

age boys owned most of the clothing items studied.
were the only items studied which fewer than half of
wing list indicates the percentage of boys who said
item in each clothing category:

	Percent
or trousers.	99
. . . .	98
. . . .	98
ks or trousers.	96
short coats	89
. . . .	85
or trousers.	78
ks or trousers.	71
. . . .	65
both dry and rainy weather)	52
. . . .	42
. . . .	28

same winter slacks or trousers for both everyday and
rth used the same summer slacks or trousers for
s 119 and 152). For the purpose of this study, the
everyday and dress occasions are considered everyday
egory in all tables.[5]

is selected for this study, cotton was the fiber most
nage boys. Tables 3 and 4 summarize the information
nces for all fibers studied.

port of the interviews held with teenage boys, ages 14
robes and the factors affecting the purchasing of these

/INTER SPORT SHIRTS

enage boys owned readymade winter sport shirts, de-
sually worn without a tie, but is not a knitted shirt or

when it came to winter sport shirts. Eighty-seven per-
sport shirts said they had at least one made of cotton.
ownership, and cotton-polyester ranked third with 10

the words pants, slacks, and trousers are used interchangeably.

19

Table 4.--Teenage boys who owned certain items of clothing: Material liked best by 10 percent or more

Items of clothing	Cotton	Wool	Cotton-polyester	Nylon	Acrylic	Plastic	Cases
	Percent	Percent	Percent	Percent	Percent	Percent	Number
Winter:							
Sport shirts. . . .	65	10	--	--	--	--	1,613
Sport coats	11	41	--	--	--	--	1,073
Dress-up pants .	24	23	--	--	--	--	1,283
Everyday pants .	69	--	--	--	--	--	1,631
Outer jackets or							
short coats. . .	20	23	--	10	--	--	1,466
Summer:							
Sport shirts. . . .	61	--	--	--	--	--	1,612
Sport coats	32	--	16	--	--	--	689
Dress-up pants .	40	--	17	--	--	--	1,142
Everyday pants .	76	--	--	--	--	--	1,583
Sweaters	--	39	--	--	14	--	1,403
Rainwear.	20	--	--	--	--	16	1,127

Almost three-fourths of the boys who owned winter sport shirts said most of them were made of cotton. Only 13 percent said most were made of wool. Cotton was preferred by 65 percent of the sport-shirt owners, and wool by 10 percent (table 109).

The percentage who owned and preferred cotton was lowest among boys from the West. Although the ownership of and preference for wool were consistently lower than those of cotton, wool was more frequently mentioned by the boys from the West (tables 110 and 111).

ences

he major factor in cotton's popularity--44 percent of the boys who
its comfortable weight, and 38 percent preferred it because it doe
helming reason for choosing wool was that it is warm (89 percent)

referred material

(55 percent) of the wool advocates mentioned no disadvantages for
shirts. However, over one-fourth of the boys who preferred wool sa
ing to the skin. Cotton received no criticisms from about three-fou
eferred it; the criticisms that were given were scattered (table 113

ho usually wore cotton winter sport shirts, 86 percent reported tha
nerally machine washed at home. Among the boys whose winter spc
ere mainly wool, 62 percent thought that most of their shirts were
able 179).

had winter sport shirts that were not cared for by a commercial
d if their shirts were pressed before wearing. Regardless of the fi
ts were made of, practically all (98 percent) of the boys reported tl
generally pressed before wearing (table 182).

WINTER SPORT COATS

coats were owned by 65 percent of the teenage boys.

and preferred

leading fiber in winter sport coats. Over half (55 percent) of the bo
sport coats had one made of wool. Wool's closest competitors were
:; wool-polyester, 9 percent; and wool-cotton, 8 percent. The propo
all or most of their winter sport coats were made of these material
: pattern (table 114).

o the most widely preferred fiber for winter sport coats. About 4 o
liked wool the best, and about 1 out of 10 preferred cotton.

sport coats were most popular with the boys living in the Northeast
oys said they liked wool the best. In the other regions, the percenta
wool best for winter sport coats ranged from 34 to 37 percent (tabl

rences

ison for liking wool--mentioned by 64 percent of the boys who pre-
at it is warm. Of the boys who preferred cotton, 27 percent liked it
too warm, and 21 percent liked it because it does not irritate the sl
ster advocates, 33 percent preferred it because it does not wrinkle
ecause it does not irritate the skin (table 117).

preferred material

ticized by 43 percent of the boys who preferred it for winter sport
:-tenths of the cotton and wool-polyester advocates mentioned a

21

The two criticisms of wool made most often by those boys who preferred it were that it irritates the skin (20 percent) and that it is too warm (9 percent); 6 percent of the boys who indicated a preference for cotton said that they thought it was not warm enough; 6 percent of the wool polyester advocates complained that it collects lint (table 118).

Methods of care

Almost all (93 percent) of the winter sport coat owners sent most of their coats to the commercial cleaners; none of the boys reported either hand washing or machine washing (table 179).

WINTER DRESS-UP PANTS

Boys who had readymade winter slacks or trousers were asked if they got some of their winter pants for everyday wear and others for Sunday and special occasions, or if they got the same kind of pants for both. The majority of the boys owned different winter pants for the different occasions. Altogether, pants that were worn only for special dress-up occasions were owned by 78 percent of the teenage boys (table 119).

Materials owned and preferred

Wool and cotton were the most frequently owned materials in boys' winter dress-up slacks--48 percent of the owners had wool slacks and 36 percent had cotton slacks. Wool-polyester (14 percent) and cotton-polyester (11 percent) were also important materials. Wool predominated in 36 percent of the wardrobes, and cotton in 22 percent. Despite the fact that more boys owned wool dress pants than cotton, cotton and wool were almost equally preferred--cotton by 24 percent and wool by 23 percent. Wool-polyester was the favorite of 9 percent of the boys, and 8 percent preferred cotton-polyester. Fourteen percent of the boys did not express a preference (tables 120, 121, and 122).

Reasons for preference

Two out of five who preferred cotton for dress slacks did so because it does not irritate the skin, and less frequently because it was considered to be warm enough for winter wear, or not too warm. Wool was preferred mainly because of its warmth; about three out of five boys gave this reason for preferring wool. Wool was also preferred because it holds a press and crease well, and because it is considered more formal or dressy in appearance. Dress pants made of polyester, or polyester blended with wool or cotton, were liked best generally because they do not irritate the skin and because they hold their press and crease well (table 123).

Disadvantages of preferred material

Wool was more frequently criticized by its adherents than cotton was by its followers (57 percent and 35 percent, respectively). The major fault attributed to wool was lack of comfort--it irritates, scratches, or itches. The major criticism of cotton was against its performance (such as wrinkles easily, or soils and stains easily) and durability. A combination of these two criticisms was made against polyester and polyester blends by the boys who preferred these materials (table 124).

Methods of care

The majority (82 percent) of the boys reported that most of their winter dress pants were commercially cleaned. However, 28 percent of the boys with dress pants wardrobes in which cotton predominated, and 16 percent of the boys with wardrobes in which cotton-polyester predominated, said their slacks were machine washed; only 4 percent of the boys with wardrobes in which either wool or wool-polyester dress pants predominated said that their pants were machine washed (table 179).

22

Practically all (97 percent) of the boys said that their winter dress pants that were ot commercially cleaned were pressed (table 182).

WINTER EVERYDAY PANTS

Practically every boy (99 percent) owned a pair of winter everyday slacks or rousers.

aterials owned and preferred

The major fiber for boys' everyday winter pants was cotton--84 percent of the boys wned at least one pair made of cotton, 76 percent had only or mostly cotton, and 69 ercent said that cotton was their first choice of material for these pants. Less frequently owned fibers were wool (14 percent) and cotton-polyester (9 percent). They tied or second in popularity, each being preferred by 6 percent of the boys (table 125).

There were some differences among the population subgroups in ownership of and reference for cotton everyday winter pants. For example, 92 percent of the boys from he town and farm areas owned cotton pants, compared with 75-percent ownership by the oys from the large cities. The preference for cotton pants followed the same pattern. More of the boys from the South, West, and North Central areas than from the Northeast owned and preferred cotton for their everyday winter pants (tables 126 and 127).

Reasons for preferences

The leading reasons for the preference for cotton in everyday winter pants were that cotton wears well, it is washable or easy to wash, and it doesn't irritate the skin. Cotton-polyester was popular because it doesn't wrinkle, holds its shape, and wears well.

Most of the boys (77 percent) who preferred wool for their everyday winter pants stressed warmth as the main reason for their preference; the only other reason mentioned by a substantial proportion (19 percent) was its retention of crease and press (table 128).

Disadvantages of preferred material

Only about three-tenths of the boys who preferred each of these three materials for their everyday winter pants had any criticism of their preferred fiber. Two-tenths of the boys who preferred wool pants criticized wool because it irritates, itches, and scratches. Cotton was criticized by roughly one-tenth of its adherents because they said cotton everyday pants fade. Although no one disadvantage was mentioned with any frequency by cotton-polyester advocates, their criticisms centered around performance and durability characteristics (table 129).

Methods of care

In wardrobes where these materials predominated, about 9 out of 10 boys had most of their cotton or cotton-polyester pants machine washed; only 3 out of 10 boys reported that most of their wool pants were similarly cared for (table 179). Regardless of the materials, 90 percent of the boys owning winter everyday pants not commercially cleaned reported that their pants were pressed before wearing (table 182).

Ownership of "permanently" creased winter pants

Only one boy in five (18 percent) said they owned at least one pair of "permanently" creased winter pants--those which have been processed or treated so that the creases stay in. Pants of wool or wool mixtures were owned by over half of the boys with "permanently" creased pants (table 130).

23

Reaction to idea of per.anently creased wool pants

All the boys were asked what they thought of the idea of permanently creased wool pants--that is, wool pants which have been processed or treated so that the creases stay in without pressing, even when the pants are washed or cleaned. A large majority (84 percent) regarded this as a good idea; the percentages were even higher among the boys who owned wool pants or "permanently" creased wool pants (table 131).

The reasons most frequently given by the boys for liking the idea of permanently creased wool pants were that the pants would require little or no ironing and that the creases would always stay in. The reasons for the favorable attitudes were basically the same whether or not the boys owned "permanently" creased wool pants (table 132).

The few boys (15 percent) who thought permanent creasing of wool pants was not a good idea felt mainly that the pants would look artificial, or that nothing would be gained since wool pants would still have to be commercially cleaned. Some boys who did not like wool pants or objected to any crease in pants did not think permanently creased wool pants a good idea (table 133).

The boys were asked to rate the importance of permanent creasing in their decision to buy a pair of wool pants. They were shown a rating scale (see 8a of questionnaire) and asked to give a rating from 1 to 5. The highest rating possible was 5 (next to it was written "most important"), and 1 was the lowest (next to it was written "not important at all"). About one-half (48 percent) of the boys gave this process a high rating, either 5 or 4. These boys based their ratings primarily on the attractive aspects of creases always staying in and little or no ironing being required to keep the pants neat. The ratings varied little between boys who owned wool pants and the other boys (tables 134, 135, and 136).

The boys (51 percent) who thought this process was not important at all or not very important (ratings of 1, 2, or 3), felt for the most part that other features would be more important, mainly the style and color of the pants. Some boys' dislike of wool pants or opinion that creases are not important also contributed to the low ratings (table 136).

RESPONSIBILITY FOR HAND WASHING AND IRONING

Those boys who said that any of their winter sport shirts, dress pants, or everyday pants were hand washed were then asked who generally did the hand washing; the majority of the boys (83 percent) reported that their mothers generally did it (table 180).

Boys who owned winter sport shirts, dress pants, or everyday pants that were pressed by other than a commercial cleaner were asked who usually did most of the pressing. As with hand washing, the majority of the boys (81 percent) reported that their mothers generally did most of it. Only a few (7 percent) of the boys said that they generally pressed their own clothes (table 183).

WINTER OUTER JACKETS AND SHORT COATS

Winter outer jackets or short coats were owned by 89 percent of the teenage boys.

Materials owned and preferred

Wool and cotton were the leading materials reported by the owners of coats and jackets--35 percent had wool outer jackets and 31 percent had cotton. Fewer of the boys had nylon (13 percent) and suede or leather (11 percent) outer jackets. Boys' choices of the fibers they liked best for outer jackets ranked in the same order--wool (23 percent), cotton (20 percent), nylon (10 percent), and suede or leather (9 percent). However, 11 percent of the outer-jacket owners indicated no fiber preference for these coats (table 137). Ownership of and preference for outer jackets made of wool was highest in the

preference for cotton was highest in the South.
the West (tables 138 and 139).

in considerations mentioned by the boys for select-
best for their winter outer jackets. The boys who
armth, and the boys who preferred nylon said it is
choice of material to a lesser degree were appear-
d durability (table 140).

r winter outer jackets drew some criticisms from
lyester were a little less likely to be criticized
cates generally cited tearing and snagging, wool
itation, and cotton advocates mentioned "not warm
polyester, and suede or leather stated staining and
eferred fiber (table 141).

MER SPORT SHIRTS

) owned a summer sport shirt that was neither a

ummer sport shirts. Not only was a cotton sport
rs' wardrobes, but 8 out of 10 of the boys said that
hirts were cotton. About 6 out of 10 said that they

ned were cotton-polyester (17 percent), nylon (13
, and polyester (10 percent). None of these fibers
nt of the boys. Eleven percent reported no prefer-
· (table 142).

ie same regardless of the boys' ages, family income,
However, the preference for cotton summer sport
: boys from the urban nonmetropolitan areas than
ible 144).

the largest proportion of boys said that their favorite
weight, and airy. No other reason was mentioned
Boys who preferred cotton-polyester for sport
wrinkle, and the boys who preferred nylon said they
le or no ironing (table 145).

s who preferred cotton summer sport shirts men-
percent) was the main criticism. Other criticisms

rted that most of their summer sport shirts were
10 (88 percent) said their shirts were washed by

25

machine; only 7 percent said the shirts were hand washed (table 179). Almost all (97 percent) of the boys said that their summer sports shirts were usually pressed after washing (table 183).

SUMMER SPORT COATS

About two-fifths of the boys (42 percent) owned a summer sport coat.

Materials owned and preferred

Fibers reported owned in boys' summer sport coats were many and varied. While 38 percent of the summer sport-coat owners reported they had at least one made of cotton and 21 percent had at least one cotton-polyester coat, the remainder of the market was scattered among many different fibers and fiber blends. The proportions saying that all or most of their summer sport coats were made of these materials followed the same pattern.

Cotton sport coats were preferred by 32 percent of the owners; 16 percent preferred cotton-polyester. However, 19 percent of the owners were unable to decide which one material they liked best for their summer sport coats (table 147).

The proportion of boys owning cotton sport coats was highest among those from the large cities and from the Northeast. The proportion of boys who owned and preferred cotton-polyester was highest among boys from the South (tables 148 and 149).

Reasons for preference

Three-fourths of the boys who preferred cotton or cotton-polyester sport coats liked these materials best because they are cool, lightweight, and airy. Among those who preferred cotton, 13 percent said cotton does not wrinkle; 37 percent of the cotton-polyester adherents attributed this quality to cotton-polyester (table 150).

Disadvantages of preferred material

A few of the advocates of cotton (10 percent) and cotton-polyester (5 percent) criticized the fibers because they thought their summer sport coats of these materials wrinkled easily. Some of the boys said that their cotton and cotton-polyester coats were not cool enough (table 151).

Methods of care

A large majority (88 percent) of the summer sport-coat owners said most of these articles were sent to a commercial cleaner (table 179). Of the few boys whose sport coats were not commercially cleaned, practically all (88 percent) had their coats pressed after washing (table 182).

SUMMER DRESS-UP PANTS

The boys who reported owning readymade summer slacks or trousers were asked if they got some of their summer pants for everyday wear and others for Sunday or special occasions, or if they got the same kind for both everyday and dress-up wear. The majority of these boys said that they got different pants for each. Altogether, 71 percent of the boys had summer pants that were only for dress-up wear (table 152).

Materials owned and preferred

Among the boys who had summer dress-up pants, cotton was the most frequently owned and preferred material. Over half (58 percent) of the owners had at least one pair of cotton, 46 percent had mostly or only cotton, and 40 percent selected cotton as the fiber they liked best.

26

Cotton-polyester was the second most popular material. It was owned by 23 percent of the boys who had dress pants, 18 percent owned mostly or only cotton-polyester, and percent said they preferred it over all other fibers.

Other less frequently owned and preferred fibers were polyester, rayon/acetate, tton and rayon/acetate, and wool. None of these fibers was owned or preferred by as ny as 10 percent of the dress-pants owners. Of the boys questioned, 17 percent indited no preference for a material in their dress pants (table 153).

A higher proportion of 17-year-olds than of 14- to 16-year-olds preferred cotton-lyester dress pants; the reverse was true for cotton. More of the southern boys rerted owning and preferring cotton-polyester than did boys from the other regions bles 154 and 155).

asons for preferences

Almost two-thirds of the boys preferring cotton for summer dress pants said that tton is comfortably cool, lightweight, and airy. Cotton-polyester advocates gave the me reason for their preference, and also stressed that it holds a crease or press and es not wrinkle (table 156).

sadvantages of preferred material

Cotton and cotton-polyester drew very few complaints as materials for summer ess pants. Cotton was criticized by 27 percent of the boys and cotton-polyester was iticized by only 20 percent. The main criticisms given by the adherents of both cotton d cotton-polyester concerned dissatisfaction over the performance and durability of e materials, particularly wrinkling; these were mentioned by 8 percent of the boys eferring each (table 157).

ethods of care

A majority of the summer dress pants were usually commercially cleaned--53 per-ent of the boys who owned mostly cotton, compared with 71 percent of the boys who wned mostly cotton-polyester, said that their dress pants were generally cared for by e commercial cleaners. Forty-one percent of the boys with summer dress-up pants ardrobes in which cotton predominated reported that most of their pants were machine ashed, compared with 22 percent of the boys with cotton-polyester wardrobes who said at their pants were machine washed (table 179). Regardless of the fiber, 97 percent of e boys reported that their summer dress pants were pressed when cared for at home able 183).

SUMMER EVERYDAY PANTS

Very few of the boys reported that they had either slacks or trousers for dress-up casions only or for everyday only. The vast majority had either different pants for ich or said that they wore the same kind of pants for dress-up and everyday wear.

aterials owned and preferred

Cotton had little competition in boys' summer everyday pants. Practically all (91 ercent) owned at least one pair made solely of cotton. Many of the boys (87 percent) iid that most of their summer everyday pants were cotton and over three-fourths of the ys liked cotton best. Cotton-polyester was owned by 10 percent of the boys and was referred by 6 percent (table 158). About 11 percent of the boys indicated they had no ber preference; the greater proportion of these boys were from the large cities, the ortheast, and the West (table 160).

Reasons for preferences

The boys who preferred cotton frequently mentioned its coolness as a reason for their preference. Cited less frequently were cotton's washability and durability. Those who preferred cotton-polyester gave similar reasons for their choice, but also emphasized wrinkle resistance (table 161).

Disadvantages of preferred material

There were no major complaints about either cotton or cotton-polyester, and neither was criticized by more than one-third of the boys who liked them best for their summer everyday pants. Cotton was criticized by 6 percent of these boys because it fades and runs; 7 percent of the boys who criticized cotton polyester said that it stains and soils easily (table 162).

Methods of care

The boys reported that most of their summer everyday pants were usually machine washed. Among boys who owned mostly cotton pants, 90 percent said that most of these pants were machine washed. Of the few boys who owned mostly cotton-polyester pants, 72 percent said that these pants were generally machine washed (table 179). A majority of the boys (85 percent) who owned summer everyday pants which were washed at home said that their pants were usually pressed before wearing (table 182).

RESPONSIBILITY FOR HAND WASHING AND IRONING

Those boys who said that any of their summer sport shirts, sport coats, dress pants, or everyday pants were hand washed were then asked who usually did that hand washing; 79 percent reported that their mothers generally did it (table 180).

Boys who owned summer sport shirts, sport coats, dress pants or everyday pants that were pressed by other than a commercial cleaner were asked who usually did most of the pressing. A majority of the boys (81 percent) reported that their mothers generally did it and 8 percent of the boys said that they generally pressed their own clothes (table 183).

SWEATERS

Eighty-five percent of the teenage boys owned at least one readymade sweater, not including polo shirts or T-shirts.

Materials owned and preferred

The boys who had sweaters most frequently owned and preferred wool--70 percent had at least one wool sweater, 56 percent had mostly or only wool sweaters, and 39 percent said they preferred wool over all other fibers. About one-fourth (24 percent) of the boys owning sweaters reported having at least one acrylic sweater, and 14 percent selected acrylic as their favorite fiber. Cotton and wool-acrylic sweaters were mentioned less frequently (tables 163, 164, and 165).

Reasons for preferences

Comfort was the main consideration given for preferring one sweater fiber over another. Wool adherents preferred wool primarily because it is comfortably warm, acrylic advocates preferred acrylic mainly because it doesn't irritate the skin, and cotton and wool-acrylic advocates stressed both the lack of irritation to the skin and warmth as the main reasons for finding these fibers comfortable. Acrylic, cotton, and wool-acrylic were also frequently cited because they hold their shape (table 166).

preferred material

ıre frequently criticized for sweaters than were the other three most
fibers; 55 percent of the wool advocates had some criticism of it. Only
boys who preferred cotton, 32 percent of the boys who preferred
ɛrcent of the boys who preferred wool-acrylic for their sweaters
referred fiber.

ticism against wool was that it irritates the skin. Acrylic's main draw-
)alls up, fuzzes, and sheds; cotton and wool-acrylic were criticized
 of these fibers lose their shape (table 167).

es in which wool was the predominant sweater fiber, 44 percent of the
)st of their sweaters were hand washed, 43 percent said that most were
ercial cleaners, and only 11 percent said that most of their sweaters
shed. However, for wardrobes in which acrylic was the predominant
 of the boys said that most of their sweaters were hand washed, only 25
 most were commercially cleaned, and 24 percent said that most were
(table 179). Regardless of the fiber, 69 percent of the boys said that
hich were not commercially cleaned were usually pressed before wear-
 large majority (87 percent) of the boys said that their mothers usually
hing and pressing of their sweaters (tables 180 and 184).

)f machine-washable wool sweaters

o owned sweaters were asked their opinions concerning a development
e possible the safe machine washing of wool sweaters without special

rcent) of the sweater owners thought machine-washable wool sweaters
idea. There were only slight differences between the answers from all
ied readymade sweaters and those who owned wool sweaters (table 168).
s the boys approved of the idea were that it would save time and money,
 be nice to have a wool sweater that retained its shape after washing

:ent of the boys who owned sweaters said they thought machine wash-
good idea. For the most part, these boys felt that a wool sweater would not
 be safe in a washing machine regardless of the claim. One-fifth of the
vorable opinion of the process because they do not like wool in sweaters
 .

re then asked to rate the importance of machine washability in the deci-
/ wool sweater. They were shown a rating scale and asked to give a
to five. The highest rating possible was 5 and 1 was the lowest. Over
ʒave the new development a high rating (either 5 or 4), mainly because
ï process would save them time and money. Some boys also thought that
ers would be more readily available for use if machine washed (table

ł percent) who gave this development lower ratings (1, 2, or 3) fre-
they considered other factors, such as style and color, more important.
)t like wool sweaters at all, or took no part in the care of their
ı72).

29

RAINWEAR

About two-thirds of the boys owned some type of rainwear. Raincoats (meant only to be worn in rainy weather) were owned by 16 percent of the boys, 40 percent owned multipurpose coats (meant to be worn in any weather), and 12 percent owned both.

Multipurpose coats

Cotton was the most frequently owned material for multipurpose coats--36 percent of the boys owning such coats had at least one made of cotton, and 12 percent had at least one of cotton-polyester. Nylon and cotton-rayon/acetate were each owned by 7 percent. Twelve percent of the multipurpose coat owners could not identify the fiber in their coats (table 174).

Raincoats

Plastic was by far the leading fiber for raincoats--57 percent of the boys who owned raincoats had at least one made of plastic. Cotton was owned by 7 percent and oilskin by 6 percent of the boys with raincoats. Some raincoat owners (7 percent) had difficulty in identifying the fiber in their raincoats (table 174).

Materials preferred for rainwear

Cotton and plastic were the best liked fibers for rainwear by the teenage boys who owned either a raincoat, a multipurpose coat, or both. Cotton was preferred by 20 percent of these boys, 16 percent preferred plastic, and 9 percent preferred cotton-polyester. Almost 3 out of 10 of the boys said that they had no preference in materials for their rainwear (table 174).

Reasons for preferences

Cotton rainwear was liked primarily because it is water repellent and because it is versatile, and less frequently because it is not too warm and is lightweight. The main advantage mentioned for plastic was its waterproof quality; it was also preferred because it is lightweight (table 177).

Disadvantages of preferred material

Only about one-third of the cotton advocates, compared with about two-thirds of the plastic advocates, mentioned any criticism of the fiber they preferred for rainwear. The major complaints about plastic were that it tears and rips easily (mentioned by 29 percent), and is too hot (mentioned by 12 percent). The disadvantages attributed to cotton were scattered; the main criticism was that it soils and stains easily (mentioned by 8 percent) (table 178).

OVERALL OPINIONS OF SELECTED FIBERS

The boys were asked to indicate which of six fibers used in clothing they thought was best for each of a number of characteristics. The fibers asked about were cotton, rayon, nylon, Orlon, Dacron, and wool. The trademark names of Orlon and Dacron were used, as in the girls' questionnaire, rather than the generic names of acrylic and polyester, to provide comparable data.

Best for hot weather

Two-thirds of the boys thought cotton was the best fiber to wear in hot weather. Dacron and nylon tied for second with 11 percent of the boys naming each. The proportion preferring cotton for hot weather was highest among the oldest boys, and the boys from the Northeast and South. Nylon was favored by more of the boys from the lower income families than those from other groups (table 186).

30

cold weather

er 7 out of 10 of the boys chose wool as the best fiber to wear in cold weather; 2
0 selected cotton. Wool was especially liked in the Northeast; 81 percent of the
om that area said it was best for cold weather (table 187).

he longest

tton and wool were about evenly rated as fibers which last the longest; they were
by 29 percent and 27 percent respectively. Nylon was mentioned by 15 percent,
percent said Dacron. Boys from lower income families and from the South most
itly said cotton, while wool was mentioned more often by boys living in large cities
the Northeast (table 188).

shape the best

tton was named by 36 percent of the boys as the fiber which keeps its shape best,
:ent said wool, 16 percent said Dacron, and 9 percent named nylon. The propor-
:ntioning cotton was highest among the southern boys, the town and farm boys,
rs from the lower income families (table 189).

t to care for

e majority (61 percent) of the boys reported that cotton was the easiest fiber to
·r. Dacron followed with 9 percent, and nylon was mentioned by 8 percent of the
·gain, cotton was selected more frequently by the town and farm boys and the
rn boys (table 190).

likely to wrinkle

·ere was more difference of opinion about which fiber wrinkles the least than on
er characteristics investigated. Wool was chosen as least likely to wrinkle by 24
t, 18 percent said Dacron, 17 percent said cotton, and 14 percent said nylon.
· percent of the boys said they did not know which fiber would wrinkle the least
191).

alue for the money

most half of the boys selected cotton as the best value for the money. Wool was
17 percent thought it was the best value--and Dacron was chosen by 9 percent.
12 percent of the boys did not express an opinion about which of these six fibers
· best value. Cotton received its largest support from the southern boys, and its
upport from the boys from the Northeast (table 192).

THE TEENAGER'S ROLE IN CLOTHING SELECTION

PLANNING THE SHOPPING

t in clothes

st over half of the teenage boys expressed considerable interest in what kinds of
; they wear--52 percent said they were very interested; 38 percent described
·lves as fairly interested, and 10 percent said they were not very interested. The
rners, the older boys, and boys from urban areas and the higher income families
·ore apt to describe themselves as being very interested in the kinds of clothes
ear (table 193).

· even greater percentage of the boys reported that they were very interested in
ection of their clothes--66 percent indicated they were very interested; 25 percent

said fairly interested, and 9 percent said they were not very interested. Again, the older boys, boys from urban areas, and those from the higher income families were more interested in selecting their own clothes (table 194).

The boys were very interested in selecting their own clothing for a variety of reasons. Mainly they said that they were particular and preferred their own taste in clothes, that they wanted to be stylish and wear what other boys wear, or that appearance in clothes is very important for a teenage boy.

The main reason some boys described themselves as being only fairly interested was that they were satisfied with the clothes their mothers bought for them.

The few boys who said they were not very interested in choosing their own clothes said that they were satisfied that their mothers did a good job in selecting their clothing, or that they did not care about clothes (table 195).

Sources of ideas

The teenage boys picked up ideas about clothing from several sources--friends, shopping, and formal media (table 196). Half of the boys credited their friends with giving the most helpful ideas. Only 17 percent found that looking in stores was the best way to get ideas about clothing, and 9 percent of the boys claimed that their parents were the most helpful source of ideas (table 197).

Decision to buy

The conclusions which follow concerning buying practices are based on the information provided by the boys themselves, and were not checked with their families.

The teenage boys said they were usually the ones who first suggested a need to buy important clothing items such as outer jackets and sport coats, or shirts and sweaters. However, according to the boys, their mothers were the ones who actually had the most to say as to whether there would be a purchase. The older boys were more likely to say that they were responsible for suggesting the need to buy something and that they had more to say in the final decision. About three-fifths of the boys said they usually suggested the need to purchase an outer jacket or sport coat, but only 15 percent actually had the most to say about whether it was to be bought. Mothers suggested the purchase of an outer jacket or sport coat in 37 percent of the cases, but made the final decision 59 percent of the time. Fathers made the final decision 25 percent of the time.

Although 69 percent of the teenage boys said that they usually suggested the need for a new shirt or sweater, only 23 percent felt that they decided whether it would be bought. On the other hand, while only about one-third of the mothers made the initial suggestion, about two-thirds had the most to say about the final decision (tables 198 and 199).

PURCHASING THE CLOTHES

Who makes the selection?

The boys were asked who usually shopped for and who usually made the final selection for some of their articles of clothing. About one-half of the mothers shopped either alone or with their sons; over one-half of the boys reported that they made the final selection.

Sport shirts

About one-fifth of the boys shopped with their mothers for their sport shirts, and more than two-fifths (44 percent) of the boys shopped alone. However, over three-fifths (64 percent) of the boys made the final selection. About one-third of the boys said their mothers both shopped alone and made the final selection for these shirts.

32

ıger boys were less likely to shop alone than the older boys--proportions
23 percent of the 14-year-olds to 68 percent of the 17-year-olds. The final
₃ made by 48 percent of the younger boys, compared with 79 percent of the
ables 200 and 201).

ıe-third of the boys shopped for sport coats alone, and about one-fourth
their mothers. The mothers shopped alone 22 percent of the time. Over
ent) of the boys said that they made the final selection of which coat to buy.
ird of the mothers and one-tenth of the fathers had the most to say about the
ın of their sons' sport coats.

percent of the 14-year-old boys, but 57 percent of the 17-year-old boys,
e. The final selection was made by 42 percent of 14-year-olds; 73 percent
ır-olds had the most to say about the selection (tables 200 and 201).

nts

half of the boys shopped alone for their everyday pants and about two-thirds
al selection. About one-third of the mothers shopped alone and made the
ın. Only one-fourth of the 14-year-olds shopped alone, compared to almost
₅ of the 17-year-olds. The final selection was made by 5 out of 10 of the
s; 8 out of 10 of the oldest boys chose their own everyday pants (tables 200

five percent of the boys said that they shopped with their mothers for dress
rcent reported shopping alone, and 30 percent said that their mothers shopped
ıajority of the boys (57 percent) made the final selection on dress pants, but
f the mothers and 8 percent of the fathers had the most to say about the final
opping alone was reported by 15 percent of the 14-year-olds and 58 percent
ır-olds. The final selection was made by 39 percent of the 14-year-old boys
nt of the 17-year-old boys (tables 200 and 201).

ıalf (46 percent) of the boys shopped alone for their sweaters; practically the
r said either that their mothers shopped alone (17 percent) or that they
their mothers (30 percent). The final selection of sweaters was made by 64
e teenage boys. One-fourth of the youngest boys, compared with three-
₂ oldest boys, shopped alone; 48 percent of the 14-year-old boys and 80 per-
7-year-old boys made the final selection (tables 200 and 201).

₃ or short coats

ıeven percent of the boys shopped alone for outer jackets or short coats, 25
eir mothers shopped alone, and 24 percent of the mothers and sons shopped
e majority (59 percent) of the boys made the final selection; 33 percent of
and 9 percent of the fathers made the final selection.

percent of the youngest boys, compared with 65 percent of the oldest boys,
e. The privilege of making the final selection ranged from 45 percent of the
boys to 79 percent of the 17-year-old boys (tables 200 and 201).

ıing independence

ıage boys on the average indicated that at about 15 years of age a boy is old
his own shopping and pick out his own clothes by himself.

33

Generally the younger boys suggested a slightly lower age than the older boys. The median age suggested by 14-year-old boys was 15.2; by 15-year-old boys, 15.3; by 16-year-old boys, 15.6; and by 17-year-old boys, 15.9 (table 202).

BACKGROUND INFORMATION ABOUT THE BOYS

SCHOOL ENROLLMENT

Almost all (95 percent) of the teenage boys were enrolled in.school during the term between January and June, 1963. Of these only 7 percent went to all-boy schools. About three-fourths of the boys were in high school. As with the girls, there was a high correlation between boys' ages and their school grade. The majority (56 percent) of the 14-year-old boys had not entered first year of high school; only 2 percent of the 17-year-old boys were in college (table 203).

WORKING STATUS

About three-fourths of the teenage boys had worked at some job during the year; 21 percent had held regular weekly jobs, 33 percent had worked occasionally, and 22 percent had held a regular job and also had done other work occasionally. Over one-third of the 14-year-old boys and over one-half of the 17-year-old boys had held regular weekly jobs (table 204).

Delivering newspapers, acting as a salesclerk, and doing yard or farm work were the most popular occupations among teenage boys holding a regular job. The median number of hours worked by all teenage boys who had held a regular job was between 16 and 20 hours per week.

The most popular occasional jobs held by the teenage boys were yard work and farm work. Boys who had worked occasionally were more inclined to work during the summer-- about half of these boys said they had held their jobs in the summer. One-third said there was no particular time or season when they worked.

AMOUNT OF MONEY EARNED

Only 16 percent of the boys who had worked reported that they had earned less than $25 in the past year; about half had earned $100 or more. The older boys earned more than the younger boys--only 23 percent of the 14-year-old boys, but 81 percent of the 17-year-old boys, had earned $100 or more in the preceding year (table 205).

USES OF MONEY EARNED

The boys who had earned $25 or more were asked "What did you do with most of the money you earned?" and "What did you do with the rest of the money?" If the boys answered "saved it" to either question they were then asked "What are (were) you saving for?"

A majority of the boys reported that most of the money they earned was spent either for clothing or for recreation and amusement. One-third of the boys saved most of their money, mainly for their education and less frequently for a car (tables 206, 207, and 208).

APPENDIX

SAMPLE DESIGN AND SELECTION PROCEDURE

This study was designed to represent all boys and girls 14 through 17 years of age living in households in the contiguous United States. In order to obtain reliable findings

le tolerance limits, the sample was designed to assure that every household
tion as defined would have a known probability of inclusion.

tage national probability sample of 17,769 dwelling units was used, with
rations performed at three successive stages as follows:

 appropriate stratification, 121 primary sampling units (67 standard
opolitan areas and 54 nonmetropolitan counties) were selected with known
ıbility.

n the 121 primary sampling units, 600 clusters were selected with known
ıbility. The cluster, in most cases, was an entire Census Enumeration
ict except ın the larger cities, where blocks, or combinations of blocks,
used.

ı the 600 clusters, 16,769 dwelling units were selected. The clusters had
prelısted, which means that a field worker had visited each of them and
a complete listıng of all dwelling places within the cluster boundaries.
ı the listing submitted by the field workers, the specıfıc units to be in-
d in the sample from each cluster were selected by random procedures.
ıumber of units selected from each cluster was determined in such a
ıer that every household in the contiguous United States had an equal
ıbility of inclusion in the sample.

RECOVERY OF ASSIGNED INTERVIEWS

signed dwelling·units 17,769
nt 1,114
cupied dwelling units 16,655
ъed any information 35
ıe ever home 156
·enagers 13,414
useholds with one or more teenagers 3,050

ıe 3,050 households with one or more teenagers, there were a total of 3,844
,940 gırls and 1,904 boys). Of these 3,339 (1,691 girls and 1,648 boys) were
interviewed.

RELIABILITY OF RESULTS

ⱶwing tabulation of two-sigma tolerances was derived from computed sam-
for approximately 70 estimates. The computed sampling errors were esti-
on the variation found among 10 replicated subsamples.

Estimated Two-Sigma Tolerance[1]

		Number of Sample Cases				
1,700	1,500	1,250	1,00ᵘ	750	500	250
1.3	1.3	1.4	1.7	1.9	2.3	3.4
1.8	1.9	2.0	2.3	2.6	3.2	4.6
1.9	2.0	2.2	2.5	2.9	3.5	5.0
2.1	2.3	2.5	2.9	3.2	4.0	5.6
2.9	3.1	3.4	3.8	4.5	5.5	7.7
3.1	3.4	3.6	4.1	4.6	5.7	8.1
3.0	3.3	3.5	3.9	4.6	5.6	7.8
3.1	3.3	3.6	4.1	4.7	5.7	8.1
2.9	3.6	3.4	3.8	4.3	5.4	7.6
2.9	3.6	3.4	3.8	4.4	5.4	7.6

lerances shown are in percentage points. If every individual in the population
ıad been interviewed, the chances are 19 out of 20 that the results obtained
fer from the reported figure by more than the tolerances shown.

35

FIELD INTERVIEWING OPERATIONS

Field work on this study began early in June, 1963, and was completed by mid-July, 1963. Interviewer training included complete written instructions on both sampling and interviewing procedures, a discussion of techniques for recovering interviews with "difficult" respondents, and a detailed explanation of the specific questioning procedure to be used. Interviewers also were required to conduct two practice interviews with strangers outside the sample areas. These interviews were checked and evaluated and each interviewer was informed of any errors or inadequacy revealed in her work. Only after satisfactory evidence had been submitted indicating that she thoroughly understood all aspects of the assignment was the interviewer allowed to start any field work on the sample.

QUESTIONNAIRES

Several versions of the questionnaires were drafted and tried out in whole or in part with small numbers of teenage girls and boys before the forms were designed for pre-testing. Pretesting was conducted in and around Englewood-Teaneck, N.J. and Atlanta, Ga. The final forms of the questionnaires were simplified somewhat as the result of these pretests, the questions were reworded where improvements were needed, and specific probes for additional answers and for clarification of general responses were inserted. The questionnaires are reproduced at the end of this report without the check-box material, office record information, and free-answer spaces.

EXPLANATION OF TABLES

The background characteristics for which separate percentages are shown are defined as follows:

Age

The exact age of the respondent was asked for each interview; the teenagers with whom this study was concerned were 14 through 17 years of age.

Family income group

The income group in which the family was placed was based on an indication by the respondent's parent or guardian of the code letter on a card which corresponded with the total annual family income before taxes. The question concerning family income was not asked of the teenagers. In some cases it was estimated by the interviewer. No information on family income was obtained from seven of the interviews (six for the girls and one for the boys). The income categories were:

> Lower--$4,999 and under
> Middle--$5,000 to $7,999
> Upper--$8,000 and over

Size of place

The urban metropolitan, urban nonmetropolitan, and farm and town classifications used to describe community size in this study were based on the designations used by the Bureau of the Census for the 1960 census. The urban metropolitan classification corresponds to the Standard Metropolitan Statistical Areas (SMSA's) of more than 1 million population. The urban nonmetropolitan classification was used for the SMSA's of less than 1 million population, plus all other urban territory as defined for Census purposes. The town and farm classification represents rural territory as defined for Census purposes, other than any rural territory that might be included in the SMSA's.

Regions

id-July
ng and
:th
)cedure
with
ed and

:er:tood
/ to the

t :t part
: :re-
:cta,

:n' spe-
:3 in-
::ch-

The regional classifications correspond to those used by the Bureau of the Census. States included in each of the four regions were:

Northeast	Iowa	Tennessee
	Missouri	Alabama
Maine	North Dakota	Mississippi
New Hampshire	South Dakota	Delaware
Vermont	Nebraska	Maryland
Massachusetts	Kansas	District of Colur
Rhode Island		
Connecticut	South	West
New York		
New Jersey	North Carolina	Montana
Pennsylvania	South Carolina	Arizona
	Virginia	Colorado
North Central	Georgia	Idaho
	Florida	Wyoming
Ohio	West Virginia	Utah
Michigan	Arkansas	Nevada
Indiana	Louisiana	New Mexico
Illinois	Oklahoma	California
Wisconsin	Texas	Oregon
Minnesota	Kentucky	Washington

37

Table 5.--All girls were asked: "Are most of your readymade winter clothes dresses, or skirt and blouse or sweater combinations?"

Background characteristics	Mostly combinations	Only combinations	About even	Mostly dresses	Only dresses	No winter readymades	Cases
	Percent	Percent	Percent	Percent	Percent	Percent	Number
United States total-----	63	24	5	7	1	(*)	1,691
Age:							
14 years--------------	61	26	5	7	1	---	519
15 years--------------	60	27	5	7	1	---	405
16 years-------------	64	21	6	8	1	(*)	454
17 years-------------	68	20	6	5	1	(*)	313
Family income group:							
Lower----------------	59	26	4	10	1	(*)	601
Middle---------------	61	26	5	6	2	---	656
Upper----------------	72	17	7	4	(*)	---	428
Size of place:							
Urban metropolitan----	67	20	7	5	1	---	561
Urban nonmetropolitan-	63	25	5	6	1	---	734
Town and farm--------	56	27	4	11	2 .	(*)	396
Region:							
Northeast------------	72	19	7	2	(*)	---	441
North Central--------	63	28	4	4	1	---	456
South----------------	61	21	5	12	1	(*)	564
West-----------------	53	32	6	8	1	---	230

*Less than 1 percent.

Table 6.--Girls who had readymade winter skirts: "What material are most of your readymade winter skirts made of?" "What other materials are your readymade winter skirts made of?" "What material do you like best for winter skirts?"[1]

Material	Materials in winter skirt wardrobe	Material most winter skirts made of	Material preferred for winter skirts
	Percent	Percent	Percent
Wool--------------------------------------	93	85	75
Cotton------------------------------------	43	8	11
Wool-polyester---------------------------	9	3	4
Wool-acrylic-----------------------------	5	1	2
Wool-rayon/acetate-----------------------	3	1	1
Cotton-polyester-------------------------	3	1	1
Rayon/acetate----------------------------	3	(*)	(*)
Polyester--------------------------------	2	(*)	(*)
Other materials--------------------------	10	1	2
Unspecified------------------------------	4	(*)	(*)
No preference----------------------------	-	-	4
Not ascertained--------------------------	(*)	(*)	---
Number of cases--------------------------	1,671	1,671	1,671

[1] Percentages may add to more than 100 because some respondents named more than 1 material.
* Less than 1 percent.

ool-yester	Wool-acrylic	Wool-rayon/acetate	Cotton-poly-ester	Rayon/acetate	All other	Unspeci-fied	Cases
rcent	Percent	Percent	Percent	Percent	Percent	Percent	Number
9	5	3	3	3	13	4	1,671
9	4	2	3	3	11	3	512
10	5	3	4	2	14	4	400
9	6	4	3	3	13	4	449
11	7	3	2	3	14	5	310
7	4	3	3	4	12	2	593
11	7	4	3	2	14	5	646
9	6	1	3	3	13	3	426
8	4	2	3	3	15	4	557
11	7	4	4	2	13	4	727
9	5	3	3	5	11	3	387
6	2	2	1	3	11	3	439
10	6	2	2	4	15	5	450
9	5	3	4	3	12	3	554
15	10	4	7	1	14	3	228

some respondents named more than 1 material.

Vool	Cotton	Wool-polyester	All other	No preference	Cases
ercent	Percent	Percent	Percent	Percent	Number
75	11	4	6	4	1,671
72	15	3	5	5	512
73	12	4	7	4	400
78	8	5	6	3	449
77	7	5	8	3	310
66	20	3	7	4	593
78	. 7	5	6	4	646
83	4	4	6	3	426
81	8	3	4	4	557
74	10	4	8	4	727
68	16	6	6	4	387
84	7	3	3	3	439
79	7	4	7	3	450
66	20	5	7	2	554
70	6	7	9	8	228

Table 9.--Girls who had readymade winter skirts and said they liked certain materials best: "Why do you prefer (material liked best) for winter skirts?"[1]

Reasons for preference	Material liked best for winter skirts[2]		
	Wool	Cotton	Wool-polyester
	Percent	Percent	Percent
COMFORT AND WEIGHT	80	69	67
Warm	75	10	21
Doesn't irritate, scratch, itch	4	41	37
Doesn't cling, stick, bind	2	8	3
Wind resistant	2	--	--
Not too warm; lightweight, airy	1	19	13
Comfortable (general)	1	3	1
Lightweight but warm	1	2	4
Weight just right	(*)	3	3
Year-round weight	(*)	3	--
Miscellaneous	(*)	1	--
PERFORMANCE AND DURABILITY	47	22	60
Doesn't wrinkle	22	6	24
Doesn't soil, stain easily	13	5	13
Holds shape; doesn't shrink, stretch	13	3	19
Durable, wears well	8	6	4
Holds pleats, press	7	2	14
Holds colors; doesn't fade, run	2	3	--
Miscellaneous	2	3	6
APPEARANCE AND STYLING	46	24	37
Good colors, prints, patterns available	9	9	4
Fits, hangs well	9	5	10
Stylish, popular, fashionable	9	2	4
Variety of styles available	7	2	3
Goes well with other clothes	5	2	3
Looks nice, pretty (general)	3	3	6
Like texture (general)	3	2	4
Looks neat, fresh, crisp	3	2	3
Looks expensive	3	1	1
Dressier, more adult-looking	2	1	3
Good for everyday, casual wear	2	--	1
Versatile, can wear anywhere, for all occasions	1	--	1
Miscellaneous	4	2	--
CARE AND LAUNDERING	13	43	36
Can be drycleaned; no washing required	5	--	7
Easy to iron, press	3	21	11
Easy to wash and care for	2	16	6
Little or no ironing required	2	2	6
Washable; no drycleaning required	(*)	14	6
Machine washable	--	9	3
Dries quickly	--	2	--
Miscellaneous	2	1	4
OTHER:			
Inexpensive	(*)	5	1
All other	2	1	--
Not ascertained	(*)	--	--
Number of cases	1,252	183	70

[1] Percentages add to more than their group totals and these add to more than 100 because some respondents gave more than 1 answer.
[2] Numbers preferring other materials too small for separate analysis.
* Less than 1 percent.

Table 10.--Girls who had readymade winter skirts and said they liked certain materials best: "Is there anything that you don't like so well about (material liked best) for winter skirts?"[1]

Criticisms of preferred material	Material liked best for winter skirts[2]		
	Wool	Cotton	Wool-polyester
	Percent	Percent	Percent
COMFORT AND WEIGHT-----------------------	37	16	14
Irritates, scratches, itches------------	32	1	12
Clings, sticks, binds-------------------	4	1	1
Too warm, not cool enough---------------	3	1	--
Not warm enough-------------------------	(*)	13	--
Miscellaneous---------------------------	1	1	1
CARE AND LAUNDERING----------------------	16	2	6
Not washable, has to be drycleaned------	14	--	6
Hard to iron, has to be ironed----------	1	2	--
Miscellaneous---------------------------	1	(*)	--
PERFORMANCE AND DURABILITY---------------	15	10	9
Collects lint---------------------------	4	1	1
Doesn't hold shape; shrinks, stretches--	4	1	3
Soils, stains easily--------------------	3	--	3
Doesn't hold pleats, creases------------	1	3	1
Wrinkles easily-------------------------	1	5	1
Not colorfast; fades, runs--------------	(*)	2	--
Miscellaneous---------------------------	5	1	--
OTHER:			
Appearance and styling------------------	2	5	3
All other-------------------------------	1	1	--
Not ascertained-------------------------	1	3	3
NO CRITICISM OF MATERIAL-----------------	40	66	71
Number of cases-------------------------	1,252	183	70

[1] Percentages may add to more than their group totals and these may add to more than 100 because some respondents gave more than 1 answer.
[2] Numbers preferring other materials too small for separate analysis.
* Less than 1 percent.

41

Table 11.--Girls who had pleated winter skirts: "What materials are your
"permanently" pleated skirts made of?" "What materials are your other
pleated winter skirts made of?"[1]

Material	All pleated skirts	"Permanently" pleated skirts	Other (not specially processed) pleated skirts
	Percent	Percent	Percent
Wool------------------	85	81	68
Cotton----------------	21	6	25
Wool-polyester--------	9	9	5
Wool-acrylic----------	4	3	.3
Cotton-polyester------	3	2	3
Rayon/acetate---------	3	2	3
Wool-rayon/acetate----	2	2	2
Polyester-------------	2	1	2
Other fibers----------	5	2	5
Unspecified-----------	(*)	(*)	1
Not ascertained-------	3	2	2
Number of cases-------	1,478	940	1,089

[1] Percentages add to more than 100 because some respondents named more than
1 material.
  * Less than 1 percent.

	Percent	Percent	Percent	Percent	Number	Percent	Percent	Percent	Percent	Number
United States total-----	93	7	94	6	1 556	95	5	96	4	757
Age:										
14 years----------------	94	6	94	6	477	96	4	98	2	215
15 years----------------	94	6	95	5	370	97	3	97	3	202
16 years----------------	92	8	93	7	418	94	6	94	6	202
17 years----------------	93	7	93	7	291	94	6	96	4	138
Family income group:										
Lower-------------------	94	6	95	5	529	96	4	97	3	248
Middle------------------	92	8	92	8	614	95	5	95	5	290
Upper-------------------	94	6	94	6	407	95	5	96	4	215
Size of place:										
Urban metropolitan-----	93	7	93	7	519	95	5	95	5	226
Urban nonmetropolitan--	94	6	94	6	685	96	4	97	3	362
Town and farm----------	92	8	93	7	352	95	5	96	4	169
Region:										
Northeast--------------	92	8	92	8	419	94	6	94	6	170
North Central----------	93	7	93	7	427	96	4	97	3	233
South------------------	94	6	94	6	508	95	5	97	3	238
West-------------------	92	8	94	6	202	96	4	97	3	116

Table 13.--Girls who had readymade winter skirts (winter wool skirts, "permanently" pleated winter skirts, "permanently" pleated winter wool skirts) and said they thought that permanent pleating in wool skirts was a good idea: "Why do you say that?"[1]

Reasons for favorable opinion	Owners of winter skirts	Owners of winter wool skirts	Owners of "permanently" pleated winter skirts	Owners of "permanently" pleated winter wool skirts
	Percent	Percent	Percent	Percent
CARE AND LAUNDERING------------------	64	64	62	62
Little or no ironing required-------	36	36	35	36
Easy to iron, press-----------------	12	9	12	11
Saves money; less expensive to care for----------------------------	8	4	8	8
Washable; pleats stay in when washed-----------------------------	8	7	8	8
Easy to care for--------------------	4	12	4	4
Repleating unnecessary--------------	3	3	3	3
Miscellaneous-----------------------	1	1	2	2
PERFORMANCE AND DURABILITY-----------	52	52	56	56
Pleats, creases always stay in------	38	39	42	41
Wrinkle free; wouldn't crush--------	7	7	8	8
Less frequent cleaning--------------	3	2	3	3
Holds shape, doesn't get baggy------	2	2	2	2
Stays neater longer-----------------	2	3	1	1
Miscellaneous-----------------------	5	3	6	6
APPEARANCE--------------------------	15	15	16	18
Would look neater-------------------	5	5	5	5
Would look nicer, more attractive---	4	4	4	5
Fits better; pleats would hang better------------------------------	4	4	4	5
Miscellaneous-----------------------	3	3	4	4
OTHER:				
Just like them, no specific reason--	1	1	1	1
All other---------------------------	1	1	1	1
Number of cases---------------------	1,556	1,455	896	729

[1] Percentages add to more than their group totals and these add to more than 100 because some respondents gave more than 1 answer.

Table 14.--Girls who had readymade winter skirts (winter wool skirts) and said they thought that permanent pleating in wool skirts was not such a good idea: "Why do you say that?"[1]

Reasons for unfavorable opinion	Owners of winter skirts	Owners of winter wool skirts
	Percent	Percent
PERFORMANCE AND DURABILITY----------------------------	38	39
Pleats don't stay in, last long-----------------------	31	32
Wrinkles--	4	4
Weakens material; not durable-------------------------	3	2
Gets double creases when pressed----------------------	2	2
Miscellaneous---	--	--
APPEARANCE--	26	27
Don't like style in permanent pleated skirts--------	8	8
Don't like looks, appearance-------------------------	5	5
Looks artificial, stiff------------------------------	5	5
Doesn't fit, hang well-------------------------------	4	7
Miscellaneous--	6	7
CARE AND LAUNDERING----------------------------------	21	20
Have to be ironed anyway-----------------------------	11	10
Still have to be drycleaned--------------------------	4	5
Requires more care-----------------------------------	3	2
Miscellaneous--	4	4
OTHER:		
Don't like pleated skirts----------------------------	10	4
Hard to alter--	6	11
Don't like wool--------------------------------------	4	6
Expensive--	3	2
All other--	8	7
Not ascertained--------------------------------------	2	2
Number of cases--------------------------------------	115	101

[1] Number of owners of "permanently" pleated skirts who thought that permanent pleating was not a good idea was too small to permit separate analysis. Percentages add to more than their group totals and these add to more than 100 because some respondents gave more than 1 answer.

44

Table 15.--Girls who had readymade winter skirts (winter wool skirts): "...tell me how you would feel about permanent pleating in deciding whether to buy a pleated wool skirt. You can give a rating anywhere from "Most important" which is number 5 to "Not important at all" which is number 1. Which block number best tells how important permanent pleating would be to you in deciding whether or not to buy a particular pleated skirt made of wool?"

Background characteristics	Owners of winter skirts gave rating of--					
	5 (most important)	4	3	2	1 (not important at all)	Cases
	Percent	Percent	Percent	Percent	Percent	Number
United States total----------------	41	25	21	5	8	1,671
Age:						
14 years-------------------------	38	26	24	5	7	512
15 years-------------------------	39	30	21	4	6	400
16 years-------------------------	.45	21	22	4	8	449
17 years-------------------------	45	24	17	4	10	310
Family income group:						
Lower--------------------------	49	22	19	4	6	593
Middle-------------------------	37	26	24	5	8	646
Upper--------------------------	38	28	21	5	8	426
Size of place:						
Urban metropolitan-------------	41	26	19	7	7	557
Urban nonmetropolitan----------	40	25	24	3	8	727
Town and farm------------------	45	.24	19	4	8	387
Region:						
Northeast----------------------	40	25	19	6	10	439
North Central------------------	41	27	21	6	5	450
South--------------------------	43	24	23	3	7	.554
West---------------------------	40	26	22	3	9	228

Background characteristics	Owners of winter wool skirts gave rating of--					
	5 (most important)	4	3	2	1 (not important at all)	Cases
	Percent	Percent	Percent	Percent	Percent	Number
United States total----------------	41	26	21	5	7	1,556
Age:						
14 years-------------------------	38	26	24	5	7	477
15 years-------------------------	39	30	21	5	5	370
16 years-------------------------	45	22	22	4	7	418
17 years-------------------------	45	25	17	4	9	291
Family income group:						
Lower--------------------------	48	24	18	4	6	529
Middle-------------------------	38	25	24	6	7	614
Upper--------------------------	37	29	21	5	8	407
Size of place:						
Urban metropolitan-------------	41	26	19	8	6	519
Urban nonmetropolitan----------	40	25	24	3	8	685
Town and farm------------------	.45	26	19	3	7	352
Region:						
Northeast----------------------	42	25	19	6	8	419
North Central------------------	41	27	21	6	5	427
South--------------------------	42	25	23	3	7	508
West---------------------------	41	26	22	3	8	202

Table 16.--Girls who had readymade "permanently" pleated winter skirts ("permanently" pleated winter wool skirts): "...tell me how you would feel about permanent pleating in deciding whether to buy a pleated wool skirt. You can give a rating anywhere from "Most important" which is number 5 to "Not important at all" which is number 1. Which block number best tells how important permanent pleating would be to you in deciding whether or not to buy a particular pleated skirt made of wool?"

Background characteristics	Owners of "permanently" pleated winter skirts gave rating of--					
	5 (most important)	4	3	2	1 (not important at all)	Cases
	Percent	Percent	Percent	Percent	Percent	Number
United States total---------------	44	28	20	4	4	940
Age:						
14 years-------------------------	39	30	24	4	3	273
15 years-------------------------	40	36	18	3	3	234
16 years-------------------------	51	21	20	4	4	253
17 years-------------------------	51	25	14	4	6	180
Family income group:						
Lower----------------------------	54	26	16	2	2	317
Middle---------------------------	40	28	24	4	4	367
Upper----------------------------	38	32	20	4	6	251
Size of place:						
Urban metropolitan--------------	41	29	19	7	4	281
Urban nonmetropolitan-----------	44	27	23	2	4	443
Town and farm-------------------	50	30	15	2	3	216
Region:						
Northeast------------------------	39	30	22	4	5	201
North Central-------------------	47	29	17	5	2	284
South---------------------------	45	27	21	3	4	311
West----------------------------	46	28	21	1	4	144

Background characteristics	Owners of "permanently" pleated winter wool skirts gave rating of--					
	5 (most important)	4	3	2	1 (not important at all)	Cases
	Percent	Percent	Percent	Percent	Percent	Number
United States total---------------	43	30	20	4	3	757
Age:						
14 years-------------------------	37	33	25	3	2	215
15 years-------------------------	39	35	19	4	3	202
16 years-------------------------	51	23	19	3	4	202
17 years-------------------------	49	27	15	5	4	138
Family income group:						
Lower----------------------------	51	28	16	3	2	248
Middle---------------------------	40	28	24	4	4	290
Upper----------------------------	38	34	20	4	4	215
Size of place:						
Urban metropolitan--------------	41	28	20	8	3	226
Urban nonmetropolitan-----------	44	28	23	2	3	362
Town and farm-------------------	46	35	14	2	3	169
Region:						
Northeast------------------------	38	31	21	4	6	170
North Central-------------------	47	29	17	4	3	233
South---------------------------	43	29	21	4	3	238
West----------------------------	44	31	21	2	2	116

Table 17.--Girls who had readymade winter skirts gave a rating as to the importance of permanent pleating in the decision to buy a pleated wool skirt· "Why do you say that?"[1]

Reasons for rating of importance	5 (most important)	4	3	2	1 (not important at all)
	Percent	Percent	Percent	Percent	Percent
POSITIVE REASONS					
CARE AND LAUNDERING-----------------------	60	37	13	5	1
Little or no ironing required-------------	34	21	7	4	1
Saves money; less expensive to care for----	13	6	2	--	--
Washable; pleats stay in when washed-------	8	3	1	--	--
Easy to care for--------------------------	6	7	3	--	--
Easy to iron, press-----------------------	6	3	2	--	.--
Repleating unnecessary--------------------	3	1	(*)	--	--
Miscellaneous-----------------------------	1	1	--	1	--
PERFORMANCE AND DURABILITY------------------	52	32	8	4	1
Pleats, creases always stay in-------------	37	24	6	4	1
Wrinkle free, wouldn't crush--------------	8	4	2	--	1
Holds shape, doesn't get baggy-------------	3	2	--	--	--
Stays neater longer-----------------------	3	2	1	--	--
Less frequent cleaning required------------	3	2	(*)	--	--
Always ready to wear----------------------	2	1	(*)	--	--
Material more durable---------------------	2	1	(*)	--	--
Miscellaneous-----------------------------	2	1	--	--	--
APPEARANCE-------------------------------	19	14	3	--	--
Would look neater------------------------	7	5	1	--	--
Would look nicer, more attractive---------	4	3	(*)	--	--
Fits better, pleats would hang better------	4	3	1	--	--
Stylish, popular--------------------------	1	2	--	--	--
Miscellaneous-----------------------------	3	3	1	--	--
OTHER:					
Just like them; a good idea---------------	3	2	1	--	--
Would influence decision to buy-----------	(*)	2	1	1	--
All other--------------------------------	(*)	1	1	---	--
NEGATIVE REASONS					
APPEARANCE--------------------------------	--	1	3	5	19
Don't like looks, appearance--------------	--	--	(*)	--	3
Don't like the style----------------------	--	1	1	3	3
Don't fit, hang well----------------------	---	--	(*)	1	2
Looks artificial, stiff-------------------	--	(*)	(*)	--	2
Not stylish, popular----------------------	--	--	(*)	--	2
Miscellaneous-----------------------------	--	1	1	1	7
CARE AND LAUNDERING-----------------------	--	1	5	11	7
Have to be ironed, pressed anyway----------	--	1	3	7	3
Still have to be drycleaned---------------	--	1	1	4	2
Miscellaneous-----------------------------	--	--	1	--	2
PERFORMANCE AND DURABILITY------------------	--	(*)	3	7	6
OTHER FACTORS HAVE TO BE CONSIDERED----------	(*)	35	56	44	26
Style-------------------------------------	--	14	25	15	10
Fit---------------------------------------	--	3	8	9	5
Color, print, pattern---------------------	(*)	12	24	15	4
Looks-------------------------------------	--	3	6	9	4
Material----------------------------------	(*)	6	9	8	2
Cost--------------------------------------	--	2	2	3	2
Miscellaneous-----------------------------	--	11	17	11	12
OTHER:					
Don't like pleated skirts-----------------	--	1	3	8	18
Don't like wool---------------------------	(*)	(*)	1	3	12
Don't care for own clothes----------------	--	--	2	1	3
Hard to alter----------------------------	--	1	1	--	3
Costs too much---------------------------	--	(*)	1	1	2
Just not important-----------------------	--	--	6	8	4
Just don't like the idea (general)--------	--	--	--	3	2
All other--------------------------------	(*)	1	1	7	6
Not ascertained--------------------------	(*)	1	2	4	2
Number of cases[2]----------------------------	697	420	351	76	126

[1] Percentages may add to more than their group totals and these may add to more than 100 because some respondents gave more than 1 answer.
[2] 1 respondent did not answer.
*Less than 1 percent.

Table 18.--Girls who had readymade winter blouses: "What material are <u>most</u> them (winter blouses) made of?" "What other materials are your winter blouses made of?" "What material do you like <u>best</u> for winter blouses?"

Material	Materials in winter blouse wardrobe	Material most winter blouses made of	Materia preferi for win blouse
	Percent	Percent	Perce
Cotton-------------------------	95	87	7
Cotton-polyester---------------	24	7	1
Polyester----------------------	13	2	
Silk---------------------------	10	(*)	
Rayon/acetate------------------	9	1	
Nylon--------------------------	8	1	
Wool---------------------------	5	1	
Acrylic------------------------	5	(*)	
Other materials----------------	5	1	
Unspecified--------------------	1	--	(*)
No preference------------------		--	
Not ascertained----------------	--	(*)	
Number of cases----------------			

[1] Percentages may add to more than 100 because some respondents named m than 1 material.
*Less than 1 percent.

Background characteristics	Cotton	Cotton-polyester	Polyester	Silk	Rayon/acetate	Nylon	Wool	Acryl
	Percent	Percent	Percent	Percent	Percent	Percent	Percent	Percen
United States total----	95	24	13	10	9	8	5	5
Age:								
14 years-------------	96	22	11	10	9	8	6	5
15 years-------------	95	21	11	7	9	10	4	6
16 years-------------	95	26	14	11	8	6	4	5
17 years-------------	96	27	15	10	11	8	6	3
Family income group:								
Lower----------------	96	13	12	8	8	9	5	5
Middle---------------.	95	28	10	10	9	8	5	4
Upper----------------	96	32	17	11	8	8	4	5
Size of place:								
Urban metropolitan---	95	24	15	14	10	12	7	4
Urban nonmetropolitan	96	26	12	9	8	6	4	5
Town and farm-------	95	19	10	5	9	6	4	5
Region:								
Northeast------------	97	24	16	14	10	10	6	4
North Central--------	96	28	15	8	7	9	3	5
South----------------	96	22	10	8	9	6	6	4
West-----------------	91	21	8	9	9	8	5	8

[1] Percentages add to more than 100 because some respondents named more than 1 material.

Background characteristics	Cotton	Cotton-polyester	Polyester	All other	N pref
	Percent	Percent	Percent	Percent	Per
United States total-------------------------	74	11	3	6	
Age:					
14 years-----------------------------------	76	8	3	6	
15 years-----------------------------------	75	10	2	6	
16 years-----------------------------------	73	14	4	5	
17 years-----------------------------------	71	14	6	5	
Family income group:					
Lower--------------------------------------	77	4	4	8	
Middle-------------------------------------	74	14	2	5	
Upper--------------------------------------	70	17	4	3	
Size of place:					
Urban metropolitan-------------------------	70	11	3	7	
Urban nonmetropolitan----------------------	76	12	4	4	
Town and farm------------------------------	76	10	4	5	
Region:					
Northeast----------------------------------	73	10	3	6	
North Central------------------------------	73	15	5	2	
South--------------------------------------	76	10	3	7	
West---------------------------------------	73	8	4	6	

Table 21.--Girls who had readymade winter blouses and said they liked certain materials best: "Why do you prefer (material liked best) for winter blouses?"[1]

Reasons for preference	Material liked best for winter blouses[2]	
	Cotton	Cotton-polyester
	Percent	Percent
CARE AND LAUNDERING-------------------------------------	62	76
Easy to iron, press---------------------------------	39	49
Easy to wash and care for---------------------------	24	17
Machine washable------------------------------------	12	4
Washable; no drycleaning required-------------------	6	1
Easy to starch--------------------------------------	5	2
Good appearance after laundering--------------------	4	3
Little or no ironing required-----------------------	3	22
Requires no starch----------------------------------	2	12
Dries quickly---------------------------------------	1	3
Miscellaneous---------------------------------------	2	1
COMFORT AND WEIGHT-------------------------------------	44	35
Doesn't irritate, scratch, itch---------------------	12	15
Not too warm; lightweight, airy---------------------	12	6
Warm--	11	6
Doesn't cling, stick, bind--------------------------	7	3
Year-round weight-----------------------------------	4	4
Comfortable (general)-------------------------------	3	3
Weight just right-----------------------------------	2	1
Miscellaneous---------------------------------------	1	1
APPEARANCE AND STYLING---------------------------------	36	26
Looks neat, fresh, crisp----------------------------	7	5
Goes well with other clothes------------------------	7	4
Variety of styles available-------------------------	7	3
Fits, hangs well------------------------------------	6	4
Good colors, prints, patterns available-------------	5	1
Stylish, popular, fashionable-----------------------	4	1
Looks nice, pretty (general)------------------------	3	3
Like texture (general)------------------------------	1	2
Dressier; more adult-looking------------------------	1	2
Looks expensive-------------------------------------	(*)	3
Miscellaneous---------------------------------------	4	2
PERFORMANCE AND DURABILITY-----------------------------	26	57
Doesn't wrinkle-------------------------------------	10	38
Durable, wears well---------------------------------	6	4
Holds colors; doesn't fade, run---------------------	5	4
Holds shape; doesn't shrink, stretch----------------	5	3
Doesn't soil, stain easily--------------------------	3	7
Miscellaneous---------------------------------------	4	3
OTHER:		
Inexpensive---	3	--
All other---	2	1
Not ascertained-------------------------------------	1	1
Number of cases-------------------------------------	1,232	188

[1] Percentages add to more than their group totals and these add to more than 100 because some respondents gave more than 1 answer.
[2] Numbers preferring other materials too small for separate analysis.
* Less than 1 percent.

o had readymade winter blouses and said they liked certain
. "Is there anything that you don't like so well about
l best) for winter blouses?"[1]

| ns of preferred material | Material liked best for winter blouses[2] | |
	Cotton	Cotton-polyester
	Percent	Percent
RABILITY-----------------------	18	15
------------------------------	12	4
yellow, gray-------------------	2	6
sily---------------------------	2	1
l-----------------------------	1	2
------------------------------	3	3
G-----------------------------	7	7
------------------------------	3	4
------------------------------	2·	2
------------------------------	2	1
------------------------------	5	5
tyling------------------------	2	2
------------------------------	--	2
------------------------------	1	1
------------------------------	1	1
TERIAL------------------------	69	73
------------------------------	1,232	188

y add to more than their group totals and these may add to more
ome respondents gave more than 1 answer.
ring other materials too small for separate analysis.

de winter dresses: "Do you get some of your winter dresses for everyday wear
cial occasions, or do you get the same kind for both everyday and dress-up

	Different dresses for each	Same dresses for both	Have only everyday dresses	Have only dress-up dresses	Cases
	Percent	Percent	Percent	Percent	Number
-	60	24	2	14	1,288
-	59	27	1	13	383
-	58	27	1	14	297
-	63	23	1	13	357
-	62	16	3	19	251
-	57	29	2	12	446
-	60	24	1	15	483
-	64	19	1	16	355
-	63	19	1	17	452
-	61	25	(*)	14	551
-	54	29	4	13	285
-	65	20	1	14	359
-	55	23	1	21	330
-	61	26	2	11	444
-	58	27	3	12	155

51

Table 24.--Girls who had readymade everyday winter dresses: "....tell me what material most of your everyday winter dresses are made of?" "What other materials are your everyday winter dresses made of?" "What material do you like best for everyday winter dresses?"[1]

Material	Materials in everyday winter dress wardrobe	Material most everyday winter dresses made of	Material preferred for everyday winter dresses
	Percent	Percent	Percent
Cotton-----------------------	71	51	46
Wool-------------------------	56	36	31
Wool-polyester----------------	7	4	2
Cotton-polyester--------------	7	3	4
Rayon/acetate-----------------	5	2	1
Wool-acrylic------------------	4	2	1
Polyester--------------------	3	1	1
Silk-------------------------	3	(*)	(*)
Wool-rayon/acetate------------	2	1	1
Other materials--------------	9	(*)	3
Unspecified------------------	3	(*)	(*)
No preference----------------	---	---	10
Not ascertained--------------	(*)	(*)	(*)
Number of cases--------------			

[1] Percentages may add to more than 100 because some respondents named more than 1 material.
*Less than 1 percent.

Table 25.--Girls who had readymade everyday winter dresses: Material in everyday winter dresses[1]

Background characteristics	Cotton	Wool	Wool-polyester	Cotton-polyester	Rayon/acetate	Other wool mixtures	All other	Not ascertained	Cases
	Percent	Percent	Percent	Percent	Percent	Percent	Percent	Percent	Number
States total-----	71	56	7	7	5	5	16	(*)	1,101
ars-------------	77	50	5	7	4	4	16	(*)	332
ars-------------	74	49	8	5	4	3	13	(*)	255
ars-------------	67	65	7	7	6	6	17	(*)	311
ars-------------	67	60	8	8	5	9	13	---	203
income group:									
-----------------	80	47	6	4	6	6	16	---	393
e----------------	60	58	8	8	6	6	16	(*)	409
-----------------	67	65	6	8	2	4	17	(*)	295
place:									
a metropolitan----	60	72	7	6	6	5	20	(*)	377
n nonmetropolitan-	75	53	8	9	4	5	15	(*)	475
and farm--------	81	38	3	5	5	7	13	(*)	249
:									
heast-------------	60	72	5	3	5	4	21	1	309
h Central--------	68	58	7	6	5	7	13	(*)	260
h----------------	84	44	6	8	5	5	14	---	396
-----------------	68	49	12	15	5	7	17	---	136

rcentages add to more than 100 because some respondents named more than 1 material.
is than 1 percent.

Table 26.--Girls who had readymade everyday winter dresses: Material preferred for everyday winter dresses

Background characteristics	Cotton	Wool	Wool mixtures	Cotton-polyester	All other	No preference	Not ascertained	Cases
	Percent	Percent	Percent	Percent	Percent	Percent	Percent	Number
i States total-----	46	31	4	4	5	10	(*)	1,101
years-------------	52	25	2	3	5	13	(*)	332
years-------------	51	30	5	4	3	6	1	255
years-------------	39	35	6	3	5	12	(*)	311
years-------------	41	36	7	5	4	7	---	203
y income group:								
er----------------	56	24	4	2	5	9	---	393
ile---------------	40	33	6	5	5	11	(*)	409
er----------------	42	37	3	4	3	10	1	295
of place:								
an metropolitan----	30	47	6	2	5	10	(*)	377
an nonmetropolitan-	50	26	4	5	4	11	(*)	475
n and farm--------	62	16	4	4	5	8	1	249
n:								
theast-------------	30	46	6	2	4	11	1	309
th Central--------	44	34	6	3	6	7	(*)	260
th----------------	62	20	3	5	3	7	---	396
t-----------------	39	22	5	6	5	23	---	136

ss than 1 percent.

53

Table 27.--Girls who had everyday winter dresses, and said they liked certain materials best: "Why do you prefer (material liked best) for everyday winter dresses?"[1]

Reasons for preference	Material liked best for everyday winter dresses[2]	
	Cotton	Wool
	Percent	Percent
CARE AND LAUNDERING------------------------------------	57	9
Easy to iron, press---------------------------------	28	1
Easy to wash and care for---------------------------	20	1
Washable; no drycleaning required-------------------	17	1
Machine washable------------------------------------	14	--
Easy to starch--------------------------------------	2	--
Little or no ironing required-----------------------	1	3
Can be drycleaned; no washing required--------------	--	4
Miscellaneous---------------------------------------	4	1
COMFORT AND WEIGHT-------------------------------------	48	76
Doesn't irritate, scratch, itch---------------------	20	4
Not too warm; lightweight, airy---------------------	16	2
Warm---	8	70
Doesn't cling, stick, bind--------------------------	6	1
Weight just right-----------------------------------	5	2
Year-round weight-----------------------------------	2	--
Miscellaneous---------------------------------------	3	3
APPEARANCE AND STYLING---------------------------------	27	41
Variety of styles available-------------------------	5	9
Good colors, prints, patterns available-------------	5	3
Fits, hangs well------------------------------------	4	10
Stylish, popular, fashionable-----------------------	4	7
Looks neat, fresh, crisp----------------------------	3	3
Looks nice, pretty (general)------------------------	3	2
Good for everyday, casual wear----------------------	2	3
Versatile; can wear anywhere, for all occasions-----	2	2
Dressier; more adult-looking------------------------	1	6
Like texture (general)------------------------------	1	3
Miscellaneous---------------------------------------	1	7
PERFORMANCE AND DURABILITY-----------------------------	21	38
Doesn't wrinkle-------------------------------------	6	21
Holds colors; doesn't fade, run---------------------	5	2
Doesn't soil, stain easily--------------------------	4	9
Holds shape; doesn't shrink, stretch----------------	4	8
Durable, wears well---------------------------------	3	7
Miscellaneous---------------------------------------	1	1
OTHER:		
Inexpensive---	6	--
All other---	2	1
Not ascertained-------------------------------------	1	1
Number of cases-------------------------------------	508	341

[1] Percentages add to more than their group totals and these add to more than 100 because some respondents gave more than 1 answer.
[2] Numbers preferring other materials too small for separate analysis.

54

yday winter dresses and said they like certain
e anything that you don't like so well about
everyday winter dresses?"[1]

erred material	Material liked best for everyday winter dresses[2]	
	Cotton	Wool
	Percent	Percent
----------------------	19	10
----------------------	12	1
----------------------	3	(*)
----------------------	1	4
3, stretches----------	1	2
----------------------	(*)	2
----------------------	2	2
----------------------	12	28
----------------------	11	--
----------------------	(*)	5
es--------------------	(*)	21
----------------------	(*)	2
----------------------	--	3
----------------------	1	(*)
----------------------	3	14
oned------------------	3	1
ycleaned--------------	(*)	14
----------------------	2	1
----------------------	(*)	1
----------------------	(*)	--
----------------------	66	50
----------------------	506	341

ore than their group totals and these add to more
dents gave more than 1 answer.
materials too small for separate analysis.

Table 29.--Girls who had winter outer jackets or short coats: "What materials are your outer jackets or short coats made of?" "What material do you like best for outer jackets or short coats?"[1]

Material	Materials in outer jacket or short coat wardrobe	Material preferred for outer jackets or short coats
	Percent	Percent
Wool---	46	37
Cotton---	33	19
Suede, leather-----------------------------------	16	13
Nylon--	6	3
Cotton-polyester---------------------------------	5	3
Plastic--	5	2
Wool-cotton--------------------------------------	3	2
Acrylic--	2	1
Other wool mixtures------------------------------	4	3
Other materials----------------------------------	8	4
Unspecified--------------------------------------	3	1
No preference------------------------------------	--	11
Not ascertained----------------------------------	3	1
Number of cases----------------------------------	1,416	1,416

[1] Percentages may add to more than 100 because some respondents named more than 1 material.

d winter outer jackets or short coats: Materials in winter outer jackets or short coats[1]

1,416

427
347
382
260

486
561
365

468
619
329

378
383
478
177

100 because some respondents named more than 1 material.

inter outer jackets or short coats: Material preferred for winter outer jackets or short coats

.1	Cotton	Suede, leather	Wool mixtures	Nylon	Cotton-polyester	All other	No preference	Not ascertained	Cases
ent	Percent	Percent	Percent	Percent	Percent	Percent	Percent	Percent	Number
7	19	13	5	3	3	8	11	1	1,416
5	19	11	5	5	3	6	14	1	427
7	17	13	6	4	4	8	10	1	347
7	23	14	3	2	2	9	10	(*)	382
0	15	17	4	2	1	14	7	--	260
4	22	15	5	2	3	9	9	1	486
0	16	13	4	3	3	8	12	1	561
9	19	12	3	5	2	9	11	(*)	365
4	14	13	3	3	2	9	12	(*)	468
4	20	14	4	4	3	8	12	1	619
7	24	13	6	2	3	9	5	1	329
1	10	12	4	4	1	7	11	(*)	378
1	20	11	3	4	2	8	11	(*)	383
8	23	19	5	1	4	10	9	1	478
7	20	9	8	5	5	11	14	1	177

Table 32.--Girls who had winter outer jackets or short coats and said they liked certain materials best: "Why do you prefer (material liked best) for winter outer jackets or short coats?"[1]

Reasons for preference	Material liked best for winter outer jackets or short coats[2]		
	Wool	Cotton	Suede, leather
	Percent	Percent	Percent
COMFORT AND WEIGHT----------------------------------	89	69	61
Warm--	83	25	35
Wind resistant-----------------------------------	5	2	12
Lightweight, but warm----------------------------	3	14	7
Water repellent----------------------------------	3	7	9
Doesn't irritate, scratch, itch-----------------	2	11	9
Not too warm; lightweight, airy-----------------	1	16	3
Doesn't cling, stick, bind----------------------	1	4	2
Weight just right-------------------------------	--	4	2
Year-round weight-------------------------------	--	2	1
Miscellaneous-----------------------------------	2	(*)	2
PERFORMANCE AND DURABILITY--------------------------	35	29	47
Doesn't soil, stain easily----------------------	12	9	32
Durable, wears well-----------------------------	10	8	11
Doesn't wrinkle---------------------------------	10	5	4
Holds shape; doesn't shrink, stretch------------	7	5	3
Holds colors; doesn't fade, run----------------	2	2	--
Miscellaneous-----------------------------------	3	6	4
APPEARANCE AND STYLING------------------------------	27	34	52
Stylish, popular, fashionable-------------------	5	8	16
Variety of styles available---------------------	5	7	3
Good colors, prints, patterns available--------	5	3	1
Looks nice, pretty (general)--------------------	3	3	5
Looks expensive---------------------------------	3	2	8
Goes well with other clothes--------------------	2	3	4
Fits, hangs well--------------------------------	2	3	4
Versatile; can wear anywhere, for all occasions-----	2	2	5
Dressier, more adult-looking--------------------	2	2	4
Like texture (general)--------------------------	2	2	3
Good for everyday, casual wear------------------	1	5	5
Looks neat, fresh, crisp------------------------	(*)	2	3
Miscellaneous-----------------------------------	1	2	3
CARE AND LAUNDERING---------------------------------	5	26	11
Washable; no drycleaning required---------------	1	12	4
Easy to wash and care for-----------------------	1	5	3
Dries quickly-----------------------------------	(*)	2	1
Little or no ironing required-------------------	(*)	2	--
Good appearance after laundering----------------	(*)	2	--
Machine washable--------------------------------	--	5	1
Easy to iron, press-----------------------------	--	2	--
Miscellaneous-----------------------------------	3	3	3
OTHER:			
Inexpensive-------------------------------------	(*)	2	1
All other---------------------------------------	--	--	2
Not ascertained---------------------------------	--	(*)	--
Number of cases---------------------------------	530	265	189

[1] Percentages add to more than their group totals and these add to more than 100 because some respondents gave more than 1 answer.

[2] Numbers preferring other materials too small for separate analysis.

* Less than 1 percent.

r outer jackets or short coats and said they liked
s there anything that you don't like so well about
inter outer jackets or short coats?"[1]

	Material liked best for winter outer jackets or short coats[2]		
	Wool	Cotton	Suede, leather
	Percent	Percent	Percent
.-	17	11	6
;-	9	---	---
.-	5	1	2
.-	2	(*)	2
.-	1	1	1
.-	(*)	8	2
.-	1	1	1
--	13	24	37
--	5	10	18
--	4	1	---
--	2	---	---
--	1	4	2
--	1	2	5
--	(*)	4	3
--	(*)	2	---
ay	---	(*)	2
--	3	3	12
--	7	3	7
--	2	2	3
--	1	---	5
--	(*)	3	6
--	1	2	1
--	64	60	46
--	530	265	189

re than their group totals and these may add to
spondents gave more than 1 answer
naterials too small for separate analysis.

Table 34.--All girls were asked: "Are most of your readymade summer clothes dresses, or blouse and skirt combinations?"

Background characteristics	Mostly combinations	Only combinations	About even	Mostly dresses	Only dresses	No summer readymades	Cases
	Percent	Percent	Percent	Percent	Percent	Percent	Number
United States total----	45	10	15	25	5	(*)	1,691
Age:							
14 years-------------	50	11	13	23	3	--	519
15 years-------------	45	9	17	24	4	1	405
16 years-------------	41	10	15	28	5	1	454
17 years-------------	41	9	16	27	7	--	313
Family income group:							
Lower----------------	43	10	13	28	6	(*)	601
Middle---------------	46	12	14	24	4	(*)	656
Upper----------------	45	7	20	24	4	(*)	428
Size of place:							
Urban metropolitan---	54	8	18	17	3	--	561
Urban nonmetropolitan	43	10	15	27	5	(*)	734
Town and farm--------	36	12	13	33	6	(*)	396
Region:							
Northeast------------	59	7	17	15	2	--	441
North Central--------	46	12	15	24	3	(*)	456
South---------------	35	8	16	34	7	(*)	564
West----------------	37	15	12	27	9	(*)	230

* Less than 1 percent.

Table 35.--Girls who had readymade summer skirts: "What material are most of your readymade summer skirts made of?" "What other materials are your readymade summer skirts made of?" "What material do you like best for summer skirts?"[1]

Material	Materials in summer skirt wardrobe	Material most summer skirts made of	Material preferred for summer skirts
	Percent	Percent	Percent
Cotton------------------------	95	88	74
Cotton-polyester--------------	17	6	9
Rayon/acetate-----------------	17	1	5
Polyester--------------------	8	1	1
Linen------------------------	5	(*)	1
Nylon------------------------	4	1	1
Cotton-rayon/acetate----------	4	1	1
Silk-------------------------	3	(*)	(*)
Other materials--------------	5	2	1
Unspecified------------------	1	(*)	(*)
No preference----------------	--	--	7
Not ascertained--------------	(*)	(*)	--
Number of cases--------------	1,605	1,605	1,605

[1] Percentages may add to more than 100 because some respondents named more than 1 material.
* Less than 1 percent.

60

ɔtton-ɔoly-ɛster	Rayon/acetate	Poly-ester	Linen	Nylon	Cotton-rayon/acetate	Silk	All other	Cases
ɛrcent	Percent	Percent	Percent	Percent	Percent	Percent	Percent	Number
17	17	8	5	4	4	3	6	1,605
15	16	9	4	5	3	3	5	501
16	14	5	6	4	3	4	9	384
18	20	8	6	3	4	3	4	428
20	19	7	7	3	5	3	8	292
12	14	7	4	5	3	5	7	560
19	18	8	7	4	3	3	6	628
21	20	9	6	3	5	2	6	411
18	24	13	6	7	4	3	6	540
19	15	6	5	2	3	4	6	694
13	11	4	5	3	4	3	6	371
17	24	13	7	6	3	2	5	432
18	15	5	5	2	3	3	7	440
17	13	6	5	4	3	5	6	524
17	18	6	5	4	6	3	10	209

00 because some respondents named more than 1 material.

had readymade summer skirts: Material preferred for summer skirts

	Cotton	Cotton-polyester	Rayon/acetate	All other	No preference	Cases
	Percent	Percent	Percent	Percent	Percent	Number
-------	74	9	5	5	7	1,605
-------	71	7	6	7	9	501
-------	77	9	4	5	5	384
-------	74	9	6	4	7	428
-------	73	10	5	5	7	292
-------	78	5	4	7	6	560
-------	73	10	5	5	7	628
-------	69	11	6	6	8	411
-------	67	9	7	6	11	540
-------	75	9	5	6	5	694
-------	82	6	2	5	5	371
-------	64	7	9	7	13	432
-------	81	9	4	4	2	440
-------	77	9	3	6	5	524
-------.	69	10	6	5	10	209

Table 38.--Girls who had readymade summer skirts and said they liked certain materials best:
"Why do you prefer (material liked best) for summer skirts?"[1]

Reasons for preference	Material liked best for summer skirts[2]		
	Cotton	Cotton-polyester	Rayon/acetate
	Percent	Percent	Percent
COMFORT AND WEIGHT-----------------------------------	68	44	50
Cool, lightweight, airy------------------------------	62	33	38
Doesn't cling, stick, bind---------------------------	10	9	8
Doesn't irritate, scratch, itch---------------------	4	9	6
Weight just right-----------------------------------	1	3	--
Miscellaneous---------------------------------------	1	1	1
CARE AND LAUNDERING---------------------------------	67	63	53
Easy to iron, press--------------------------------	39	32	21
Easy to wash and care for--------------------------	26	25	13
Machine washable-----------------------------------	18	6	6
Washable; doesn't have to be drycleaned------------	9	2	7
Easy to starch-------------------------------------	5	1	--
Little or no ironing required----------------------	4	20	20
Good appearance after laundering-------------------	4	2	--
Dries quickly--------------------------------------	3	7	6
Requires no starch---------------------------------	1	6	--
Miscellaneous--------------------------------------	1	--	--
APPEARANCE AND STYLING-----------------------------	22	17	25
Good colors, prints, patterns available-----------	8	1	4
Variety of styles available-----------------------	6	4	2
Stylish, popular, fashionable---------------------	3	4	1
Looks neat, fresh, crisp--------------------------	3	3	4
Fits, hangs well----------------------------------	2	3	9
Looks nice, pretty (general)----------------------	2	1	4
Like texture (general)----------------------------	1	2	--
Miscellaneous-------------------------------------	3	2	4
PERFORMANCE AND DURABILITY-------------------------	21	59	64
Doesn't wrinkle-----------------------------------	7	44	40
Holds colors; doesn't fade, run-------------------	6	4	1
Holds shape; doesn't shrink, stretch--------------	4	9	6
Durable, wears well-------------------------------	4	4	5
Doesn't soil, stain easily------------------------	2	4	9
Holds pleats, press-------------------------------	1	7	16
Miscellaneous-------------------------------------	1	2	--
OTHER:			
Inexpensive---------------------------------------	5	3	1
All other---	1	1	--
Not ascertained-----------------------------------	1	--	--
Number of cases-----------------------------------	1,183	138	80

[1] Percentages add to more than their group totals and these add to more than 100 because some respondents gave more than 1 answer.
[2] Numbers preferring other materials too small for separate analysis.

eadymade summer skirts and said they liked certain materials best: "Is there
don't like so well about (material liked best) for summer skirts?"[1]

preferred material	Material liked best for summer skirts[2]		
	Cotton	Cotton-polyester	Rayon/acetate
	Percent	Percent	Percent
	34	17	14
-------------------------------	27	8	9
-------------------------------	4	2	4
-------------------------------	3	1	--
-------------------------------	2	1	--
ray---------------------------	(*)	2	--
-------------------------------	3	4	1
-------------------------------	6	11	7
-------------------------------	3	1	1
-------------------------------	2	6	1
-------------------------------	1	3	2
-------------------------------	1	1	3
-------------------------------	2	4	6
-------------------------------	1	2	2
-------------------------------	1	1	4
-------------------------------	4	1	--
-------------------------------	1	3	1
-------------------------------	(*)	1	1
-------------------------------	1	--	1
-------------------------------	59	68	71
-------------------------------	1,183	138	80

more than their group totals and these may add to more than 100 because some
answer.
r materials too small for separate analysis.

adymade summer blouses: "What material are most of your summer blouses made
ials are your summer blouses made of?" "What material do you like best for

aterial	Materials in summer blouse wardrobe	Material most summer blouses made of	Material preferred for summer blouses
	Percent	Percent	Percent
-------------------------------	95	85	68
-------------------------------	24	8	13
-------------------------------	14	1	2
-------------------------------	12	2	4
-------------------------------	11	1	2
-------------------------------	9	2	2
-------------------------------	2	1	1
-------------------------------	2	(*)	1
-------------------------------	2	(*)	(*)
-------------------------------	2	(*)	(*)
-------------------------------	1	(*)	(*)
-------------------------------	(*)	--	(*)
-------------------------------	--	--	7
-------------------------------	--	--	--
-------------------------------	1,645	1,645	1,645

more than 100 because some respondents named more than 1 material.

Table 41.--Girls who had readymade summer blouses: Materials in summer blouses[1]

Background characteristics	Cotton	Cotton-polyester	Nylon	Polyester	Silk	Rayon/acetate	Other cotton mixtures	All other	Cases
	Percent	Percent	Percent	Percent	Percent	Percent	Percent	Percent	Number
United States total------	95	24	14	12	11	9	3	5	1,645
Age:									
14 years---------------	95	22	15	12	10	9	3	4	507
15 years---------------	95	26	14	8	12	8	3	6	392
16 years---------------	95	24	11	13	10	8	3	5	440
17 years---------------	95	25	15	15	10	10	4	7	306
Family income group:									
Lower------------------	95	16	19	11	13	9	3	5	574
Middle-----------------	95	27	11	11	10	9	4	5	648
Upper------------------	96	32	9	15	8	8	4	5	417
Size of place:									
Urban metropolitan-----	96	25	16	16	13	11	2	6	546
Urban nonmetropolitan--	96	27	12	11	10	8	4	5	716
Town and farm----------	95	17	14	8	8	7	4	5	383
Region:									
Northeast--------------	97	25	16	17	12	10	3	4	436
North Central----------	96	28	10	13	10	6	3	4	452
South------------------	95	23	15	9	11	9	4	5	540
West-------------------	93	19	12	8	9	11	4	10	217

[1] Percentages add to more than 100 because some respondents named more than 1 material.

Table 42.--Girls who had readymade summer blouses: Material preferred for summer blouses

Background characteristics	Cotton	Cotton-polyester	Polyester	Silk	Nylon	All other	No preference	Cases
	Percent	Percent	Percent	Percent	Percent	Percent	Percent	Number
United States total------	68	13	4	2	2	4	7	1,645
Age:								
14 years---------------	69	11	4	3	2	3	8	507
15 years---------------	69	14	3	1	2	3	8	392
16 years---------------	67	14	4	3	1	5	6	440
17 years---------------	66	14	7	2	3	3	5	306
Family income group:								
Lower------------------	70	9	3	3	3	4	8	574
Middle-----------------	69	15	4	1	1	3	7	648
Upper------------------	62	18	6	3	1	3	7	417
Size of place:								
Urban metropolitan-----	61	14	6	2	2	4	11	546
Urban nonmetropolitan--	68	14	4	2	2	3	7	716
Town and farm----------	75	11	2	2	3	4	3	383
Region:								
Northeast--------------	64	12	6	3	1	3	11	436
North Central----------	69	17	5	1	1	2	5	452
South------------------	71	13	2	2	3	4	5	540
West-------------------	66	11	2	2	3	5	11	217

Table 43.--Girls who had readymade summer blouses and said they liked certain materials best: "Why do you prefer (material liked best) for summer blouses?"[1]

Reasons for preference	Material liked best for summer blouses[2]	
	Cotton	Cotton-polyester
	Percent	Percent
COMFORT AND WEIGHT--------------------------------------	66	55
Cool, lightweight, airy-----------------------------	59	42
Doesn't cling, stick, bind--------------------------	9	4
Doesn't irritate, scratch, itch--------------------	5	12
Year-round weight----------------------------------	2	2
Miscellaneous--------------------------------------	·6	1
CARE AND LAUNDERING------------------------------------	62	75
Easy to iron, press--------------------------------	34	38
Easy to wash and care for--------------------------	29	22
Machine washable-----------------------------------	15	6
Washable; no drycleaning required------------------	6	1
Little or no ironing required----------------------	5	31
Easy to starch-------------------------------------	3	1
Good appearance after laundering-------------------	3	1
Dries quickly--------------------------------------	2	10
Requires no starch---------------------------------	1	10
Miscellaneous--------------------------------------	2	1
APPEARANCE AND STYLING---------------------------------	28	21
Variety of styles available------------------------	7	4
Looks neat, fresh, crisp---------------------------	6	6
Good colors, prints, patterns available-----------	6	2
Goes well with other clothes-----------------------	4	2
Fits, hangs well-----------------------------------	3	3
Looks nice, pretty (general)-----------------------	2	1
Stylish, fashionable, popular----------------------	2	1
Looks expensive------------------------------------	(*)	2
Miscellaneous--------------------------------------	4	2
PERFORMANCE AND DURABILITY-----------------------------	21	48
Doesn't wrinkle------------------------------------	6	34
Durable, wears well--------------------------------	5	5
Holds colors; doesn't fade, run-------------------	4	4
Doesn't soil, stain easily-------------------------	3	4
Holds shape; doesn't shrink, stretch--------------	3	3
Miscellaneous--------------------------------------	1	1
OTHER:		
Inexpensive--	5	1
All other--	2	1
Not ascertained-----------------------------------	(*)	---
Number of cases------------------------------------	1,109	219

[1] Percentages add to more than their group totals and these add to more than 100 because some respondents gave more than 1 answer.
[2] Numbers preferring other materials too small for separate analysis.
*Less than 1 percent.

Table 44.--Girls who had readymade summer blouses and said they like certain materials best: "Is there anything that you don't like so well about (material liked best) for summer blouses?"[1]

Criticisms of preferred material	Material liked best for summer blouses[2]	
	Cotton	Cotton-polyester
	Percent	Percent
PERFORMANCE AND DURABILITY---------------------	20	12
Wrinkles easily-----------------------------	14	2
Not colorfast; fades, runs-------------------	2	1
Soils, stains easily-------------------------	2	2
Discolors; turns yellow, gray----------------	1	6
Doesn't wear well---------------------------	1	1
Balls up, fuzzes, sheds----------------------	(*)	2
Miscellaneous-------------------------------	2	1
CARE AND LAUNDERING---------------------------	7	7
Has to be ironed----------------------------	3	--
Hard to iron--------------------------------	2	5
Miscellaneous-------------------------------	2	2
OTHER:		
Not cool enough, clings, irritates-----------	3	4
All other-----------------------------------	1	3
Not ascertained-----------------------------	1	--
NO CRITICISM OF MATERIAL----------------------	71	76
Number of cases------------------------------	1,109	219

[1] Percentages may add to more than their group totals and these add to more than 100 because some respondents gave more than 1 answer.
[2] Numbers preferring other materials too small for separate analysis.
* Less than 1 percent.

66

e summer dresses: "Do you get some of your summer dresses for
Sunday or special occasions, or do you get the same kind for both

Have onl;
everyday
dresses

Percent	Percent	Percent	Percent	Number
63	24	2	11	1,520
59	24	2	15	462
62	25	3	10	366
67	24	2	7	407
65	23	2	10	285
65	23	2	10	539
62	24	3	11	578
61	27	2	10	397
62	24	3	11	517
65	23	2	10	657
61	26	2	11	346
65	22	2	11	410
59	23	3	15	402
66	25	2	7	514
59	28	1	12	194

(ymade everyday summer dresses: "...tell me what material most of
ses are made of?" "What other materials are your everyday summer
material do you like best for everyday summer dresses?"[1]

	Materials in everyday summer dress wardrobe	Material most everyday summer dresses made of	Material preferred for everyday summer dresses
	Percent	Percent	Percent
-------------------	95	89	71
-------------------	17	5	8
-------------------	11	1	4
-------------------	8	1	2
-------------------	7	1	2
-------------------	6	(*)	1
-------------------	5	(*)	1
-------------------	4	1	1
-------------------	2	(*)	1
-------------------	3	2	(*)
-------------------	1	(*)	(*)
-------------------	--	--	9
-------------------	(*)	(*)	(*)
-------------------	1,357	1,357	1,357

)re than 100 because some respondents named more than 1 material.

Table 47.--Girls who had readymade everyday summer dresses: Materials in everyday summer dresses[1]

Background characteristics	Cotton	Cotton-polyester	Rayon/acetate	Nylon	Polyester	Linen	Silk	Cotton-rayon/acetate	All other	Cases
	Percent	Percent	Percent	Percent	Percent	Percent	Percent	Percent	Percent	Number
United States total-----	95	17	11	8	7	6	5	4	6	1,357
Age:										
14 years--------------	94	15	10	11	7	5	4	3	6	394
15 years--------------	95	15	9	8	5	5	4	3	8	331
16 years--------------	95	18	11	7	8	6	6	5	6	376
17 years--------------	95	20	16	5	9	8	5	3	5	256
Family income group:										
Lower----------------	96	14	10	11	5	3	5	2	4	482
Middle---------------	95	17	12	7	8	7	4	4	6	514
Upper----------------	94	21	12	6	8	8	5	5	10	355
Size of place:										
Urban metropolitan----	94	19	15	12	12	8	6	2	5	459
Urban nonmetropolitan-	95	19	8	5	5	6	5	5	8	592
Town and farm---------	97	11	11	7	4	4	4	4	6	306
Region:										
Northeast-------------	94	19	18	12	14	8	6	2	7	365
North Central---------	95	16	8	3	5	6	3	4	7	343
South-----------------	98	16	9	8	4	5	6	4	4	478
West------------------	90	18	11	9	6	4	3	4	11	171

[1] Percentages add to more than 100 because some respondents named more than 1 material.

Table 48.--Girls who had readymade everyday summer dresses: Material preferred for everyday summer dresses

Background characteristics	Cotton	Cotton-polyester	Rayon/acetate	Polyester	All other	No preference	Not ascertained	Cases
	Percent	Percent	Percent	Percent	Percent	Percent	Percent	Number
United States total----------------	71	8	4	2	6	9	(*)	1,357
Age:								
14 years--------------------------	72	7	2	2	6	11	--	394
15 years--------------------------	73	7	4	2	6	8	(*)	331
16 years--------------------------	69	8	5	3	6	9	(*)	376
17 years--------------------------	68	11	3	2	6	10	--	256
Family income group:								
Lower-----------------------------	76	6	3	2	6	7	(*)	482
Middle----------------------------	69	9	4	2	6	10	--	514
Upper-----------------------------	65	10	4	3	7	11	--	355
Size of place:								
Urban metropolitan---------------	60	10	6	3	7	14	(*)	459
Urban nonmetropolitan------------	73	8	2	3	6	8	--	592
Town and farm--------------------	81	5	3	1	5	5	--	306
Region:								
Northeast-------------------------	60	8	7	3	7	15	(*)	365
North Central--------------------	77	9	1	3	6	4	--	343
South-----------------------------	78	7	2	2	5	6	--	478
West------------------------------	61	8	5	3	7	16	--	171

*Less than 1 percent.

Table 49.--Girls who had readymade everyday summer dre:
    certain materials best: "Why do you prefer (mater:
    summer dresses?"[1]

| | Mater: |
Reason for preference	
CARE AND LAUNDERING----------------------------	
Easy to iron, press--------------------------	
Easy to wash and care for--------------------	
Machine washable-----------------------------	
Washable; no drycleaning required------------	
Little or no ironing required----------------	
Good appearance after washing----------------	
Easy to starch-------------------------------	
Dries quickly--------------------------------	
Doesn't need starch--------------------------	
Miscellaneous--------------------------------	
COMFORT AND WEIGHT---------------------------	
Cool, lightweight, airy---------------------	
Doesn't cling, stick, bind------------------	
Doesn't irritate, scratch, itch-------------	
Miscellaneous-------------------------------	
APPEARANCE AND STYLING-----------------------	
Variety of styles available-----------------	
Good colors, prints, patterns available------	
Looks neat, fresh, crisp---------------------	
Versatile; can wear anywhere for all occasions----------------------------------	
Stylish, popular, fashionable----------------	
Fits, hangs well-----------------------------	
Looks nice, pretty (general)-----------------	
Like texture (general)-----------------------	
Miscellaneous--------------------------------	
PERFORMANCE AND DURABILITY--------------------	
Durable, wears well--------------------------	
Doesn't wrinkle------------------------------	
Holds colors, doesn't fade, run--------------	
Holds shape, doesn't shrink, stretch---------	
Doesn't soil, stain easily-------------------	
Miscellaneous--------------------------------	
OTHER:	
Inexpensive----------------------------------	
All other------------------------------------	
Not ascertained------------------------------	
Number of cases-------------------------------	

[1] Percentages add to more than their group totals an
because some respondents gave more than 1 answer.
[2] Numbers preferring other materials too small for s
*Less than 1 percent.

Table 50.--Girls who had readymade everyday summer dresses and said they liked
certain materials best: "Is there anything that you don't like so well about
(material liked best) for everyday summer dresses?"[1]

Criticisms of preferred material	Material liked best for everyday summer dresses[2]	
	Cotton	Cotton-polyester
	Percent	Percent
PERFORMANCE AND DURABILITY----------------------	22	13
Wrinkles easily------------------------------	18	5
Not colorfast; fades, runs-------------------	2	2
Soils, stains easily-------------------------	2	--
Doesn't hold shape; shrinks, stretches-------	1	3
Discolors; turns yellow, gray----------------	(*)	3
Miscellaneous--------------------------------	1	4
CARE AND LAUNDERING---------------------------	5	5
Hard to iron--------------------------------	2	4
Has to be ironed----------------------------	2	--
Miscellaneous-------------------------------	1	2
OTHER:		
Comfort and weight-------------------------	2	6
Appearance and styling---------------------	2	3
Expensive----------------------------------	(*)	2
All other----------------------------------	(*)	--
Not ascertained----------------------------	2	1
NO CRITICISM OF MATERIAL----------------------	69	74
Number of cases-------------------------------	958	109

[1] Percentages may add to more than their group totals and these may add to
more than 100 because some respondents gave more than 1 answer.
[2] Numbers preferring other materials too small for separate analysis.
*Less than 1 percent.

Table 51.--Girls who had readymade sweaters: "What material are most of your readymade sweaters made of?"
"What other materials are your readymade sweaters made of?" "What material do you like best for
sweaters?"[1]

Material	Materials in sweater wardrobe	Material most sweaters made of	Material preferred for sweaters
	Percent	Percent	Percent
Wool---	69	46	35
Acrylic--	46	24	22
Nylon--	20	7	7
Wool-acrylic-----------------------------------	17	8	8
Cashmere---------------------------------------	9	1	6
Cotton---	8	3	3
Polyester--------------------------------------	7	2	2
Wool-nylon-------------------------------------	5	2	1
Rayon/acetate----------------------------------	4	2	1
Mohair---	4	1	1
Wool-cotton------------------------------------	3	1	1
Angora---	2	(*)	1
Other materials--------------------------------	8	3	4
No preference----------------------------------	--	--	7
Not ascertained--------------------------------	1	(*)	1
Number of cases--------------------------------	1,641	1,641	1,641

[1] Percentages may add to more than 100 because some respondents named more than 1 material.
*Less than 1 percent

70

Table 52.--Girls who had readymade sweaters: Materials in sweaters[1]

Background characteristics	Wool	Acrylic	Nylon	Wool-acrylic	Cash-mere	Cotton	Poly-ester	Wool-nylon	Rayon/ace-tate	Mohair	Wool-cotton	Angora	All other	Not ascer-tained	Cases
	Percent	Percent	Percent	Percent	Percent	Percent	Percent	Percent	Percent	Percent	Percent	Percent	Percent	Percent	Number
United States total------	69	46	20	17	9	8	7	5	4	4	3	2	8	1	1,641
Age:															
14 years------------	68	45	19	12	8	10	8	5	5	3	5	1	5	1	503
15 years------------	67	47	20	18	9	9	7	3	6	4	2	3	7	(*)	391
16 years------------	71	45	18	21	11	7	6	5	3	4	3	2	12	--	444
17 years------------	72	47	23	18	11	8	7	5	4	5	4	4	10	--	303
Family income group:															
Lower---------------	61	44	25	15	6	13	9	3	6	2	4	1	6	--	577
Middle--------------	71	47	20	18	11	7	5	7	5	4	3	--	8	(*)	637
Upper---------------	78	47	14	18	11	4	7	3	2	6	2	5	12	(*)	421
Size of place:															
Urban metropolitan---	73	48	16	16	9	6	6	4	3	4	2	2	9	(*)	528
Urban nonmetropolitan--	71	44	20	19	11	8	7	6	4	4	3	4	9	(*)	724
Town and farm-------	61	46	25	14	7	12	7	4	7	2	6	1	6	(*)	389
Region:															
Northeast-----------	79	48	21	17	6	7	5	4	4	7	2	1	4	(*)	416
North Central-------	70	46	20	20	9	5	7	5	4	2	3	4	11	(*)	449
South---------------	64	43	23	16	11	13	7	5	5	3	5	2	8	--	555
West----------------	64	47	10	14	14	6	10	5	6	5	2	4	10	(*)	221

[1] Percentages add to more than 100 because some respondents named more than 1 material.
*Less than 1 percent.

71

Table 53.--Girls who had readymade sweaters: Material preferred for sweaters

Background characteristics	Wool	Acrylic	Wool-acrylic	Nylon	Cashmere	Cotton	All other	No preference	Not ascertained	Cases
	Percent	Percent	Percent	Percent	Percent	Percent	Percent	Percent	Percent	Number
United States total------------	35	22	8	7	6	3	11	7	1	1,641
Age:										
14 years-----------	37	22	5	7	6	4	10	8	1	503
15 years-----------	32	22	9	8	4	4	13	7	1	391
16 years-----------	36	22	9	6	7	2	11	6	1	444
17 years-----------	34	22	7	8	8	3	12	6	-	303
Family income group:										
Lower--------------	30	24	6	10	5	6	11	7	1	577
Middle-------------	34	21	10	8	6	2	11	7	1	637
Upper--------------	42	21	7	3	8	1	10	8	(*)	421
Size of place:										
Urban metropolitan-------------	37	25	7	5	7	2	9	7	1	528
Urban nonmetropolitan----------	36	18	8	7	7	3	13	8	(*)	724
Town and farm------------------	29	25	7	11	4	6	10	7	1	389
Region:										
Northeast----------	46	19	8	6	4	1	9	7	(*)	416
North Central------	31	25	10	8	5	2	15	4	(*)	449
South--------------	30	22	8	9	7	6	10	8	(*)	555
West---------------	34	23	5	3	10	2	10	12	1	221

*Less than 1 percent.

Table 54.--Girls who had readymade sweaters and said they liked certain materials best: "Why do you prefer (material liked best) for sweaters?"[1]

Reasons for preference	Material liked best for sweaters[2]				
	Wool	Acrylic	Wool-acrylic	Nylon	Cashmere
	Percent	Percent	Percent	Percent	Percent
COMFORT AND WEIGHT	74	69	69	53	78
Warm, heavy	65	14	19	9	17
Doesn't irritate, scratch, itch	8	51	46	35	73
Doesn't cling, stick, bind	5	4	1	3	4
Weight just right	2	3	4	2	2
Not too warm; cool, lightweight, airy	1	12	9	11	5
Lightweight, but warm	1	4	2	3	2
Miscellaneous	2	3	--	3	--
APPEARANCE AND STYLING	44	18	24	22	71
Variety of styles available	9	2	3	3	5
Good colors, patterns available	8	4	3	5	7
Goes well with other clothes	8	1	5	1	4
Like texture (general)	7	1	3	2	7
Stylish, popular, fashionable	7	1	2	2	4
Fits well	5	4	7	2	10
Looks nice, pretty (general)	3	2	4	5	16
Looks expensive	3	(*)	--	1	21
Looks neat, crisp, fresh	2	2	1	--	4
Good for everyday, casual wear	2	1	--	--	--
Dressier, more adult-looking	1	1	1	1	7
Versatile, can wear anywhere, for all occasions	(*)	1	2	--	4
Miscellaneous	1	1	--	3	3
PERFORMANCE AND DURABILITY	40	47	44	47	24
Holds shape; doesn't shrink, stretch	22	35	30	36	13
Durable, wears well	8	4	2	3	9
Doesn't soil, stain easily	5	4	4	5	1
Doesn't wrinkle	4	3	3	3	--
Doesn't tear, rip, snag	4	3	2	2	3
Doesn't ball up, fuzz, shed	4	3	2	5	2
Holds colors; doesn't fade, run	1	5	3	4	1
Miscellaneous	1	3	4	1	1
CARE AND LAUNDERING	13	50	39	56	7
Easy to wash and care for	6	21	17	26	3
Washable; doesn't have to be drycleaned	4	12	13	12	4
Little or no ironing required	2	5	6	13	1
Easy to iron	1	3	2	1	--
Machine washable	(*)	11	2	9	--
Dries quickly	--	9	2	12	--
Miscellaneous	1	2	2	3	--
OTHER:					
Inexpensive	1	3	4	3	--
Miscellaneous	1	--	1	--	1
Not ascertained	(*)	(*)	1	1	--
Number of cases	571	362	127	116	102

[1] Percentages add to more than their group totals and these add to more than 100 because some respondents gave more than 1 answer.

[2] Numbers preferring other materials too small for separate analysis.

* Less than 1 percent.

Table 55.--Girls who had readymade sweaters and said they liked certain materials best: "Is there anything that you don't like so well about (material liked best) for sweaters?"[1]

Criticisms of preferred material	Material liked best for sweaters[2]				
	Wool	Acrylic	Wool-acrylic	Nylon	Cashmere
	Percent	Percent	Percent	Percent	Percent
COMFORT AND WEIGHT------------------------------------	29	6	9	4	4
Irritates, scratches, itches-------------------------	21	2	4	--	2
Too warm, not cool enough----------------------------	6	(*)	2	1	--
Not comfortable (general)----------------------------	2	(*)	--	--	1
Clings, sticks, binds--------------------------------	1	2	2	2	2
Not warm enough--------------------------------------	--	2	2	2	--
Miscellaneous--	(*)	--	1	--	--
PERFORMANCE AND DURABILITY---------------------------	28	27	22	48	22
Doesn't hold shape; shrinks, stretches---------------	13	10	8	10	8
Balls up, fuzzes, sheds------------------------------	10	9	7	7	7
Tears, rips, snags-----------------------------------	3	8	6	26	5
Collects lint---------------------------------------	2	1	1	6	--
Not durable, doesn't wear well-----------------------	1	1	1	1	3
Soils, stains easily---------------------------------	1	(*)	--	2	4
Wrinkles easily-------------------------------------	(*)	1	2	3	--
Miscellaneous--	5	2	1	2	2
CARE AND LAUNDERING----------------------------------	14	3	6	3	21
Not washable, has to be drycleaned-------------------	6	(*)	2	--	9
Hard to wash and care for---------------------------	5	1	2	--	10
Dries slowly---	2	1	1	--	--
Not machine washable---------------------------------	2	(*)	1	1	1
Miscellaneous--	1	1	2	3	3
OTHER:					
Appearance and styling-------------------------------	1	2	--	--	1
Expensive--	1	1	1	2	29
All other---	(*)	(*)	--	--	--
Not ascertained-------------------------------------	1	1	2	3	1
NO CRITICISM OF MATERIAL-----------------------------	40	62	63	42	41
Number of cases	571	362	127	116	102

[1] Percentages may add to more than their group totals and these may add to more than 100 because some respondents gave more than 1 answer.
[2] Numbers preferring other materials too small for separate analysis.
* Less than 1 percent.

Table 56.--Girls who had readymade sweaters (wool sweaters): "Do you think making wool sweaters that can be washed in a machine is a good idea or not such a good idea?"

Background characteristics	Owners of sweaters			Owners of wool sweaters		
	Machine-washable wool sweaters are--		Cases	Machine-washable wool sweaters are--		Cases
	A good idea	Not a good idea		A good idea	Not a good idea	
	Percent	Percent	Number	Percent	Percent	Number
United States total---------------------	89	11	1,641	88	12	1,140
Age:						
14 years-----------------------------	91	9	503	90	10	342
15 years-----------------------------	89	11	391	89	11	263
16 years-----------------------------	89	11	444	89	11	315
17 years-----------------------------	84	16	303	83	17	218
Family income group:						
Lower--------------------------------	90	10	577	90	10	350
Middle-------------------------------	89	11	637	88	12	454
Upper--------------------------------	88	12	421	88	12	329
Size of place:						
Urban metropolitan-------------------	87	13	528	86	14	385
Urban nonmetropolitan----------------	88	12	724	88	12	515
Town and farm------------------------	92	8	389	93	7	238
Region:						
Northeast----------------------------	88	12	416	88	12	327
North Central------------------------	88	12	449	86	14	315
South--------------------------------	92	8	555	92	8	354
West---------------------------------	85	15	221	84	15	142

	Owners of sweaters	Owners of wool sweaters
	Percent	Percent
---------------------	84	85
---------------------	51	51
---------------------	37	38
---------------------	8	8
---------------------	4	4
---------------------	2	2
---------------------	3	3
---------------------	23	25
---------------------	14	15
---------------------	7	7
---------------------	4	4
leaners--------------	7	8
---------------------	5	5
---------------------	2	2
---------------------	1	1
---------------------	1	1
---------------------	3	3
---------------------	1	1
---------------------	1,454	1,006

p totals and these add to more than 100 because some respondents

	Owners of sweaters	Owners of wool sweaters
	Percent	Percent
---------------------	56	58
h--------------------	34	38
---------------------	8	8
---------------------	6	7
---------------------	6	5
---------------------	5	5
---------------------	4	5
---------------------	3	3
---------------------	6	6
---------------------	48	51
---------------------	33	38
---------------------	8	7
---------------------	5	5
clean as hand		
---------------------	4	5
---------------------	4	4
---------------------	4	2
---------------------	2	3
---------------------	2	2
---------------------	2	2
---------------------	5	5
---------------------	1	1
---------------------	186	133

p totals and these add to more than 100 because some respondents

Table 59.--Girls who had readymade sweaters (wool sweaters): "... tell me if you think machine washability would be important to you or not in deciding whether to buy a particular new wool sweater?"

Background characteristics	Owners of sweaters gave rating of--					
	5 (most important)	4	3	2	1 (not important at all)	Cases
	Percent	Percent	Percent	Percent	Percent	Number
United States total----------------	40	19	17	7	17	1,641
Age:						
14 years-------------------------	42	20	18	6	14	503
15 years-------------------------	40	19	18	8	15	391
16 years-------------------------	40	20	16	7	17	444
17 years-------------------------	36	16	16	9	23	303
Family income group:						
Lower----------------------------	49	16	15	6	14	577
Middle---------------------------	39	20	18	7	16	637
Upper----------------------------	31	22	19	8	20	421
Size of place:						
Urban metropolitan---------------	32	21	19	8	20	528
Urban nonmetropolitan------------	38	19	18	7	18	724
Town and farm--------------------	53	17	12	6	12	389
Region:						
Northeast------------------------	39	19	15	8	19	416
North Central--------------------	36	22	20	8	14	449
South----------------------------	45	18	15	5	17	555
West-----------------------------	37	16	19	11	17	221

Background characteristics	Owners of wool sweaters gave rating of--					
	5 (most important)	4	3	2	1 (not important at all)	Cases
	Percent	Percent	Percent	Percent	Percent	Number
United States total----------------	37	20	19	7	17	1,140
Age:						
14 years-------------------------	37	21	20	6	16	343
15 years-------------------------	37	20	21	9	13	263
16 years-------------------------	38	23	17	6	16	316
17 years-------------------------	34	16	16	9	25	218
Family income group:						
Lower----------------------------	47	17	16	6	14	351
Middle---------------------------	36	21	19	7	17	455
Upper----------------------------	28	23	20	8	21	329
Size of place:						
Urban metropolitan---------------	30	22	20	9	19	386
Urban nonmetropolitan------------	36	20	19	7	18	516
Town and farm--------------------	52	18	14	5	11	238
Region:						
Northeast------------------------	37	20	16	8	19	328
North Central--------------------	32	23	23	7	15	315
South----------------------------	41	20	17	5	17	355
West-----------------------------	34	18	18	10	20	142

*Less than 1 percent.

Table 60.--Girls who had readymade sweaters and gave a rating as to the importance of machine washability in the decision to buy a wool sweater: "Why is that?"[1]

Reasons for rating of importance	5 (most important)	4	3	2	1 (not important at all)
	Percent	Percent	Percent	Percent	Percent
POSITIVE REASONS					
CARE AND LAUNDERING-------------------------	75	54	15	4	3
Saves time, easier to care for------------	50	32	11	1	1
Saves money: less expensive to care for---	31	23	5	3	1
No special care required------------------	6	3	2	--	(*)
Would be cleaner if machine washed--------	4	3	--	--	(*)
Dries gently------------------------------	2	2	--	1	--
Miscellaneous-----------------------------	1	1	1	--	1
PERFORMANCE AND DURABILITY------------------	26	16	4	1	(*)
Retains shape after washing---------------	11	9	2	1	(*)
Could wear sweaters more often------------	9	6	2	--	--
More durable------------------------------	5	1	(*)	--	--
Miscellaneous-----------------------------	2	1	--	--	--
OTHER:					
More convenient; do not have to take to cleaners------------------------------	6	3	1	--	--
Nice idea---------------------------------	5	2	1	1	--
Conditional; it depends-------------------	4	4	2	1	--
Less expensive----------------------------	3	1	(*)	--	--
Could have more sweaters------------------	3	1	1	1	(*)
Appearance--------------------------------	3	1	1	--	(*)
Comfort and weight------------------------	1	1	(*)	--	--
All other---------------------------------	1	1	--	1	--
NEGATIVE REASONS					
CARE AND LAUNDERING-------------------------	(*)	2	8	18	28
Machine washability not safe------;-------	(*)	2	5	11	22
Wouldn't look good after washing----------	(*)	--	1	1	4
Wool needs special care-------------------	--	--	1	3	2
Miscellaneous-----------------------------	--	(*)	1	3	2
PERFORMANCE AND DURABILITY------------------	(*)	4	8	15	18
Might/or would lose shape, shrink, stretch----------------------------------	--	3	3	6	7
Prefer to send to drycleaners-------------	--	1	2	3	5
Not colorfast-----------------------------	--	(*)	1	3	3
Might/or would not be durable-------------	(*)	(*)	1	3	1
Miscellaneous-----------------------------	(*)	--	1	2	4
OTHER FACTORS MORE IMPORTANT----------------	2	29	51	44	23
Color-------------------------------------	1	10	18	21	8
Style-------------------------------------	1	14	21	20	7
Appearance--------------------------------	--	4	5	7	3
Fit---------------------------------------	--	2	4	7	3
Material, texture-------------------------	1	4	6	9	3
Price-------------------------------------	1	3	5	4	1
Miscellaneous-----------------------------	1	8	18	12	10
OTHER:					
Machine washability not important--------	--	2	11	10	7
Someone else cares for clothes------------	(*)	--	2	7	6
Don't like wool---------------------------	1	2	4	7	15
Would cost more---------------------------	--	--	1	3	1
All other---------------------------------	(*)	(*)	3	3	5
Not ascertained---------------------------	1	1	1	1	3
Number of cases---------------------------	652	312	280	117	278

[1] Percentages may add to more than their group totals and these add to more than 100 because some respondents gave more than 1 answer.
*Less than 1 percent.

Table 61.--Girls who had half slips and regular (full-length) slips: "Which would you say you wear most often--half slips or regular (full-length) slips?"

Background characteristics	Half slip	Regular slip	Not ascertained	Cases
	Percent	Percent	Percent	Number
United States total-----------------	59	40	1	1,239
Age:				
14 years----------------------------	60	40	(*)	356
15 years----------------------------	57	42	1	297
16 years----------------------------	59	39	2	354
17 years----------------------------	58	41	1	232
Family income group:				
Lower-------------------------------	61	38	1	440
Middle------------------------------	58	41	1	486
Upper-------------------------------	56	43	1	311
Size of place:				
Urban metropolitan------------------	66	33	1	379
Urban nonmetropolitan---------------	53	46	1	557
Town and farm----------------------	59	40	1	303
Region:				
Northeast---------------------------	66	33	1	306
North Central-----------------------	51	47	2	321
South-------------------------------	55	45	(*)	457
West--------------------------------	71	28	1	155

*Less than 1 percent.

Table 62.--Girls who had half slips: "What material are most of them made of?" "What other materials are your half slips made of?" "What material do you like best for them?"[1]

Material	Materials in half slip wardrobe	Material most half slips made of	Material preferred for half slips[2]
	Percent	Percent	Percent
Nylon-------------------------------	68	56	49
Cotton------------------------------	44	17	17
Silk--------------------------------	15	8	8
Rayon/acetate-----------------------	11	6	5
Cotton-polyester--------------------	7	3	3
Polyester---------------------------	6	3	3
Polyester-nylon-cotton--------------	4	3	3
Acetate-nylon-----------------------	2	1	1
Other materials---------------------	7	3	3
No preference-----------------------	--	--	8
Not ascertained--------------------	1	(*)	(*)
Number of cases--------------------	1,500	1,500	988

[1] Percentages may add to more than 100 because some respondents named more than 1 material.
[2] Only respondents who owned mostly or only half slips were asked material liked best for this type slip.
* Less than 1 percent.

78

who had regular (full-length) slips: "What material are <u>most</u>
of? What other materials are your regular full-length slips
at material do you like best for them?"[1]

ial	Materials in full-length slip wardrobe	Material most full-length slips made of	Material preferred for full-length slips[2]
	<u>Percent</u>	<u>Percent</u>	
-----------	66	55	51
-----------	40	20	19
-----------	10	7	6
-----------	8	5	3
-----------	6	3	6
-----------	6	3	4
-cotton------	3	3	3
-----------	6	3	3
-----------			5
-----------	1	1	(*)
-----------	1,424	1,424	685

may add to more than 100 because some respondents named more
.
ients who owned mostly or only regular (full-length) slips were
: they liked best for this type slip.
percent.

79

Table 64.--Girls who had half slips: Materials in half slips[1]

Background characteristics	Nylon	Cotton	Silk	Rayon/ acetate	Cotton-polyester	Polyester	Polyester-nylon-cotton	All other	Not ascer-tained	Cases
	Percent	Percent	Percent	Percent	Percent	Percent	Percent	Percent	Percent	Number
United States total-----	68	44	15	11	7	6	4	7	1	1,500
Age:										
14 years--------------	67	46	16	12	5	6	5	7	1	439
15 years--------------	66	46	15	10	9	7	3	6	1	357
16 years--------------	71	43	13	10	7	6	5	6	1	417
17 years--------------	70	39	14	12	8	5	4	9	1	287
Family income group:										
Lower-----------------	65	52	18	12	5	5	4	4	1	537
Middle----------------	68	41	13	11	7	6	5	9	1	586
Upper-----------------	73	37	12	10	10	8	4	7	1	373
Size of place:										
Urban metropolitan----	69	44	18	12	8	8	4	8	1	508
Urban nonmetropolitan-	70	41	13	9	7	5	4	7	1	648
Town and farm---------	66	50	13	12	4	6	5	6	1	344
Region:										
Northeast-------------	66	50	16	13	8	9	4	5	(*)	402
North Central---------	65	39	16	12	9	6	4	9	1	396
South-----------------	72	47	14	8	5	5	4	6	1	509
West------------------	68	33	11	13	5	3	8	8	2	193

[1] Percentages may add to more than 100 because some respondents named more than 1 material.
* Less than 1 percent.

Table 65.--Girls who had regular (full-length) slips: Materials in regular slips[1]

Background characteristics	Nylon	Cotton	Silk	Rayon/ acetate	Cotton-polyester	Polyester	Polyester-nylon-cotton	All other	Not ascer-tained	Cases
	Percent	Percent	Percent	Percent	Percent	Percent	Percent	Percent	Percent	Number
United States total-----	66	40	10	8	6	6	3	6	1	1,424
Age:										
14 years--------------	61	47	11	8	7	5	4	6	1	435
15 years--------------	66	43	11	8	5	6	3	6	1	342
16 years--------------	71	35	9	8	7	5	3	4	1	389
17 years--------------	66	34	10	10	6	7	3	6	1	258
Family income group:										
Lower-----------------	62	46	13	9	4	5	4	3	1	504
Middle----------------	68	38	9	8	7	5	3	8	--	552
Upper-----------------	69	35	7	7	10	7	4	6	1	364
Size of place:										
Urban metropolitan----	65	37	13	7	7	7	2	6	1	430
Urban nonmetropolitan-	69	39	8	8	6	5	4	6	--	639
Town and farm---------	61	47	11	9	6	6	3	5	1	355
Region:										
Northeast-------------	63	40	12	9	6	10	4	4	1	344
North Central---------	63	41	11	8	11	5	3	7	1	378
South-----------------	72	41	11	7	4	4	3	5	--	512
West------------------	63	37	6	11	5	4	4	7	2	190

[1] Percentages add to more than 100 because some respondents gave more than 1 answer.

Table 66.--Girls who had half slips and regular (full-length) slips: Preferred material by kind of slip owned

Material	Girls owning--			
	Mostly half slips	Mostly regular slips	Only half slips	Only regular slips
	Percent	Percent	Percent	Percent
Nylon--------------------------------	51	52	47	49
Cotton-------------------------------	17	18	18	22
Silk---------------------------------	7	5	9	6
Cotton-polyester---------------------	4	7	2	4
Rayon/acetate------------------------	4	3	5	3
Polyester----------------------------	3	4	2	3
Polyester-nylon-cotton---------------	4	3	1	2
Other materials----------------------	4	3	3	2
No preference------------------------	6	4	12	9
Not ascertained----------------------	--	1	1	(*)
Number of cases[1]--------------------	727	500	261	185

[1] 12 girls could not classify the type of slip worn most often.
*Less than 1 percent.

Table 67.--Girls who had half slips and/or regular (full-length) slips: Material preferred for slips

Background characteristics	Nylon	Cotton	Silk	Cotton-polyester	Rayon/acetate	Polyester	Polyester-nylon-cotton	All other	No prefer-ence	Not ascer-tained	Cases
	Percent	Percent	Percent	Percent	Percent	Percent	Percent	Percent	Percent	Percent	Number
United States total-------	51	18	7	4	4	3	3	3	7	(*)	1,685
Age:											
14 years----------------	47	21	8	4	3	3	2	3	9	--	518
15 years----------------	53	19	6	3	3	4	2	3	7	--	402
16 years----------------	53	17	6	6	5	2	3	3	5	--	452
17 years----------------	50	14	6	6	5	4	4	4	6	1	313
Family income group:											
Lower-------------------	52	18	9	3	5	3	2	2	5	1	601
Middle------------------	49	19	6	5	3	2	3	5	8	(*)	652
Upper-------------------	50	16	5	6	4	5	3	2	8	1	426
Size of place:											
Urban metropolitan------	46	16	8	4	4	3	2	4	12	1	559
Urban nonmetropolitan---	54	19	5	5	3	3	3	3	5	--	730
Town and farm-----------	50	18	8	5	5	4	3	3	4	--	396
Region:											
Northeast---------------	43	20	6	5	5	3	3	3	12	(*)	440
North Central-----------	49	18	8	7	3	4	2	4	4	1	453
South-------------------	58	18	7	4	3	3	2	2	3	--	564
West--------------------	49	15	4	2	6	3	3	5	13	--	228

*Less than 1 percent.

Table 68.--Girls who had half slips and/or regular (full-length) slips and said they liked certain materials best: "Why do you prefer (material liked best) for slips?"[1]

Reasons for preference	Material liked best for slips[2]				
	Nylon	Cotton	Silk	Cotton-polyester	Rayon/acetate
	Percent	Percent	Percent	Percent	Percent
COMFORT AND WEIGHT-----------------------	60	91	65	89	59
Cool, lightweight, airy-------------------	20	31	28	47	26
Doesn't cling, stick, bind---------------	18	67	16	59	24
Feels soft, smooth-----------------------	14	10	25	5	16
Doesn't climb or bunch up----------------	13	7	11	17	8
Doesn't irritate, scratch, itch----------	2	3	3	1	3
Heavy------------------------------------	2	2	2	--	2
Comfortable (general)--------------------	2	(*)	--	--	--
Thin, sheer------------------------------	2	--	5	--	--
Doesn't create static electricity--------	1	8	3	13	2
Weight just right; year round------------	1	3	--	1	--
Not transparent, has body----------------	1	3	--	--	--
Miscellaneous----------------------------	3	2	1	3	2
CARE AND LAUNDERING----------------------	53	25	24	33	36
Little or no ironing required------------	34	4	12	20	23
Washes easily---------------------------	22	10	9	15	12
Dries fast-------------------------------	18	3	6	9	5
Machine washable-------------------------	7	8	5	4	11
Irons easily-----------------------------	2	5	2	3	3
No special care required-----------------	2	1	--	1	--
Miscellaneous----------------------------	2	2	--	--	--
PERFORMANCE AND DURABILITY----------------	22	13	13	13	18
Durable----------------------------------	8	5	3	1	6
Doesn't wrinkle--------------------------	7	1	5	4	8
Doesn't shrink, stretch------------------	5	4	2	5	5
Stays white, doesn't turn yellow, gray---	4	3	--	4	--
Doesn't tear, fray, snag-----------------	1	2	1	--	--
Miscellaneous----------------------------	3	2	4	--	--
APPEARANCE AND STYLING--------------------	17	3	22	2	12
Fits better, nicer; fits tight-----------	6	2	3	1	8
Looks nice, pretty (general)-------------	5	--	5	--	2
More feminine---------------------------	3	--	9	--	2
Miscellaneous----------------------------	5	2	7	1	3
OTHER:					
Only kind worn---------------------------	2	1	3	--	6
Inexpensive------------------------------	1	(*)	--	--	6
All other--------------------------------	2	2	4	4	2
Not ascertained-------------------------	1	--	2	--	6
Number of cases--------------------------	851	303	115	75	66

[1] Percentages add to more than their group totals and these add to more than 100 because some respondents gave more than 1 answer.
[2] Numbers preferring other materials too small for separate analysis.
*Less than 1 percent.

preferred material	Nylon Percent	Cotton Percent	Silk Percent	Cotton-polyester Percent	Rayon/acetate Percent
COMFORT AND WEIGHT	38	7	33	11	21
Sticks, clings	27	3	27	7	17
Creates static electricity	7	(*)	5	--	5
Not year-round weight	5	1	2	3	--
Too warm, heavy	3	2	2	--	2
Climbs, bunches up	2	1	2	1	2
Miscellaneous	1	1	2	--	3
PERFORMANCE AND DURABILITY	10	9	4	16	12
Discolors; turns yellow, gray	4	1	--	7	--
Tears, frays, snags easily	2	1	2	1	3
Doesn't hold shape, shrinks, stretches	1	1	1	3	9
Wrinkles easily	(*)	4	--	1	--
Not soil resistant	(*)	(*)	1	3	--
Miscellaneous	3	3	2	3	--
OTHER:					
Care and laundering	1	8	2	4	3
Appearance and styling	1	2	--	1	--
All other	1	--	2	--	1
Not ascertained	2	2	4	1	1
NO CRITICISM OF MATERIAL	51	73	55	67	62
Number of cases	851	303	115	75	66

[1] Percentages may add to more than their group totals and these may add to more than 100 because some respondents gave more than 1 answer.

Table 70.--All girls were asked: "Do you have a raincoat--one that's meant to be worn only in rainy weather?" "Do you have a coat that is meant to be worn in dry as well as rainy weather and is specially treated so that it is water repellent?"

Background characteristics	Only raincoats	Only multipurpose coats	Have both	Have neither	Cases
	Percent	Percent	Percent	Percent	Number
United States total----------------------------	12	52	12	24	1,691
Age:					
14 years-----------------------------------	13	50	12	25	519
15 years-----------------------------------	11	52	13	24	405
16 years-----------------------------------	11	52	14	23	454
17 years-----------------------------------	12	56	10	22	313
Family income group:					
Lower--------------------------------------	14	40	11	35	601
Middle-------------------------------------	13	56	13	18	656
Upper--------------------------------------	8	62	14	16	428
Size of place:					
Urban metropolitan-------------------------	12	56	13	19	561
Urban nonmetropolitan----------------------	14	53	13	20	734
Town and farm------------------------------	9	43	10	38	396
Region:					
Northeast----------------------------------	11	65	12	12	441
North Central------------------------------	8	57	10	25	456
South--------------------------------------	17	40	16	27	564
West---------------------------------------	11	42	10	37	230

Table 71.--Girls who had rainwear: "What material is this coat (meant to be worn only in rainy weather) made of?" "What material is this coat (meant to be worn in dry as well as rainy weather) made of?" "What material do you like best for rainwear?"[1]

Material	Material rainwear made of		Material preferred for rainwear
	Raincoats	Multipurpose coats	
	Percent	Percent	Percent
Plastic---	58	2	13
Cotton--	17	51	37
Cotton-polyester--------------------------------------	3	11	9
Cotton-rayon/acetate----------------------------------	3	7	4
Rayon/acetate---	3	4	3
Oilskin---	3	(*)	1
Polyester---	1	2	1
Nylon---	1	1	1
Wool, wool mixtures-----------------------------------	--	2	1
Other materials---------------------------------------	3	7	4
Unspecified---	1	1	1
No preference---	--	--	24
Not ascertained---------------------------------------	8	12	1
Number of cases---------------------------------------	414	1,086	1,289

[1] Percentages may add to more than 100 because some respondents named more than 1 material.
*Less than 1 percent.

84

Cotton-polyester	Cotton-rayon/acetate	Rayon/acetate	All other	Not ascertained	Cases
Percent	Percent	Percent	Percent	Percent	Number
11	7	4	15	12	1,086
10	8	4	19	13	318
13	8	5	13	12	261
9	4	4	17	12	300
13	9	5	14	9	207
11	7	4	19	9	303
9	7	5	16	15	455
13	7	3	12	11	323
9	7	7	13	14	387
12	6	3	16	11	487
10	10	2	21	9	212
,8	8	8	11	12	341
12	9	2	10	12	308
14	5	3	21	10	317
8	4	3	31	13	120

wned in raincoats (ones meant only to be worn in rainy weather) has been
rs of raincoats to be significant. Percentages may add to more than 100
h 1 material.

Plastic	Cotton-polyester	Cotton-rayon/acetate	Rayon/acetate	All other	No preference	Not ascertained	Cases
Percent	Percent	Percent	Percent	Percent	Percent	Percent	Number
13	9	4	3	9	24	1	1,289
15	9	4	4	10	24	1	387
15	10	5	3	6	25	1	307
12	8	4	3	9	24	1	350
9	9	5	3	10	22	(*)	245
21	9	3	4	10	21	(*)	387
11	8	4	3	9	27	1	538
7	11	5	3	7	25	(*)	358
8	8	4	4	9	30	1	456
14	10	3	2	9	24	1	587
20	10	7	3	9	13	(*)	246
4	8	5	5	7	29	1	388
8	12	6	2	5	19	1	343
24	10	3	3	11	19	(*)	412
18	5	1	2	17	35	1	146

Table 74.--Girls who had rainwear (raincoats and/or multipurpose coats) and said they liked certain materials best: "Why do you prefer (material liked best) for rainwear?"[1]

Reasons for preference	Material liked best for rainwear[2]		
	Cotton	Plastic	Cotton-polyester
	Percent	Percent	Percent
APPEARANCE AND STYLING---------------------------------------	50	11	60
Versatile; can wear for more than one purpose or occasion-	27	1	35
Stylish, popular, fashionable----------------------------	10	1	11
Like appearance; looks better---------------------------	4	4	9
Variety of styles available-----------------------------	4	1	6
Fits well; well tailored--------------------------------	3	1	5
Looks neat, fresh---------------------------------------	3	1	2
Good colors available-----------------------------------	2	2	3
Dressier; more adult-looking----------------------------	2	--	3
Like texture (general)----------------------------------	1	1	--
Miscellaneous---	2	1	2
PERFORMANCE AND DURABILITY-------------------------------	43	79	59
Water repellent; sheds water well-----------------------	21	64	37
Doesn't wrinkle easily when wet-------------------------	10	5	17
Doesn't tear, rip, snag--------------------------------	4	1	2
Holds shape; doesn't sag, shrink-----------------------	4	--	6
Doesn't soil, stain easily-----------------------------	4	11	7
Dries quickly---	4	12	2
More durable, lasts longer------------------------------	3	3	8
Doesn't fade---	2	1	3
Wind breaker---	(*)	2	1
Miscellaneous---	3	1	3
COMFORT AND WEIGHT--------------------------------------	39	27	39
Not too warm, cool-------------------------------------	16	2	14
Lightweight--	10	15	5
Warm, heavyweight--------------------------------------	6	1	7
Doesn't stick, cling-----------------------------------	5	--	6
Not bulky; can be worn over other coat-----------------	3	6	2
Year-round weight--------------------------------------	2	2	5
Doesn't irritate, scratch, itch------------------------	2	1	3
Comfortable (general)----------------------------------	1	1	1
Lightweight but warm-----------------------------------	(*)	--	1
Miscellaneous--	1	1	2
CARE AND LAUNDERING------------------------------------	15	5	17
Washable; no drycleaning required----------------------	9	--	9
Easy to care for; cleans easily------------------------	4	4	3
Easy to iron---	1	--	5
Miscellaneous--	2	1	2
-OTHER:			
Unfamiliar with any other material---------------------	3	1	1
Inexpensive--	1	5	--
Can be rolled, folded---------------------------------	--	17	--
All other---	1	1	--
Not ascertained---------------------------------------	3	1	1
Number of cases---------------------------------------	474	169	117

[1] Percentages add to more than their group totals and these add to more than 100 because some respondents gave more than 1 answer.
[2] Numbers preferring other materials too small for separate analysis.
* Less than 1 percent.

and said they liked certain materials best:
like so well about (material liked best) for

material	Cotton	Plastic	Cotton-polyester
	Percent	Percent	Percent
-----------------	26	37	21
-----------------	10	3	9
-----------------	5	2	7
-----------------	4	--	7
-----------------	4	--	6
-----------------	(*)	24	--
-----------------	(*)	4	--
-----------------	--	4	--
-----------------	--	3	--
-----------------	3	2	1
-----------------	5	20	3
-----------------	2	4	3
-----------------	1	10	--
-----------------	1	4	1
-----------------	1	3	--
-----------------	1	2	--
-----------------	4	1	3
-----------------	(*)	5	2
-----------------	1	4	1
-----------------	3	1	1
-----------------	65	43	74
-----------------			

than their group totals and these may add to
ndents gave more than 1 answer.
erials too small for separate analysis.

87

Table 76.--Girls who had readymade winter skirts (winter blouses, winter everyday dresses, summer skirts, summer blouses, summer everyday dresses, slips, sweaters): "Would you say that most of yours are washed at home by hand, by machine, or taken to the drycleaners, or just what?"

Owners, by material predominating in wardrobe[1]	Commercial cleaner	Machine washed	Hand washed	All other[2]	Cases
	Percent	Percent	Percent	Percent	Number
Winter skirt owners-----------	78	9	8	5	1,671
Mostly wool-----------------	83	6	6	5	1,417
Mostly cotton---------------	31	43	24	2	131
Winter blouse owners----------	3	77	20	(*)	1,666
Mostly cotton---------------	2	80	18	(*)	1,451
Mostly cotton-polyester-----	2	71	27	(*)	124
Winter everyday dress owners--	20	59	19	2	1,101
Mostly cotton---------------	14	66	19	1	560
Mostly wool-----------------	81	10	6	3	397
Summer skirt owners-----------	4	79	17	(*)	1,605
Mostly cotton---------------	4	81	16	(*)	1,417
Mostly cotton-polyester-----	2	75	22	1	90
Summer blouse owners----------	--	84	15	1	1,645
Mostly cotton---------------	--	86	13	1	1,401
Mostly cotton-polyester-----	--	80	19	1	137
Summer everyday dress owners--	7	76	17	(*)	1,357
Mostly cotton---------------	7	77	16	(*)	1,208
Mostly cotton-polyester-----	4	72	24	--	71
Sweater owners----------------	26	10	62	2	1,641
Mostly wool-----------------	37	5	56	2	750
Mostly acrylic--------------	11	19	68	2	391
Mostly wool-acrylic---------	25	5	65	5	124
Mostly nylon----------------	11	13	75	1	112
Slip owners-------------------	--	70	30	--	1,685
Mostly nylon----------------	--	68	32	--	1,102
Mostly cotton---------------	--	75	25	--	455
Mostly silk-----------------	--	72	28	--	172
Mostly rayon/acetate--------	--	70	30	--	122

[1] Numbers owning other materials too small for separate analysis.
[2] Mainly coin-operated cleaner.
* Less than 1 percent.

Table 77.--Girls owning winter (summer) clothes that were hand washed: "Who would you say generally does most of the hand washing of your winter (summer) clothes?"[1]

Background characteristics	Person doing most hand washing of winter clothes				Cases	Person doing most hand washing of summer clothes				Cases
	Mother	Respondent	Other	Not ascertained		Mother	Respondent	Other	Not ascertained	
	Percent	Percent	Percent	Percent	Number	Percent	Percent	Percent	Percent	Number
United States total-------	49	46	4	2	470	45	50	4	1	425
Age:										
14 years---------------	60	33	4	3	134	58	36	4	2	110
15 years---------------	49	45	7	--	121	45	47	4	4	102
16 years---------------	41	56	2	2	120	34	62	4	--	121
17 years---------------	41	54	3	3	95	43	53	4	--	92

[1] Percentages may add to more than 100 because some respondents named more than 1 person.

Table 78.--Girls owning sweaters (slips) that were hand washed: "Who would you say generally does most of the hand washing of your sweaters (slips)?"

Background characteristics	Person doing most hand washing of sweaters				Cases	Person doing most hand washing of slips				Cases
	Mother	Respondent	Other	Not ascertained		Mother	Respondent	Other	Not ascertained	
	Percent	Percent	Percent	Percent	Number	Percent	Percent	Percent	Percent	Number
United States total-------	49	48	2	1	1,017	36	60	3	1	505
Age:										
14 years---------------	60	36	3	1	317	45	49	4	2	144
15 years---------------	47	51	1	1	250	35	61	2	2	125
16 years---------------	47	48	3	2	267	32	62	4	2	130
17 years---------------	35	62	1	2	189	26	73	1	--	106

Table 79.--Girls who had readymade winter skirts (winter blouses, winter everyday dresses, summer skirts, summer blouses, summer everyday dresses, slips, sweaters) that were cared for by a method other than by commercial cleaner: "Are most of them usually pressed or not?"[1]

Owners, by material predominating in wardrobe	Pressed	Not pressed	Not ascertained	Cases
	Percent	Percent	Percent	Number
Winter skirt owners-----------------------	92	7	1	376
Mostly wool-----------------------------	88	10	2	242
Mostly cotton---------------------------	98	2	--	91
Winter blouse owners----------------------	99	1	(*)	1,624
Mostly cotton---------------------------	99	(*)	1	1,422
Mostly cotton-polyester-----------------	99	1	--	122
Winter everyday dress owners--------------	97	2	1	635
Mostly cotton---------------------------	99	1	(*)	484
Mostly wool-----------------------------	94	3	3	74
Summer skirt owners-----------------------	99	1	(*)	1,536
Mostly cotton---------------------------	100	(*)	(*)	1,365
Mostly cotton-polyester-----------------	99	--	1	88
Summer blouse owners----------------------	99	1	(*)	1,625
Mostly cotton---------------------------	99	1	(*)	1,385
Mostly cotton-polyester-----------------	99	1	--	136
Summer everyday dress owners--------------	99	1	(*)	1,260
Mostly cotton---------------------------	99	1	(*)	1,130
Mostly cotton-polyester-----------------	100	--	--	68
Sweater owners----------------------------	65	34	1	1,213
Mostly wool-----------------------------	64	34	2	472
Mostly acrylic--------------------------	64	35	1	346
Mostly wool-acrylic---------------------	67	32	1	93
Mostly nylon----------------------------	71	28	1	100
Slip owners-------------------------------	38	62	(*)	1,685
Mostly nylon----------------------------	31	69	(*)	1,102
Mostly cotton---------------------------	56	44	(*)	455
Mostly silk-----------------------------	45	54	1	172
Mostly rayon/acetate--------------------	34	66	(*)	122

[1] Numbers owning other materials too small for separate analysis.
* Less than 1 percent.

89

Table 80.--Girls owning winter (summer) clothes that were pressed other than by commercial cleaner: "Who would you say generally does most of the pressing of your winter (summer) clothes?"[1]

Background characteristics	Person doing most pressing of winter clothes					Cases	Person doing most pressing of summer clothes					Cases
	Respondent	Mother	Maid	Other	Not ascertained		Respondent	Mother	Maid	Other	Not ascertained	
	Percent	Percent	Percent	Percent	Percent	Number	Percent	Percent	Percent	Percent	Percent	Number
United States total	52	41	4	3	1	1,624	61	33	4	2	(*)	1,657
Age:												
14 years---------	41	52	4	3	1	495	50	43	4	3	(*)	510
15 years---------	53	41	4	3	1	392	62	32	4	2	--	397
16 years---------	55	37	5	2	2	440	67	27	5	2	--	445
17 years---------	63	32	3	1	1	297	68	27	3	2	(*)	305

[1] Percentages may add to more than 100 because some respondents named more than 1 person.
* Less than 1 percent.

Table 81.--Girls owning sweaters (slips) that were pressed other than by commercial cleaner. "Who would you say generally does most of the pressing of your sweaters (slips)?"[1]

Background characteristics	Person doing most pressing of sweaters				Cases	Person doing most pressing of slips				Cases
	Respondent	Mother	Other	Not ascertained		Respondent	Mother	Other	Not ascertained	
	Percent	Percent	Percent	Percent	Number	Percent	Percent	Percent	Percent	Number
United States total------------------	56	40	3	1	411	52	42	6	(*)	639
Age:										
14 years----------------------------	41	53	4	2	126	42	52	5	1	202
15 years----------------------------	59	38	2	1	114	60	36	3	1	151
16 years----------------------------	64	33	3	--	100	48	42	10	--	170
17 years----------------------------	68	28	4	--	71	63	34	2	1	116

[1] Percentages may add to more than 100 because some respondents named more than 1 person.
* Less than 1 percent.

Table 62.--All girls were asked: "Which one of the six materials listed on this card would you say Is the best to wear in hot weather? Is the best to wear in cold weather? Lasts the longest? Keeps its shape best? Is easiest to care for? Is least likely to wrinkle? Is the best value for the money?"

Question answered	Cotton	Rayon	Nylon	Acrylic (Orlon)	Polyester (Dacron)	Wool	Not ascertained	Cases
	Percent	Percent	Percent	Percent	Percent	Percent	Percent	Number
Best to wear in hot weather?----------	78	13	5	2	1	(*)	1	1,691
Best to wear in cold weather?----------	5	(*)	1	1	1	92	(*)	1,691
Lasts the longest?---------------------	28	2	5	2	7	49	7	1,691
Keeps its shape best?-------------------	41	2	7	4	13	28	5	1,691
Easiest to care for?-------------------	61	2	11	3	13	7	3	1,691
Least likely to wrinkle?---------------	7	4	19	6	21	38	5	1,691
Best value for the money?-------------	43	1	3	2	11	32	8	1,691

* Less than 1 percent.

Table 83.--All girls were asked: "Which one of the six materials listed on this card would you say is the best to wear in hot weather?"

Background characteristics	Cotton	Polyester (Dacron)	Nylon	Rayon	Acrylic (Orlon)	Wool	Not ascertained	Cases
	Percent	Percent	Percent	Percent	Percent	Percent	Percent	Number
United States total------	78	13	5	2	1	(*)	1	1,691
Age:								
14 years---------------	80	10	7	1	1	--	1	519
15 years---------------	79	12	5	1	1	(*)	2	405
16 years---------------	78	15	4	2	(*)	(*)	1	454
17 years---------------	74	15	5	3	1	--	2	313
Family income group:								
Lower------------------	76	10	9	3	1	--	1	601
Middle-----------------	81	11	3	2	1	(*)	2	656
Upper------------------	76	18	3	2	(*)	(*)	1	428
Size of place:								
Urban metropolitan-----	78	12	3	2	1	--	4	561
Urban nonmetropolitan--	78	14	5	2	1	(*)	(*)	734
Town and farm---------	77	10	9	3	1	--	(*)	396
Region:								
Northeast------*-------	74	15	3	2	1	--	5	441
North Central----------	77	16	4	2	1	(*)	(*)	456
South------------------	81	8	8	2	1	(*)	--	564
West-------------------	80	13	5	2	(*)	--	(*)	230

*Less than 1 percent.

Table 84.--All girls were asked: "Which one of the six materials listed on this card would you say is the best to wear in cold weather?"

Background characteristics	Wool	Cotton	Acrylic (Orlon)	Polyester (Dacron)	Nylon	Rayon	Not ascertained	Cases
	Percent	Percent	Percent	Percent	Percent	Percent	Percent	Number
United States total------	92	5	1	1	1	(*)	(*)	1,691
Age:								
14 years---------------	92	5	1	1	1	--	(*)	519
15 years---------------	93	3	1	2	1	(*)	(*)	405
16 years---------------	92	5	2	(*)	(*)	(*)	1	454
17 years---------------	92	5	1	1	(*)	--	1	313
Family income group:								
Lower------------------	89	7	1	1	1	(*)	1	601
Middle-----------------	93	4	2	1	--	(*)	(*)	656
Upper------------------	96	2	1	1	(*)	--	(*)	428
Size of place:								
Urban metropolitan-----	92	3	2	2	(*)	(*)	1	561
Urban nonmetropolitan--	93	5	1	1	(*)	(*)	(*)	734
Town and farm---------	90	6	2	(*)	2	(*)	--	396
Region:								
Northeast--------------	94	3	1	(*)	(*)	(*)	2	441
North Central----------	95	3	1	1	(*)	--	(*)	456
South------------------	89	8	1	1	1	(*)	--	564
West-------------------	92	3	3	2	(*)	--	(*)	230

*Less than 1 percent.

Table 85.--All girls were asked: "Which one of the six materials listed on this card would you say lasts the longest?"

Background characteristics	Wool	Cotton	Polyester (Dacron)	Nylon	Acrylic (Orlon)	Rayon	Not ascertained	Cases
	Percent	Percent	Percent	Percent	Percent	Percent		Number
United States total-------	49	28	7	5	2	2		1,691
Age:								
14 years----------------	44	31	7	4	3	2	9	519
15 years----------------	51	28	6	6	1	1	7	405
16 years----------------	51	28	7	5	1	1	7	454
17 years----------------	53	25	7	7	3	1	4	313
Family income group:								
Lower-------------------	43	35	7	5	2	1	7	601
Middle------------------	52	26	6	5	2	2	7	656
Upper-------------------	52	22	9	6	1	2	8	428
Size of place:								
Urban metropolitan------	52	24	7	5	2	2	8	561
Urban nonmetropolitan---	50	28	7	5	2	1	7	734
Town and farm-----------	44	34	6	6	2	2	6	396
Region:								
Northeast---------------	52	26	7	4	2	2	7	441
North Central-----------	50	26	7	6	2	2	7	456
South-------------------	47	34	6	5	1	1	6	564
West--------------------	47	21	8	9	3	3	9	230

Table 86.--All girls were asked: "Which one of the six materials listed on this card would you say keeps its shape best?"

Background characteristics	Cotton	Wool	Polyester (Dacron)	Nylon	Acrylic (Orlon)	Rayon	Not ascertained	Cases
	Percent	Percent	Percent	Percent	Percent	Percent	Percent	Number
United States total-------	41	28	13	7	4	2	5	1,691
Age:								
14 years----------------	43	26	12	5	5	3	6	519
15 years----------------	43	29	10	7	4	2	5	405
16 years----------------	40	28	13	7	4	2	6	454
17 years----------------	37	28	15	8	4	3	5	313
Family income group:								
Lower-------------------	45	25	10	7	5	4	4	601
Middle------------------	40	29	12	6	5	2	6	656
Upper-------------------	37	29	18	6	3	1	6	428
Size of place:								
Urban metropolitan------	33	34	13	6	4	2	8	561
Urban nonmetropolitan---	43	26	14	6	5	2	4	734
Town and farm-----------	49	23	10	8	4	3	3	396
Region:								
Northeast---------------	36	32	12	6	4	2	8	441
North Central-----------	41	29	13	7	4	3	3	456
South-------------------	45	26	12	6	4	3	4	564
West--------------------	41	22	14	7	6	1	9	230

Cotton	Polyester (Dacron)	Nylon	Wool	Acrylic (Orlon)	Rayon	Not ascertained	Cases
Percent	Percent	Percent	Percent	Percent	Percent	Percent	Number
61	13	11	7	3	2	3	1,691
64	10	11	8	2	2	3	519
65	12	10	6	3	1	3	405
61	16	10	5	4	2	2	454
52	18	14	10	2	2	2	313
65	8	14	5	3	3	2	601
61	15	9	8	2	1	4	656
55	19	11	7	4	2	2	428
55	15	10	8	3	2	7	561
62	15	11	7	3	1	1	734
69	8	12	6	2	2	1	396
55	17	7	8	4	2	7	441
60	17	11	8	2	2	(*)	456
66	10	14	6	2	1	1	564
62	11	12	7	3	1	4	230

Wool	Polyester (Dacron)	Nylon	Cotton	Acrylic (Orlon)	Rayon	Not ascertained	Cases
Percent	Percent	Percent	Percent	Percent	Percent	Percent	Number
38	21	19	7	6	4	5	1,691
39	19	19	9	4	4	6	519
41	19	19	5	6	5	5	405
36	22	19	7	7	4	5	454
35	27	18	4	7	5	4	313
34	15	22	10	8	5	6	601
41	23	17	6	5	3	5	656
38	27	16	4	5	5	5	428
38	23	16	6	5	5	7	561
39	23	17	7	5	5	4	734
36	15	26	7	7	4	5	396
37	23	13	7	6	6	8	441
42	25	19	4	5	2	3	456
36	18	22	9	6	5	4	564
36	21	19	6	7	4	7	230

Table 89.--All girls were asked: "Which one of the six materials listed on this card would you say is the best value for the money?"

Background characteristics	Cotton	Wool	Polyester (Dacron)	Nylon	Acrylic (Orlon)	Rayon	Not ascertained	Cases
	Percent	Percent	Percent	Percent	Percent	Percent	Percent	Number
United States total------	43	32	11	3	2	1	8	1,691
Age:								
14 years---------------	45	31	9	3	3	1	8	519
15 years---------------	41	33	9	3	3	1	10	405
16 years---------------	42	31	12	3	2	2	8	454
17 years---------------	43	31	12	3	2	(*)	9	313
Family income group:								
Lower------------------	48	29	8	4	2	2	7	601
Middle-----------------	39	37	11	2	1	1	9	656
Upper------------------	40	29	14	3	3	1	10	428
Size of place:								
Urban metropolitan-----	36	35	11	2	2	1	13	561
Urban nonmetropolitan--	44	31	12	2	2	2	7	734
Town and farm---------	50	29	9	4	2	1	5	396
Region:								
Northeast--------------	34	35	12	3	3	1	12	441
North Central----------	42	34	11	3	2	1	7	456
South------------------	48	29	9	3	2	2	7	564
West-------------------	48	26	10	3	2	--	11	230

*Less than 1 percent.

Table 90.--All girls were asked: "Would you say that you are very interested, fairly interested, or not very interested in what kinds of clothes you wear?"

Background characteristics	Very interested	Fairly interested	Not very interested	Cases
	Percent	Percent	Percent	Number
United States total--------------	81	17	2	1,691
Age:				
14 years-----------------------	77	21	2	519
15 years-----------------------	82	15	3	405
16 years-----------------------	84	14	2	454
17 years-----------------------	81	17	2	313
Family income group:				
Lower--------------------------	80	17	3	601
Middle-------------------------	80	18	2	656
Upper--------------------------	83	15	2	428
Size of place:				
Urban metropolitan-------------	82	16	2	561
Urban nonmetropolitan----------	81	17	2	734
Town and farm------------------	79	19	2	396
Region:				
Northeast----------------------	80	18	2	441
North Central------------------	83	16	1	456
South--------------------------	81	17	2	564
West---------------------------	78	20	2	230

Background characteristics	Very interested	Fairly interested	Not very interested	Cases
	Percent	Percent	Percent	Number
d States total-------------------------------------	89	9	2	1,691
years---	86	11	3	519
years---	88	9	3	405
years---	92	7	1	454
years---	91	8	1	313
y income group:				
er--	88	9	3	601
dle---	89	9	2	656
er--	90	9	1	428
of place:				
an metropolitan-------------------------------------	88	10	2	561
an nonmetropolitan----------------------------------	90	8	2	734
n and farm--	89	9	2	396
n:				
theast--	89	9	2	441
th Central--	91	7	2	456
th--	89	9	2	564
t---	86	12	2	230

Table 92.--Girls who said they were very interested or fairly interested in selecting the clothes they wear: "Why is that?"[1]

	Percent	Percent
ositive reasons:		
Clothes and appearance are important-----------------------------------	28	13
Particular, fussy; prefer own taste------------------------------------	23	7
Want to be certain of fit, size--	18	10
Want to be stylish, want to wear what other teenagers wear-------------	17	12
Want to select color, patterns---	17	7
Want to select style---	16	7
Enjoy clothes, fashions, shopping---------------------------------------	9	2
Want good value, quality---	7	4
People judge you by your clothes; clothes affect personality, character---	6	--
Want to select fabrics---	5	2
Want clothes that are easy to care for----------------------------------	2	5
Good experience--	2	1
Want clothes suitable for the occasion---------------------------------	2	1
Want inexpensive clothes---	1	2
All other--	5	2
Not ascertained--	1	--
egative reasons:		
Mother does a good job---	--	17
Don't care about clothes---	--	8
Don't like to shop---	--	8
No choice; mother does it---	--	7
Like to shop with mother---	--	6
Conditional; it depends---	--	3
Clothes mostly gifts, hand-me-downs------------------------------------	--	--
All other--	--	2
Not ascertained--	--	5
umber of cases---		

[1] Too few girls said "not very interested" to permit separate analysis. Percentages add to more than 100 ecause some respondents gave more than 1 answer.

Table 93.--All girls were asked: "Where do you pick up ideas about what clothes you'd like to get?"[1]

Sources of ideas	U.S. total	Age of girls				Family income group			Size of place			Region			
		14 years	15 years	16 years	17 years	Lower	Middle	Upper	Urban metro-politan	Urban non-metro-politan	Town and farm	North-east	North Central	South	West
	Percent	Percent	Percent	Percent	Percent	Percent	Percent	Percent	Percent	Percent	Percent	Percent	Percent	Percent	Percent
FORMAL MEDIA----------	73	70	73	73	78	70	74	75	68	77	73	69	77	74	71
Fashion magazines------	44	37	43	48	51	36	47	51	45	48	35	44	46	42	43
Catalogs--------------	26	27	27	23	25	32	25	17	15	25	41	13	33	28	30
Other magazines-------	19	16	20	20	21	19	18	20	18	19	20	20	22	18	14
Newspapers------------	14	13	13	14	14	13	14	14	20	12	7	21	13	10	9
Television------------	11	12	10	10	13	12	12	9	10	10	14	9	13	10	14
Movies----------------	4	3	4	4	5	4	3	5	5	3	3	3	4	3	6
FRIENDS AND RELATIVES-----	72	74	74	70	67	68	74	73	73	72	70	71	74	69	75
Friends---------------	66	68	67	64	62	62	68	67	66	65	66	66	69	62	68
Parents---------------	15	15	17	14	13	12	16	16	19	14	9	20	13	13	14
Sisters or brothers------	6	7	7	4	5	7	5	5	6	6	5	7	6	5	6
Other relatives-------	(*)	(*)	1	(*)	(*)	1	(*)	(*)	--	1	--	1	--	1	--
STORES AND SHOPPING-----	61	58	56	65	68	62	61	61	67	59	57	68	58	59	62
Looking in stores------	45	44	42	46	52	46	44	47	49	45	41	51	42	45	43
Window shopping-------	38	36	35	41	40	40	38	34	44	35	35	46	35	35	38
OTHER PEOPLE----------	26	27	27	23	25	32	25	17	15	25	41	13	33	28	30
COURSES AT SCHOOL, TEACHER-	2	1	3	2	2	3	2	1	1	2	3	1	2	4	1
ALL OTHERS------------	2	2	2	1	2	1	1	2	1	2	1	1	1	2	3
NOT ASCERTAINED-------	(*)	(*)	--	(*)	--	(*)	--	1	(*)	(*)	--	1	(*)	--	--
Number of cases-------	1,691	519	405	454	313	601	656	428	561	734	396	441	456	564	230

[1] Percentages add to more than their group totals and these add to more than 100 because some respondents named more than one source.
*Less than 1 percent.

96

Table 94.--All girls were asked: "Which one of these (sources of ideas) do you think is most helpful?"

Sources of ideas	U.S. total	Age of girls				Family income group			Size of place			Region			
		14 years	15 years	16 years	17 years	Lower	Middle	Upper	Urban metro-politan	Urban non-metro-politan	Town and farm	North-east	North Central	South	West
	Percent	Percent	Percent	Percent	Percent	Percent	Percent	Percent	Percent	Percent	Percent	Percent	Percent	Percent	Percent
FRIENDS AND RELATIVES-------	36	40	39	33	29	33	40	36	40	36	34	38	39	35	35
Friends-----------	29	31	32	28	23	26	32	29	31	28	29	29	32	27	29
Parents-----------	5	7	6	4	4	5	6	6	7	6	4	7	5	6	5
Sisters-----------	2	2	1	1	2	2	2	1	2	2	1	2	2	2	1
Other relative----------	(*)	(*)	(*)	--	(*)	(*)	--	(*)	(*)	(*)	--	(*)	--	(*)	--
FORMAL MEDIA----------	31	31	30	30	31	31	31	29	23	33	36	24	32	34	29
Fashion magazines-----------	17	15	14	19	19	14	17	19	15	20	13	15	15	20	15
Catalogs----------	9	12	10	8	6	12	10	6	5	8	17	6	12	9	11
Other magazines----------	3	2	4	2	3	3	2	3	1	3	4	1	3	3	2
Other media----------	2	2	2	1	3	2	2	1	2	2	2	2	2	2	1
STORES AND SHOPPING----------	29	24	26	31	34	32	24	30	33	27	24	35	26	25	28
Looking in stores----------	20	17	17	22	23	22	16	22	22	19	18	23	19	17	19
Window shopping----------	9	7	9	9	11	10	8	8	11	8	6	12	7	8	9
ALL OTHERS----------	2	1	2	3	3	2	2	2	1	2	3	1	2	4	1
NO PARTICULAR SOURCE------	2	2	2	3	--	2	3	2	3	2	3	2	1	2	6
NOT ASCERTAINED----------	(*)	2	(*)	--	--	(*)	(*)	1	(*)	--	(*)	(*)	(*)	--	1
Number of cases----------	1,691	519	405	454	313	601	656	428	561	734	396	441	456	564	230

* Less than 1 percent.

97

Table 95.--All girls were asked: "Are you usually the one who suggests that you need a dress or coat, or does someone else suggest it first?" "How about other clothing items such as blouses and skirts--are you usually the one who suggests that you need things like this, or does someone else suggest it first?"[1]

Clothing items	Respondent	Mother	Father	All others	Not ascertained	Cases
	Percent	Percent	Percent	Percent	Percent	Number
Dresses and coats						
Total-------------	76	24	1	1	--	1,691
14 years--------	70	30	1	1	--	519
15 years--------	76	24	1	1	--	405
16 years--------	79	21	1	1	--	454
17 years--------	83	15	1	1	--	313
Blouses and skirts						
Total-------------	85	15	(*)	1	(*)	1,691
14 years--------	79	22	(*)	1	(*)	519
15 years--------	84	17	(*)	1	--	405
16 years--------	88	13	(*)	(*)	--	454
17 years--------	93	7	1	(*)	(*)	313

[1] Percentages add to more than 100 because some respondents named more than 1 person.
*Less than 1 percent.

Table 96.--All girls were asked: "Who has the most to say about whether or not you might get a dress or a coat?...such articles as blouses or skirts?"

Clothing items	Mother	Father	Respondent	All others	Not ascertained	Cases
	Percent	Percent	Percent	Percent	Percent	Number
Dresses and coats						
Total-------------	74	13	10	2	1	1,691
14 years--------	77	18	4	1	(*)	519
15 years--------	80	12	5	2	1	405
16 years--------	72	11	15	2	(*)	454
17 years--------	67	10	20	3	(*)	313
Blouses and skirts						
Total-------------	71	8	20	1	(*)	1,691
14 years--------	76	11	12	1	(*)	519
15 years--------	78	10	10	2	(*)	405
16 years--------	66	7	26	1	(*)	454
17 years--------	58	5	34	2	1	313

*Less than 1 percent.

.--All girls were asked: "Who usually shops for your skirts?...how about blouses?...your everyday dresses?...your sweaters?...your outer jackets or t coats?"

othing items	Girls shopping alone	Mothers shopping alone	Mothers and daughters both shopping	Other	Not ascer-tained	Cases
	Percent	Percent	Percent	Percent	Percent	Number
-----------------	55	10	31	3	1	1,684
ears--------------	39	16	43	2	(*)	518
ears--------------	52	10	34	3	1	403
ears--------------	66	6	24	3	1	452
ears--------------	73	7	17	2	1	311
-----------------	60	11	27	2	(*)	1,691
ears--------------	43	18	37	2	(*)	' 519
ears--------------	58	11	28	3	(*)	405
ears--------------	69	7	21	2	1	454
ears--------------	77	6	16	1	(*)	313
dresses						
-----------------	54	11	31	2	2	1,472
ears--------------	33	19	43	2	3	440
ears--------------	49	12	34	3	2	350
ears--------------	65	7	24	2	2	409
ears--------------	76	5	18	1	(*)	273
:						
-----------------	54	15	28	3	(*)	1,641
ears--------------	36	22	39	3	--	503
ears--------------	50	16	30	4	(*)	391
ears--------------	64	10	22	4	--	444
ears--------------	70	9	19	2	--	303
ckets or oats						
-----------------	35	20	38	6	1	1,416
ears--------------	19	27	46	7	1	427
ears--------------	30	23	40	6	1	347
ears--------------	44	17	32	6	1	382
ears--------------	53	10	32	4	1	260

than 1 percent.

Table 98.--All girls were asked: "Who usually has the most to say about the skirt that is finally selected?...the blouse?...the everyday dress?...the sweater?...the outer jacket or short coat?"[1]

Clothing items	Girls	Mothers	Fathers	All others	Not ascertained	Cases
	Percent	Percent	Percent	Percent	Percent	Number
Skirts						
Total------------------	68	30	1	1	(*)	1,684
14 years-------------	59	38	2	2	(*)	518
15 years-------------	64	35	1	(*)	(*)	403
16 years-------------	74	25	1	1	--	452
17 years-------------	79	18	1	1	1	311
Blouses						
Total------------------	76	24	1	1	1	1,691
14 years-------------	67	32	1	1	1	519
15 years-------------	73	26	1	1	(*)	405
16 years-------------	80	19	(*)	1	(*)	454
17 years-------------	86	12	1	1	1	313
Everyday dresses						
Total------------------	70	28	1	1	(*)	1,472
14 years-------------	58	39	2	1	--	440
15 years-------------	67	31	1	1	1	350
16 years-------------	77	22	(*)	1	(*)	409
17 years-------------	82	16	1	1	(*)	273
Sweaters						
Total------------------	68	31	1	2	(*)	1,641
14 years-------------	58	40	2	2	1	503
15 years-------------	65	35	1	1	(*)	391
16 years-------------	74	25	(*)	2	(*)	444
17 years-------------	78	20	1	2	1	303
Outer jackets or short coats						
Total------------------	56	41	3	2	(*)	1,416
14 years-------------	44	50	4	2	--	427
15 years-------------	56	44	2	2	(*)	347
16 years-------------	59	39	3	1	--	382
17 years-------------	69	27	2	2	--	260

[1] Percentages may add to more than 100 because some respondents gave more than 1 answer.

* Less than 1 percent.

e 99.--All girls were asked: "Generally speaking, at what age do you think a girl is old
enough to go shopping and pick out her own clothing by herself?"

Suggested age at which girl is old enough to shop	U.S. total	Age of girls			
		14 years	15 years	16 years	17 years
	Percent	Percent	Percent	Percent	Percent
14 years---------------------------------	14	19	14	11	9
ars-------------------------------------	28	31	30	25	24
ars-------------------------------------	24	20	24	28	24
ars-------------------------------------	24	21	21	26	33
ars-------------------------------------	5	5	5	5	7
ars-------------------------------------	4	3	5	4	2
ars or over-----------------------------	1	1	--	1	1
scertained------------------------------	(*)	--	1	(*)	(*)
n age named (years)---------------------	15.3	15.0	15.2	15.4	15.7
r of cases------------------------------	1,691	519	405	454	313

ess than 1 percent.

e 100.--All girls were asked: "Are you still enrolled in school?" "What grade are you in
now?" "What was the last grade of school you completed?"

School status	U.S. total	Age of girls			
		14 years	15 years	16 years	17 years
	Percent	Percent	Percent	Percent	Percent
nrolled---------------------------------	4	(*)	1	5	15
t grade completed:					
Jnder first year high school-------------	1	(*)	1	2	3
'irst year high school-------------------	1	--	(*)	1	2
econd year high school------------------	1	--	--	1	3
hird year high school-------------------	(*)	--	--	1	2
ourth year high school------------------	1	--	--	(*)	5
lled------------------------------------	96	100	99	95	85
Jnder first year high school-------------	19	55	9	2	(*)
'irst year high school-------------------	26	41	49	5	1
econd year high school------------------	22	4	36	39	9
hird year high school-------------------	20	(*)	5	44	40
ourth year high school------------------	8	--	--	5	33
ollege freshman-------------------------	1	--	--	(*)	2
)ther and not ascertained---------------	(*)	(*)	(*)	--	(*)
r of cases------------------------------	1,691	519	405	454	313

ess than 1 percent.

Table 101.--All girls were asked: "Have you done any kind of work at all for pay in the past 12 months?" "Do you have a regular job that you go to every week?"

Work status	U.S. total	Age of girls			
		14 years	15 years	16 years	17 years
	Percent	Percent	Percent	Percent	Percent
Have not worked in past year-----------------	36	40	37	36	30
Have worked in past year---------------------	64	60	63	64	70
Have regular job--------------------------	16	11	12	20	20
Do not have regular job-------------------	41	45	45	33	42
Both regular and nonregular job-----------	7	4	6	11	8
Number of cases-----------------------------	1,691	519	405	454	313

Table 102.--Girls who worked in the past year: "About how much money did you earn in the past year from working?"

Amount of money earned	U.S. total	Age of girls			
		14 years	15 years	16 years	17 years
	Percent	Percent	Percent	Percent	Percent
Less than $25--------------------------------	34	50	40	24	19
$25 to $99-----------------------------------	39	37	41	44	31
$100 to $199---------------------------------	13	10	12	17	14
$200 to $299---------------------------------	6	2	5	4	13
$300 to $399---------------------------------	3	1	2	4	7
$400 to $499---------------------------------	2	--	--	3	4
$500 or more---------------------------------	3	(*)	--	3	11
Not ascertained-----------------------------	(*)	(*)	(*)	1	1
Number of cases-----------------------------	1,073	310	256	289	218

* Less than 1 percent.

Table 103.--Girls who worked in the past year and earned $25 or more: Uses of money earned[1]

Uses of money earned	U.S. total	Age of girls			
		14 years	15 years	16 years	17 years
	Percent	Percent	Percent	Percent	Percent
Clothing---------------------------------	87	84	89	87	89
Recreation and amusement------------------	47	46	53	44	48
Gifts-------------------------------------	24	22	22	23	29
Accessories, makeup-----------------------	23	20	21	24	27
School supplies---------------------------	22	20	22	21	25
Board, family expenses--------------------	7	9	5	7	9
Trip--------------------------------------	4	3	3	2	6
Luxuries (beauty shop, records, etc.)-----	3	5	3	3	2
Miscellaneous-----------------------------	5	1	2	4	10
Saved it----------------------------------	40	43	39	40	38
Education--------------------------------	20	16	20	21	21
Clothing---------------------------------	6	10	6	5	4
Trip-------------------------------------	3	5	3	2	1
Emergency-rainy day---------------------	2	3	2	2	1
Gifts------------------------------------	2	2	2	1	2
Car--------------------------------------	2	1	1	1	3
Miscellaneous---------------------------	2	4	3	1	3
No special reason-----------------------	6	7	6	8	7
Not ascertained--------------------------	4	5	3	4	3
Number of cases--------------------------	700	153	154	218	175

[1] Percentages add to more than 100 (or more than the subtotal shown) because some respondents named more than 1 use of money earned.

Table 104.--Girls who worked in the past year and earned $25 or more: "What did you do with most of the money you earned?"[1]

Primary uses of money earned	U.S. total	Age of girls			
		14 years	15 years	16 years	17 years
	Percent	Percent	Percent	Percent	Percent
Clothing---------------------------------	68	61	70	70	68
Recreation and amusement------------------	8	14	7	7	6
Gifts-------------------------------------	4	2	3	5	4
School supplies---------------------------	4	3	3	4	5
Board, family expenses--------------------	4	5	3	4	2
Accessories, makeup-----------------------	2	1	3	2	3
Miscellaneous-----------------------------	3	4	3	3	4
Saved it----------------------------------	18	21	20	15	19
Education--------------------------------	11	9	11	10	13
Clothing---------------------------------	3	6	3	3	1
Gifts------------------------------------	2	4	3	1	1
Emergency-rainy day---------------------	1	--	2	(*)	--
Car--------------------------------------	(*)	--	--	(*)	1
Miscellaneous---------------------------	1	1	1	--	1
No special reason-----------------------	1	1	1	1	3
Number of cases--------------------------	700	153	154	218	175

[1] Percentages add to more than 100 (or more than the subtotal shown) because some respondents named more than 1 use of money earned.
*Less than 1 percent.

103

Table 105.--Girls who worked in the past year and earned $25 or more: "What did you do with the rest of money you earned?"[1]

Uses of money earned	U.S. total	Age of girls			
		14 years	15 years	16 years	17 years
	Percent	Percent	Percent	Percent	Percent
Recreation and amusement-----------------	39	32	47	37	42
Accessories, makeup----------------------	21	19	18	23	24
Gifts------------------------------------	21	20	20	18	25
Clothing---------------------------------	20	24	20	17	21
School supplies--------------------------	18	16	20	17	20
Board, family expenses-------------------	4	4	2	3	6
Trip-------------------------------------	3	3	1	2	5
Luxuries, (beauty shop, records, etc.)----	2	2	1	1	2
Miscellaneous----------------------------	4	1	2	3	8
Saved it---------------------------------	22	24	20	26	20
Education-----------------------------	9	7	9	11	8
Clothing------------------------------	3	4	3	3	3
Gifts---------------------------------	1	1	2	1	1
Car-----------------------------------	1	1	1	1	2
Trip----------------------------------	1	2	1	1	1
Emergency-rainy day--------------------	1	3	--	1	1
Miscellaneous-------------------------	2	3	2	1	2
No special reason---------------------	5	6	5	7	3
Not ascertained-------------------------	4	5	3	4	3
Number of cases--------------------------	700	153	154	218	175

[1] Percentages add to more than 100 (or more than the subtotal shown) because some respondents named more than 1 use of money earned.

Table 106.--Interviewers' report on whether or not any other person was present during the girls' interviews besides the respondent, and if so, who[1]

Person present	Percentage of cases
	Percent
No other person present----------	58
Other person present-------------	42
Mother------------------------	28
Sister-------------------------	10
Girl friend--------------------	4
Other female relative----------	2
Brother------------------------	3
Father-------------------------	2
Male friend--------------------	1
Other male relative------------	(*)
All others--------------------	1
Number of cases------------------	1,691

[1] Subtotals add to more than total because interviews indicated that more than 1 person was present during interviews.
*Less than 1 percent.

Table 107.--Interviewers' impressions about whether the presence of other persons seemed to have a great influence, some influence, or no influence on girl respondents' answers

Amount of influence	Interviews with other persons present
	Percent
Great influence--------	3
Some influence---------	27
No influence-----------	70
Not ascertained--------	(*)
Number of cases--------	704

*Less than 1 percent.

15 years	16 years	17 years	Lower	Middle	Upper
Percent	Percent	Percent	Percent	Percent	Percent
--	--	--	30	31	30
100	--	--	26	26	18
--	100	--	24	27	31
	--	100	20	16	21
38	33	38	100	--	--
43	38	34	--	100	--
19	29	28		--	100
30	31	39	20	38	44
45	44	41	40	45	46
25	25	20	40	17	10
24	25	27	18	31	30
28	26	27	20	31	30
35	36	33	52	24	22
13	13	13	10	14	18

Background characteristics

Size of place			Region			
an ro- tan	Urban non- metro- politan	Town and farm	North- east	North Central	South	West
ent	Percent	Percent	Percent	Percent	Percent	Percent
2	31	30	34	32	27	33
L	25	26	22	25	25	23
5	27	28	25	25	29	26
2	17	16	19	18	19	18
2	33	60	24	26	55	27
4	40	30	47	45	28	40
4	27	10	29	29	17	33
J	--	--	60	37	11	29
-.	100	--	29	40	54	51
-	--	100	11	23	35	20
7	18	12	100	--	--	--
)	25	26	--	100	--	--
L	41	50	--	--	100	--
2	16	12	--	--	--	100

Table 109.--Boys who had readymade winter sport shirts (not including knitted shirts or T-shirts) "What material are most of your winter sport shirts made of?" "What other materials are your winter sport shirts made of?" "What material do you like best for winter sport shirts?"[1]

Material	Materials in winter sport shirt wardrobe	Material most winter sport shirts made of	Material preferred for winter sport shirts
	Percent	Percent	Percent
Cotton-------------------------	87	74	65
Wool---------------------------	28	13	10
Cotton-polyester---------------	10	2	4
Polyester----------------------	6	1	2
Rayon/acetate------------------	6	2	1
Nylon--------------------------	4	1	1
Wool-cotton--------------------	4	1	1
Acrylic------------------------	3	1	1
Wool-polyester-----------------	2	1	1
Other wool mixtures------------	3	1	1
Other materials---------------	1	1	1
Unspecified-------------------	3	1	1
No preference-----------------	--	--	8
Not ascertained---------------	2	2	3
Number of cases---------------	1,613	1,613	1,613

[1] Percentages may add to more than 100 because some respondents named more than 1 material.

Table 110.--Boys who had readymade winter sport shirts: Materials in winter sport shirts[1]

Background characteristics	Cotton Percent	Wool Percent	Cotton-polyester Percent	Polyester Percent	Rayon/acetate Percent	Other wool mixtures Percent	Nylon Percent	Wool-cotton Percent	Acrylic Percent	All other Percent	Unspecified Percent	Not ascertained Percent	Cases Number
United States total-----	87	28	10	6	6	4	4	4	3	1	3	2	1,613
Age:													
14 years----------------	87	30	8	6	6	4	5	5	2	1	4	2	422
15 years----------------	89	26	10	5	6	2	4	3	3	(*)	4	2	437
16 years----------------	85	27	10	5	6	5	4	4	3	1	2	2	452
17 years----------------	86	26	11	8	5	5	3	4	2	(*)	3	2	302
Family income group													
Lower-------------------	88	27	7	4	6	2	4	4	2	1	3	2	518
Middle------------------	85	30	10	7	6	4	4	4	3	1	3	2	655
Upper-------------------	87	25	13	7	6	6	5	4	3	(*)	4	2	439
Size of place:													
Urban metropolitan------	82	33	9	7	5	5	4	6	3	1	3	2	548
Urban nonmetropolitan---	89	25	10	7	7	4	4	2	2	(*)	3	1	653
Town and farm----------	90	25	10	4	6	2	4	4	3	1	3		412
Region:													
Northeast--------------	82	33	9	6	6	4	3	4	3	1	4	2	380
North Central----------	90	24	7	7	7	4	4	3	3	(*)	3	2	455
South------------------	92	20	11	5	6	2	5	2	1	(*)	3	1	526
West-------------------	77	42	12	7	5	9	4	10	4	2	2	3	252

[1] Percentages add to more than 100 because some respondents named more than 1 material.
* Less than 1 percent.

Table 111.--Boys who had readymade winter sport shirts: Material preferred for winter sports shirts

Background characteristics	Cotton	Wool	Cotton-polyester	All other	No preference	Not ascertained	Cases
	Percent	Percent	Percent	Percent	Percent	Percent	Number
United States total-------	65	10	4	10	8	3	1,613
Age:							
14 years-------------	62	11	5	12	8	2	422
15 years-------------	68	9	4	8	9	2	437
16 years-------------	67	10	4	9	7	3	452
17 years-------------	63	12	4	10	8	3	302
Family income group:							
Lower---------------	69	9	3	9	7	3	518
Middle--------------	63	13	3	9	10	2	655
Upper---------------	66	8	5	11	7	3	439
Size of place:							
Urban metropolitan---	59	15	3	11	9	3	548
Urban nonmetropolitan-	69	8	5	8	7	3	653
Town and farm--------	69	7	4	9	9	2	412
Region:							
Northeast-----------	59	13	4	11	9	4	380
North Central-------	69	7	2	9	10	3	455
South---------------	75	6	5	8	4	2	526
West----------------	46	22	5	13	12	2	252

winter sport shirts and said they liked certain materials
(material liked best) for winter sport shirts?"[1]

| | Material liked best for winter sport shirts[2] | |
	Cotton	Wool
	Percent	Percent
	79	95
----------	38	7
----------	22	89
----------	22	1
----------	9	1
----------	6	1
----------	2	2
----------	1	4
----------	4	2
	30	23
----------	10	8
----------	8	4
----------	6	2
----------	4	2
----------	3	2
----------	2	4
----------	2	2
----------	3	2
	23	4
----------	9	--
----------	7	1
----------	3	1
----------	3	1
----------	3	--
----------	2	--
----------	3	1
	19	16
----------	7	7
----------	6	4
ch--------	3	3
----------	3	1
----------	2	3
----------	2	--
----------	4	--
----------	3	1
----------	(*)	1
----------	1,053	

ir group totals and these add to more than 100 because some

ls too small for separate analysis.

109

Table 113.--Boys who had readymade winter sport shirts and said they liked
certain materials best: "Is there anything that you don't like so well
about (material liked best) for winter sport shirts?"[1]

Criticisms of preferred material	Material liked best for winter sport shirts[2]	
	Cotton	Wool
	Percent	Percent
PERFORMANCE AND DURABILITY------------------	13	9
Wrinkles easily---------------------------	5	--
Not colorfast; fades, runs----------------	3	1
Doesn't hold shape; shrinks, stretches-----	1	4
Balls up, fuzzes, sheds--------------------	--	2
Miscellaneous-----------------------------	5	3
COMFORT AND WEIGHT-------------------------	8	36
Not warm enough---------------------------	4	1
Irritates, scratches, itches--------------	2	26
Too warm, not cool enough-----------------	1	7
Clings, binds-----------------------------	1	4
Miscellaneous-----------------------------	1	1
OTHER:		
Appearance and styling--------------------	3	2
Care and laundering-----------------------	2	4
All other---------------------------------	1	--
Not ascertained---------------------------	1	1
NO CRITICISM OF MATERIAL-------------------	74	55
Number of cases---------------------------	1,053	168

[1] Percentages may add to more than their group totals and these may add to
more than 100 because some respondents gave more than 1 answer.
[2] Numbers preferring other materials too small for separate analysis.

de winter sport coats: "What material are
ats made of?" "What other materials are
of?" "What material do you like best for

	Materials in winter sport coat wardrobe	Material most winter sport coats made of	Material pre- ferred for winter sport coats
	Percent	Percent	Percent
	55	50	41
	17	13	11
	9	7	7
	8	6	4
	6	4	3
	3	2	2
	3	1	2
	2	2	1
	2	2	1
	2	1	2
	6	4	5
	2	1	1
			14
	7	8	6
	1,073	1,073	1,073

than 100 because some respondents named more

Table 115.--Boys who had readymade winter sport coats: Materials in winter sport coats[1]

Background characteristics	Wool	Cotton	Wool-poly-ester	Wool-cotton	Other wool mixtures	Cotton-poly-ester	All other	Not ascer-tained	Cases
	Percent	Percent	Percent	Percent	Percent	Percent	Percent	Percent	Number
United States total--------	55	17	9	8	6	6	12	7	1,073
Age:									
14 years-----------------	52	17	10	10	7	6	13	6	273
15 years-----------------	58	15	7	9	5	5	10	6	298
16 years-----------------	57	16	7	7	7	7	13	8	294
17 years-----------------	53	19	11	7	7	7	15	6	208
Family income group:									
Lower--------------------	51	21	6	8	6	6	15	7	305
Middle-------------------	55	15	10	9	7	6	12	5	444
Upper--------------------	58	15	10	7	7	7	11	9	323
Size of place:									
Urban metropolitan-------	63	14	5	10	7	4	13	7	378
Urban nonmetropolitan----	55	18	10	7	6	7	12	6	453
Town and farm-----------	43	19	11	7	5	7	14	7	242
Region:									
Northeast---------------	69	13	5	7	6	2	13	4	288
North Central-----------	50	11	8	9	5	6	12	11	282
South-------------------	50	21	11	6	6	10	14	6	341
West--------------------	49	25	9	13	11	6	9	6	162

[1] Percentages add to more than 100 because some respondents named more than 1 material.

Table 116.--Boys who had readymade winter sport coats: Material preferred for winter sport coats

characteristics	Wool	Cotton	Wool-poly-ester	Wool-cotton	All other	No pref-erence	Not ascer-tained	Cases
	Percent	Percent	Percent	Percent	Percent	Percent	Percent	Number
United States total---------------	41	11	7	4	17	14	6	1,073
Age:								
14 years-------------------------	38	10	7	5	16	18	6	273
15 years-------------------------	44	11	6	4	15	14	6	298
16 years-------------------------	42	12	7	3	18	11	7	294
17 years-------------------------	36	13	11	4	20	10	6	208
Family income group:								
Lower---------------------------	40	13	5	5	21	9	7	305
Middle--------------------------	38	11	8	4	16	18	5	444
Upper---------------------------	43	10	9	3	15	11	9	323
Size of place:								
Urban metropolitan--------------	46	8	4	5	15	15	7	378
Urban nonmetropolitan-----------	40	14	9	3	16	12	6	453
Town and farm-------------------	34	11	9	3	23	13	7	242
Region:								
Northeast-----------------------	54	8	4	6	13	11	4	288
North Central-------------------	37	7	9	4	17	14	12	282
South---------------------------	36	14	10	2	21	12	5	341
West----------------------------	34	19	5	3	16	19	4	162

Table 117.--Boys who had readymade winter sport coats and said they liked certain materials best: "Why do you prefer (material liked best) for winter sport coats?"[1]

Reasons for preference	Material liked best for winter sport coats[2]		
	Wool	Cotton	Wool-polyester
	Percent	Percent	Percent
COMFORT AND WEIGHT---------------------------------	77	74	72
Warm--	64	19	18
Doesn't irritate, scratch, itch-----------------	4	21	26
Not too warm; lightweight, airy----------------	3	27	19
Doesn't cling, bind----------------------------	3	9	3
Lightweight but warm---------------------------	3	6	8
Weight just right------------------------------	2	4	5
Year-round weight------------------------------	2	3	6
Miscellaneous----------------------------------	2	3	1
APPEARANCE AND STYLING---------------------------	44	42	53
Good colors, patterns available----------------	11	8	12
Variety of styles available--------------------	7	9	9
Stylish, popular, fashionable------------------	7	8	9
Fits, hangs well-------------------------------	7	6	10
Looks nice (general)---------------------------	4	7	3
Dressier; more formal--------------------------	4	2	5
Like texture (general)-------------------------	4	3	9
Goes well with other clothes-------------------	3	2	5
Good for everyday, casual wear-----------------	2	3	3
Versatile; can wear for any occasion-----------	2	2	1
Looks expensive--------------------------------	2	--	4
Miscellaneous----------------------------------	3	1	3
PERFORMANCE AND DURABILITY-----------------------	33	22	50
Doesn't wrinkle--------------------------------	14	12	33
Holds shape, doesn't shrink, stretch-----------	9	3	14
Durable, wears well----------------------------	7	4	6
Doesn't soil, stain easily---------------------	6	2	8
Holds crease, press----------------------------	5	1	9
Miscellaneous----------------------------------	2	3	--
CARE AND LAUNDERING------------------------------	4	19	3
Machine washable-------------------------------	(*)	4	--
Washable; no drycleaning required--------------	--	5	--
Easy to wash and care for----------------------	--	5	--
Easy to iron, press----------------------------	--	4	--
Miscellaneous----------------------------------	4	4	3
OTHER:			
Inexpensive------------------------------------	1	4	1
All other--------------------------------------	2	1	1
Not ascertained--------------------------------	1	--	--
Number of cases--------------------------------	434	122	78

[1] Percentages add to more than their group totals and these add to more than 100 because some respondents gave more than 1 answer.
[2] Numbers preferring other materials too small for separate analysis.
*Less than 1 percent.

113

Table 118.--Boys who had readymade winter sports coats and said they liked certain materials best: "Is there anything that you don't like so well about (material liked best) for winter sport coats?"[1]

Criticisms of preferred material	Material liked best for winter sport coats[2]		
	Wool	Cotton	Wool-polyester
	Percent	Percent	Percent
COMFORT AND WEIGHT----------------------	30	11	10
Irritates, scratches, itches----------	20	--	5
Too warm, not cool enough-------------	9	2	4
Not warm enough-----------------------	(*)	6	.1
Miscellaneous-------------------------	3	4	--
PERFORMANCE AND DURABILITY-------------	11	16	13
Collects lint-------------------------	5	1	6
Soils, stains easily------------------	2	2	1
Snags, tears easily-------------------	1	3	3
Doesn't wear well---------------------	1	3	--
Wrinkles easily-----------------------	1	3	4
Doesn't hold shape; stretches, shrinks	1	3	.1
Not colorfast; fades, runs------------	--	--	3
Miscellaneous-------------------------	2	1	1
OTHER:			
Care and laundering-------------------	3	5	5
Appearance and styling----------------	1	5	4
All other-----------------------------	1	--	1
Not ascertained-----------------------	(*)	4	--
NO CRITICISM OF MATERIAL--------------	57	64	69
Number of cases-----------------------	434	122	78

[1] Percentages may add to more than their group totals and these may add to more than 100 because some respondents gave more than 1 answer.
[2] Numbers preferring other materials too small for separate analysis.
* Less than 1 percent.

Table 119.--Boys who had readymade winter pants: "Do you get some of your winter pants for
everyday wear and others for Sunday or special occasions, or do you get the same kind for
both everyday and dress-up wear?"

Background characteristics	Different pants for each	Same pants for both	Have only everyday pants	Have only dress-up pants	Cases
	Percent	Percent	Percent	Percent	Number
United States total---------------------	77	20	2	1	1,648
Age:					
14 years------------------------------	82	16	1	1	431
15 years------------------------------	76	22	2	(*)	447
16 years------------------------------	73	24	2	1	459
17 years------------------------------	75	21	2	2	311
Family income group:					
Lower---------------------------------	73	24	2	1	534
Middle--------------------------------	77	21	1	1	664
Upper---------------------------------	82	16	1	1	449
Size of place:					
Urban metropolitan--------------------	74	23	2	1	564
Urban nonmetropolitan-----------------	77	20	2	1	664
Town and farm-------------------------	80	18	1	1	420
Region:					
Northeast-----------------------------	74	24	1	1	388
North Central-------------------------	78	19	2	1	467
South---------------------------------	78	20	1	1	535
West----------------------------------	76	19	3	2	258

* Less than 1 percent.

Table 120.--Boys who had dress-up winter pants: "What material are most of your dress-up winter
pants made of?" "What other materials are your dress-up winter pants made of?" "What material do you like best for dress-up winter pants?"[1]

Material	Materials in dress-up winter pants wardrobe	Material most dress-up winter pants made of	Material preferred for dress-up winter pants
	Percent	Percent	Percent
Wool----------------------------------	48	36	23
Cotton--------------------------------	36	22	24
Wool-polyester------------------------	14	9	9
Cotton-polyester----------------------	11	8	8
Wool-cotton---------------------------	7	5	3
Polyester-----------------------------	6	3	4
Rayon/acetate-------------------------	5	3	3
Wool-rayon/acetate--------------------	4	2	2
Wool-acrylic--------------------------	3	1	1
Other materials-----------------------	8	4	4
Unspecified---------------------------	2	1	1
No preference-------------------------	--	--	14
Not ascertained-----------------------	4	6	4
Number of cases-----------------------	1,283	1,283	1,283

[1] Percentages may add to more than 100 because some respondents named more than 1 material.

Table 121.--Boys who had dress-up winter pants: Materials in dress-up winter pants[1]

Background characteristics	Wool	Cotton	Wool-polyester	Cotton-polyester	Wool-cotton	Polyester	Rayon/acetate	Wool-rayon/acetate	Wool-acrylic	All other	Not ascertained	Cases
	Percent	Percent	Percent	Percent	Percent	Percent	Percent	Percent	Percent	Percent	Percent	Number
United States total------	48	36	14	11	7	6	5	4	3	10	4	1,283
Age:												
14 years---------------	46	41	14	8	8	5	6	4	6	12	4	359
15 years---------------	45	37	12	11	7	5	4	2	5	11	4	341
16 years---------------	49	33	12	13	8	6	5	4	2	7	5	342
17 years---------------	56	32	17	12	6	7	7	5	4	7	2	241
Family income group:												
Lower------------------	46	41	12	13	9	6	5	4	4	7	8	396
Middle-----------------	49	34	14	12	7	6	6	3	3	9	4	516
Upper------------------	50	34	15	6	6	5	5	4	3	12	6	370
Size of place:												
Urban metropolitan-----	53	33	12	8	8	5	5	3	4	12	6	424
Urban nonmetropolitan--	51	37	17	10	6	6	5	4	3	9	3	516
Town and farm----------	39	38	11	15	9	6	6	3	3	8	4	343
Region:												
Northeast--------------	52	32	14	8	8	4	5	5	3	11	4	293
North Central----------	50	35	8	9	8	6	7	2	2	10	5	367
South------------------	47	41	17	14	7	7	4	3	3	9	3	423
West-------------------	45	35	17	11	6	5	6	5	7	9	6	200

[1] Percentages add to more than 100 because some respondents named more than 1 material.

Table 122.--Boys who had dress-up winter pants: Material preferred for dress-up winter pants

Background characteristics	Cotton	Wool	Wool-polyester	Cotton-polyester	Poly-ester	Wool-cotton	Other wool mixtures	Rayon/acetate	All other	No preference	Not ascertained	Cases
	Percent	Percent	Percent	Percent	Percent	Percent	Percent	Percent	Percent	Percent	Percent	Number
United States total------	24	23	9	8	4	3	3	3	5	14	4	1,283
Age:												
14 years---------------	30	21	8	6	2	3	3	3	4	16	4	359
15 years---------------	25	21	8	8	5	3	2	3	7	14	4	341
16 years---------------	21	25	7	9	6	5	4	2	3	12	6	342
17 years---------------	19	26	12	9	5	2	5	6	3	12	1	241
Family income group:												
Lower------------------	29	24	6	9	5	4	4	3	3	10	3	396
Middle-----------------	21	24	8	9	4	3	3	4	4	16	4	516
Upper------------------	22	21	12	5	4	4	4	3	6	14	5	370
Size of place:												
Urban metropolitan-----	21	28	8	5	3	3	4	4	5	13	6	424
Urban nonmetropolitan--	24	23	11	7	5	3	3	3	4	15	2	516
Town and farm----------	28	18	6	12	4	5	4	3	3	13	4	343
Region:												
Northeast--------------	20	30	9	7	2	3	5	3	5	12	4	293
North Central----------	22	26	6	4	5	5	3	4	4	16	5	367
South------------------	27	19	10	11	6	3	3	3	4	11	3	423
West-------------------	25	16	8	7	3	4	4	3	5	4	5	200

Table 123.--Boys who had dress-up winter pants and said they liked certain materials best: "Why do you prefer (material liked best) for dress-up winter pants?"[1]

Reasons for preference	Material liked best for dress-up winter pants[2]			
	Cotton	Wool	Wool-polyester	Cotton-polyester
	Percent	Percent	Percent	Percent
COMFORT AND WEIGHT----------------------------	71	68	70	60
Doesn't irritate, scratch, itch---------------	40	6	31	30
Warm---	16	61	20	9
Not too warm; lightweight, airy---------------	15	1	13	17
Doesn't cling, bind--------------------------	9	2	4	3
Comfortable (general)------------------------	3	(*)	2	4
Weight just right---------------------------	2	2	5	3
Year-round weight---------------------------	2	1	2	--
Lightweight but warm------------------------	2	--	6	2
Miscellaneous-------------------------------	1	1	--	--
PERFORMANCE AND DURABILITY---------------------	31	48	62	48
Holds crease, press-------------------------	8	26	38	29
Doesn't wrinkle-----------------------------	8	13	15	16
Durable, wears well-------------------------	7	8	5	2
Doesn't soil, stain easily------------------	6	5	8	2
Holds shape, doesn't shrink, stretch--------	5	8	16	8
Holds colors; doesn't fade, run-------------	1	1	2	2
Miscellaneous-------------------------------	4	1	3	4
APPEARANCE AND STYLING------------------------	29	37	27	32
Fits well-----------------------------------	10	6	9	11
Looks nice (general)------------------------	5	3	2	9
Good colors, patterns available-------------	4	3	2	--
Stylish, popular, fashionable---------------	4	3	--	3
Variety of styles available-----------------	4	2	5	2
Dressier; more formal-----------------------	2	14	7	3
Goes well with other clothes----------------	2	3	1	2
Like texture (general)----------------------	2	2	3	9
Versatile; can wear for any occasion--------	2	1	--	2
Miscellaneous-------------------------------	3	6	5	--
CARE AND LAUNDERING---------------------------	18	6	16	21
Washable, no drycleaning required-----------	8	1	3	6
Easy to iron, press-------------------------	6	1	5	7
Easy to wash and care for-------------------	3	1	3	4
Little or no ironing required---------------	2	1	5	2
Machine washable---------------------------	2	--	1	2
Can be drycleaned--------------------------	1	2	--	1
Miscellaneous-----------------------------	1	1	2	3
OTHER:				
Inexpensive--------------------------------	4	--	3	1
All other----------------------------------	2	1	--	1
Not ascertained----------------------------	--	--	--	1
Number of cases----------------------------	307	297	111	98

[1] Percentages add to more than their group totals and these add to more than 100 because some respondents gave more than 1 answer.
[2] Numbers preferring other materials too small for separate analysis.
*Less than 1 percent.

117

Table 124.--Boys who had dress-up winter pants and said they liked certain materials best: "
there anything that you don't like so well about (material liked best) for dress-up wint
pants?"[1]

Criticisms of preferred material

PERFORMANCE AND DURABILITY-------------------				
Wrinkles easily----------------------------	4	2	5	1
Soils, stains easily-----------------------	4	1	--	2
Collects lint------------------------------	3	4	4	1
Doesn't hold crease------------------------	3	2	2	--
Not colorfast; fades, runs-----------------	3	2	--	--
Doesn't wear well--------------------------	3	1	3	4
Doesn't hold shape; stretches, shrinks-----	2	2	1	4
Snags, tears easily------------------------	2	--	--	3
Miscellaneous------------------------------	1	1	2	--
COMFORT AND WEIGHT-------------------------	9	39	14	7
Not warm enough----------------------------	8	1	--	5
Irritates, scratches, itches---------------	1	34	12	1
Clings, binds------------------------------	(*)	1	4	2
Too warm, not cool enough------------------	(*)	4	1	1
Miscellaneous------------------------------	(*)	2	--	--
OTHER:				
Appearance and styling---------------------	3	2	4	
Care and laundering------------------------	2	7	2	
All other----------------------------------	1	2	2	
Not ascertained----------------------------	2	1	3	
NO CRITICISM OF MATERIAL--------------------	65	43	61	80
Number of cases----------------------------				

[1] Percentages may add to more than their group totals and these may add to more than 100 because some respondents gave more than 1 answer.
[2] Numbers preferring other materials too small for separate analysis.
*Less than 1 percent.

118

everyday winter pants: "What material are most of
pants made of?" "What other materials are your every-
e of?" "What material do you like best for everyday

	Materials in everyday winter pants wardrobe	Material most everyday winter pants made of	Material preferred for everyday winter pants
	Percent	Percent	Percent
------------	84	76	69
------------	14	7	6
------------	9	5	6
------------	3	1	1
------------	3	2	1
------------	3	1	1
------------	2	1	1
------------	2	1	1
------------	5	2	2
------------	4	2	1
------------			9
------------	2	3	2
------------	1,631	1,631	1,631

to more than 100 because some respondents named more

Table 126.--Boys who had everyday winter pants: Materials in everyday winter pants[1]

Background characteristics	Cotton	Wool	Cotton-polyester	Polyester	Wool-cotton	Wool-polyester	Other wool mixtures	Rayon/acetate	All other	Unspeci-fied	Not ascer-tained	Cases
	Percent	Percent	Percent	Percent	Percent	Percent	Percent	Percent	Percent	Percent	Percent	Number
United States total------	84	14	9	3	3	3	2	2	5	4	2	1,631
Age:												
14 years----------------	86	13	7	2	4	3	2	2	5	5	3	426
15 years----------------	84	12	10	3	3	2	1	2	5	3	3	445
16 years----------------	81	15	10	3	2	2	3	3	5	4	2	455
17 years----------------	83	13	10	5	3	5	3	3	3	5	2	305
Family income group:												
Lower-------------------	87	12	7	3	2	2	2	3	4	2	2	528
Middle------------------	82	16	9	3	4	3	3	3	4	4	2	658
Upper-------------------	81	12	12	3	3	4	2	1	6	6	3	444
Size of place:												
Urban metropolitan-----	75	21	8	4	5	5	4	3	3	6	3	560
Urban nonmetropolitan--	86	11	11	3	3	3	1	2	6	3	2	657
Town and farm----------	92	8	9	1	1	1	1	2	4	3	2	414
Region:												
Northeast--------------	72	25	10	3	5	6	3	3	4	6	3	383
North Central----------	86	10	8	3	2	1	2	2	6	5	3	463
South------------------	89	11	11	3	2	2	1	2	3	2	1	531
West-------------------	87	9	9	4	4	2	4	2	5	2	2	254

[1] Percentages add to more than 100 because some respondents named more than 1 material.

Table 127.--Boys who had everyday winter pants: Material preferred for everyday winter pants

Background characteristics	Cotton	Cotton-polyester	Wool	Wool mixtures	All other	No preference	Not ascertained	Cases
	Percent	Percent	Percent	Percent	Percent	Percent	Percent	Number
United States------------	68	6	6	4	5	9	2	1,631
Age:								
14 years----------------	69	4	6	3	4	11	3	426
15 years----------------	71	7	4	3	4	9	2	445
16 years----------------	66	5	7	5	5	10	2	455
17 years----------------	67	6	5	5	6	9	2	305
Family income group:								
Lower-------------------	73	5	5	3	3	9	2	528
Middle------------------	67	5	6	4	5	11	2	658
Upper-------------------	65	7	5	6	6	8	3	444
Size of place:								
Urban metropolitan-----	57	4	11	5	6	14	3	560
Urban nonmetropolitan--	71	7	4	3	5	8	2	657
Town and farm----------	80	6	2	1	3	7	1	414
Region:								
Northeast--------------	55	5	13	7	5	12	3	383
North Central----------	71	5	4	3	5	9	3	463
South------------------	75	8	3	3	4	6	1	531
West-------------------	69	3	3	4	4	15	2	254

Table 128.--Boys who had everyday winter pants and said they liked certain materials best: "Why do you prefer (material liked best) for everyday winter pants?"[1]

Reasons for preference	Material liked best for everyday winter pants[2]		
	Cotton	Cotton-polyester	Wool
	Percent	Percent	Percent
COMFORT AND WEIGHT------------------------------	51	47	86
Doesn't irritate, scratch, itch---------------	18	11	2
Warm--	14	4	77
Not too warm; lightweight, airy---------------	11	12	1
Doesn't cling, bind--------------------------	7	10	2
Comfortable (general)-------------------------	4	4	2
Weight just right-----------------------------	3	9	--
Year-round weight-----------------------------	3	4	--
Lightweight but warm--------------------------	1	3	--
Wind resistant--------------------------------	1	--	6
Miscellaneous---------------------------------	1	1	1
PERFORMANCE AND DURABILITY----------------------	47	62	33
Durable, wears well---------------------------	23	17	8
Doesn't snag, tear easily---------------------	8	4	4
Holds crease, press---------------------------	6	19	19
Doesn't soil, stain easily--------------------	6	7	6
Doesn't wrinkle-------------------------------	5	20	8
Holds shape; doesn't shrink, stretch----------	5	10	4
Holds colors; doesn't fade, run---------------	3	8	--
Miscellaneous---------------------------------	1	2	--
APPEARANCE AND STYLING--------------------------	35	41	15
Stylish, popular, fashionable-----------------	9	4	2
Fits well-------------------------------------	8	7	3
Variety of styles available-------------------	6	3	1
Good for everyday, casual wear----------------	5	4	2
Good colors, prints available-----------------	4	3	1
Looks neat, clean, fresh----------------------	2	8	--
Looks nice (general)--------------------------	2	4	--
Dressier; more formal-------------------------	1	5	3
Like texture (general)------------------------	1	5	1
Goes well with other clothes------------------	1	3	--
Versatile; can wear for any occasion----------	1	3	--
Miscellaneous---------------------------------	1	--	6
CARE AND LAUNDERING-----------------------------	34	25	3
Machine washable------------------------------	10	9	--
Easy to wash and care for---------------------	10	5	2
Washable; no drycleaning required-------------	8	7	--
Easy to iron, press---------------------------	7	4	--
Little or no ironing required-----------------	5	7	--
Dries quickly---------------------------------	1	2	--
Miscellaneous---------------------------------	2	3	1
OTHER:			
Inexpensive-----------------------------------	7	4	--
All other-------------------------------------	3	1	1
Not ascertained-------------------------------	1	--	1
Number of cases-------------------------------	1,115	92	91

[1] Percentages add to more than their group totals and these add to more than 100 because some respondents gave more than 1 answer.
[2] Numbers preferring other materials too small for separate analysis.

121

Table 129.--Boys who had everyday winter pants and said they liked certain materials best: "Is there anything that you don't like so well about (material liked best) for everyday winter pants?"[1]

Criticisms of preferred material	Material liked best for everyday winter pants[2]		
	Cotton	Cotton-polyester	Wool
	Percent	Percent	Percent
PERFORMANCE AND DURABILITY---------------------	22	17	5
Not colorfast; fades, runs--------------------	8	1	--
Wrinkles easily-------------------------------	4	3	--
Doesn't hold shape, stretches, shrinks--------	4·	2	2
Soils, stains easily--------------------------	3	2	--
Not durable-----------------------------------	3	--	1
Doesn't hold crease, press--------------------	2	4	--
Snags, tears easily---------------------------	2	2	--
Miscellaneous---------------------------------	2	3	2
COMFORT AND WEIGHT----------------------------	7	8	25
Not warm enough-------------------------------	3	4	--
Too warm, not cool enough---------------------	1	1	2
Clings, binds---------------------------------	1	2	2
Irritates, scratches, itches-----------------	1	--	20
Miscellaneous---------------------------------	1	1	1
OTHER:			
Appearance and styling-----------------------	3	3	--
Care and laundering--------------------------	2	2	3
All other------------------------------------	(*)	1	--
Not ascertained------------------------------	1	--	4
NO CRITICISM OF MATERIAL---------------------	67	70	67
Number of cases------------------------------	1,115	92	91

[1] Percentages may add to more than their group totals and these may add to more than 100 because some respondents gave more than 1 answer.
[2] Numbers preferring other materials too small for separate analysis.
* Less than 1 percent.

Table 130.--Boys who had "permanently" creased winter pants: Materials owned in "permanently" creased winter pants[1]

Materials	"Permanently" creased winter pants
	Percent
Wool---	44
Cotton---------------------------------------	12
Cotton-polyester--- -------------------------	11
Wool mixtures--------------------------------	21
All other------------------------------------	12
Not ascertained--·--------------------------	7
Number of cases------------------------------	305

[1] Percentages add to more than 100 because some respondents named more than 1 material.

Table 131.--Boys who had readymade winter wool pants (winter wool pants, "permanently" creased winter wool pants) 'Do you think that permanent creasing in wool pants is a good idea or not such a good idea?"

Background characteristics	Owners of winter pants				Owners of winter wool pants				Owners of "permanently" creased winter wool pants			
	Permanent creasing is--		Not ascertained	Cases	Permanent creasing is--		Not ascertained	Cases	Permanent creasing is--		Not ascertained	Cases
	A good idea	Not a good idea			A good idea	Not a good idea			A good idea	Not a good idea		
	Percent	Percent	Percent	Number	Percent	Percent	Percent	Number	Percent	Percent	Percent	Number
United States total------------	84	15	1	1,648	88	12	(*)	751	90	10	--	135
Age:												
14 years-----------	84	15	1	431	88	11	1	197	78	22	--	32
15 years-----------	86	13	1	447	90	10	--	181	93	7	--	29
16 years-----------	81	17	2	459	86	13	1	212	96	4	--	44
17 years-----------	86	13	1	311	90	10	--	161	90	10	--	30
Family income group:												
Lower-----------	87	12	1	534	89	11	(*)	221	90	10	--	40
Middle----------	82	17	1	664	89	11	(*)	313	87	13	--	54
Upper-----------	84	14	2	449	87	13	(*)	217	93	7	--	41
Size of place:												
Urban metropolitan----------	84	14	2	564	87	12	1	.290	84	16	--	45
Urban nonmetropolitan-------	85	15	(*)	664	89	11	--	305	94	6	--	68
Town and farm--------------	84	15	1	420	90	9	1	156	86	14	--	22
Region:												
Northeast-------------	82	18	(*)	388	87	13	--	199	86	14	--	28
North Central---------	85	13	2	467	88	12	(*)	213	95	5	--	42
South-----------------	86	14	(*)	535	91	9	--	233	89	11	--	44
West------------------	83	14	3	258	86	12	2	106	86	14	--	21

* Less than 1 percent.

Table 132.--Boys who had readymade winter pants (winter wool pants and "permanently" creased winter pants made of wool) and said they thou that permanent creasing in wool pants was a good idea: "Why do you that?"[1]

Reasons for favorable opinion	Owners of winter pants	Owners of winter wool pants	Owners "permane creas winter pant
	Percent	Percent	Perce
CARE AND LAUNDERING----------------------	55	54	50
Little or no ironing required------------	33	33	31
Easy to iron, press----------------------	8	8	10
Saves money, less expensive to care for--	7	8	7
Easy to care for-------------------------	6	5	4
Washable, creases stay in when washed----	4	4	1
Recreasing unnecessary-------------------	2	2	--
Miscellaneous----------------------------	(*)	(*)	--
PERFORMANCE AND DURABILITY----------------	54	54	66
Creases always stay in-------------------	28	27	31
Creases always centered, straight--------	7	6	12
Holds shape; doesn't get baggy-----------	4	5	5
Stays neater longer----------------------	4	5	5
Wrinkle free-----------------------------	3	3	5
Easy to hang up--------------------------	3	4	9
Less frequent cleaning-------------------	3	3	4
Always available to wear-----------------	3	2	2
Crease stays in even when wet------------	2	2	2
Miscellaneous----------------------------	3	2	
APPEARANCE--------------------------------	16	16	6
Would look nicer, more attractive--------	6	7	9
Would look neater------------------------	5	6	3
Dressier---------------------------------	2	2	3
Miscellaneous----------------------------	3	2	2
OTHER:			
Just like them; no specific reason-------	2	1	
All other--------------------------------	(*)	--	
Not ascertained--------------------------	(*)	(*)	
Number of cases--------------------------			

[1] Percentages add to more than their group totals and these add to m 100 because some respondents gave more than 1 answer.
* Less than 1 percent.

124

Table 133.--Boys who had readymade winter pants (winter pants made of wool, and "permanently" creased winter pants made of wool) and said they thought that permanent creasing in wool pants was not such a good idea: "Why do you say that?"[1]

Reasons for unfavorable opinion	Owners of winter pants	Owners of winter wool pants	Owners of "permanently" creased winter wool pants
	Percent	Percent	Percent
APPEARANCE-------------------------------	29	37	43
Looks artificial, stiff------------------	14	11	22
Don't like looks, appearance-------------	5	7	--
Don't like style; not tight enough-------	4	5 ,	7
Not stylish, popular---------------------	3	6	7
Miscellaneous---------------------------	4	9	7
PERFORMANCE AND DURABILITY----------------	17	15	14
Creases won't stay in; no such thing as permanent creases---------------------	8	7	14
Weakens material; not durable------------	3	--	--
Gets double crease when pressed----------	3	4	--
Doesn't hold shape; gets baggy-----------	2	2	--
Miscellaneous---------------------------	3	2	--
OTHER:			
Still has to be sent to the cleaners-----	13	22	29
Don't like wool-------------------------	15	5	7
Don't like creased pants----------------	10	9	14
Hard to alter--------------------------	4	6	--
Just not important----------------------	4	4	7
Other factors are more important--------	3	4	--
Expensive------------------------------	3	2	--
Don't like the idea (general)-----------	3	4.	--
All other-----------------------------	7	7	7
Not ascertained------------------------	4	1	--
Number of cases-------------------------	243	85	14

[1] Percentages add to more than their group totals and these add to more than 100 because some respondents gave more than 1 answer.

Table 134.--Boys who had readymade winter pants:"... tell me how you would feel about permanent creases in deciding whether to buy a pair of wool pants. You can give a rating anywhere from "Most important" which is number 5 to "Not important at all" which is number 1. Which block number best tells how important permanent creases would be to you in deciding whether or not to buy a particular pair of pants made of wool?"

Background characteristics	5 (most important)	4	3	2	1 (not important at all)	Not ascer- tained	Cases
	Percent	Percent	Percent	Percent	Percent	Percent	Number
United States total--------	28	20	25	8	18	1	1,648
Age:							
14 years------------------	30	20	21	8	20	1	431
15 years------------------	26	21	24	10	18	1	447
16 years------------------	26	18	27	7	21	1	459
17 years------------------	29	22	26	9	14	--	311
Family income group:							
Lower---------------------	33	20	22	4	20	1	534
Middle--------------------	27	21	26	10	16	(*)	664
Upper---------------------	23	18	27	12	20	--	449
Size of place:							
Urban metropolitan--------	30	19	23	9	18	1	564
Urban nonmetropolitan-----	24	21	27	9	19	(*)	664
Town and farm-------------	31	21	23	7	17	1	420
Region:							
Northeast-----------------	30	17	21	9	22	1	388
North Central-------------	22	22	28	9	18	1	467
South---------------------	33	18	23	7	18	1	535
West----------------------	22	25	27	10	15	1	258

*Less than 1 percent.

Table 135.--Boys who had readymade winter pants made of wool:"... tell me how you would feel about permanent creases in deciding whether to buy a pair of wool pants. You can give a rating anywhere from "Most important" which is number 5 to "Not important at all" which is number 1. Which block number best tells how important permanent creases would be to you in deciding whether or not to buy a particular pair of pants made of wool?"

Background characteristics	5 (most important)	4	3	2	1 (not important at all)	Not ascertained	Cases
	Percent	Percent	Percent	Percent	Percent	Percent	Number
United States total--------	32	20	24	9	15	(*)	751
Age:							
14 years------------------	33	19	20	10	17	1	197
15 years------------------	31	24	22	10	13	--	181
16 years------------------	33	17	27	7	16	--	212
17 years------------------	33	20	27	9	11	--	161
Family income group:							
Lower---------------------	38	23	21	4	14	(*)	221
Middle--------------------	31	20	25	11	13	--	313
Upper---------------------	29	17	25	11	18	--	217
Size of place:							
Urban metropolitan--------	40	16	20	10	14	--	290
Urban nonmetropolitan-----	26	20	28	9	17	(*)	305
Town and farm-------------	33	26	22	8	11	--	156
Region:							
Northeast-----------------	39	17	20	9	15	--	199
North Central-------------	28	23	23	11	15	--	213
South---------------------	34	16	28	8	14	(*)	233
West----------------------	26	27	26	8	13	--	106

*Less than 1 percent.

126

Table 136.--Boys who had readymade winter pants and gave a rating as to the importance of permanent creases in the decision to buy a pair of wool pants: "Why do you say that?"[1]

Reasons for rating of importance	5 (most important)	4	3	2	1 (not important at all)
	Percent	Percent	Percent	Percent	Percent
POSITIVE REASONS					
PERFORMANCE---	49	30	10	3	1
Creases always stay in--------------------------------	25	18	6	2	--
Stays neater longer-----------------------------------	5	3	1	--	--
Always ready to wear-----------------------------------	5	2	1	--	--
Hold shape; don't get baggy at the knees--------------------	5	1	--	--	--
Creases are always centered, straight-----------------------	3	3	1	--	--
Material more durable---------------------------------	2	1	1	--	--
Crease stays in even when wet-----------------------------	2	--	--	--	--
Wrinkle free--	2	2	1	--	--
Less frequent cleaning required----------------------------	2	1	1	--	(*)
Miscellaneous--	2	1	(*)	1	1
CARE AND LAUNDERING--	43	29	10	5	1
Little or no ironing required-----------------------------	20	19	6	3	1
Saves money; less expensive to care for-------------------	12	3	1	1	--
Easy to care for--------------------------------------	7	4	2	1	(*)
Easy to iron, press-----------------------------------	4	4	1	--	(*)
Miscellaneous--	3	2	1	1	(*)
APPEARANCE---	23	9	5	--	(*)
Would look neater------------------------------------	10	4	1	--	--
Would look nicer, more attractive------------------------	7	3	2	--	--
Dressier---	3	1	1	--	--
Better fit, creases hang straighter----------------------	2	--	--	--	--
Miscellaneous--	2	1	1	--	(*)
OTHER:					
Just like them; a good idea; more practical-----------------	3	7	2	1	--
All other---	2	1	3	1	(*)
NEGATIVE REASONS					
APPEARANCE---	--	1	3	8	14
Not stylish, popular---------------------------------	--	(*)	1	1	4
Looks artificial, stiff-------------------------------	--	1	1	2	2
Don't like looks, appearance---------------------------	--	(*)	(*)	2	3
Don't like style; not tight enough-----------------------	--	--	1	1	3
Miscellaneous--	--	1	1	4	3
CARE AND LAUNDERING--	--	--	2	9	7
Still has to be ironed, pressed anyway---------------------	--	--	2	5	2
Still has to be drycleaned-----------------------------	--	--	1	1	4
Miscellaneous--	--	--	(*)	3	1
PERFORMANCE---	--	1	1	4	3
OTHER FACTORS HAVE TO BE CONSIDERED--------------------------	2	33	47	44	16
Style--	(*)	9	16	17	5
Color, print, pattern---------------------------------	1	9	15	16	6
Material---	(*)	5	11	11	4
Fit--	--	4	8	8	3
Cost--	1	6	6	4	2
Looks--	--	3	4	4	1
Miscellaneous--	(*)	11	14	9	4
OTHER:					
Don't like wool--------------------------------------	(*)	2	5	9	31
Creases not important---------------------------------	--	1	10	6	9
Don't care for own clothes-----------------------------	(*)	(*)	4	3	4
Don't like creased pants-------------------------------	--	--	1	2	7
Just don't like the idea (general)------------------------	--	--	--	4	4
Hard to alter--	--	(*)	1	1	2
All other---	--	2	8	13	8
Not ascertained--------------------------------------	(*)	1	3	1	2
Number of cases---------------------------------------	456	327	407	142	305

[1] Percentages add to more than their group totals and these add to more than 100 because some respondents gave more than 1 answer.
*Less than 1 percent.

127

Table 137.--Boys who had winter outer jackets or short coats: "What materials are your outer jackets or short coats made of?" "What material do you like best for outer jackets or short coats?"[1]

Material	Materials in outer jacket or short coat wardrobe	Material preferred for outer jackets or short coats
	Percent	Percent
Wool--	35	23
Cotton--	31	20
Nylon---	13	10
Suede, leather--------------------------------------	11	9
Cotton-polyester------------------------------------	8	6
Plastic---	5	2
Wool-cotton---	4	2
Polyester---	3	3
Rayon/acetate---------------------------------------	3	1
Acrylic---	2	1
Other wool mixtures---------------------------------	4	3
Other materials-------------------------------------	5	5
Unspecified---	3	2
No preference---------------------------------------	--	11
Not ascertained-------------------------------------	3	2
Number of cases-------------------------------------	1,466	1,466

[1] Percentages may add to more than 100 because some respondents named more than 1 material.

128

e, er	Cotton- poly- ester	Plastic	Wool- cotton	Other wool mixtures	Poly- ester	All other	Not ascer- tained	Cases
nt	Percent	Percent	Percent	Percent	Percent	Percent	Percent	Number
	8	5	4	4	3	15	3	1,466
	8	5	4	4	4	14	4	379
	9	5	3	4	4	12	3	398
	8	7	5	4	3	18	3	413
	7	4	5	4	3	16	5	276
	6	6	3	3	3	12	4	450
	7	6	4	4	3	15	2	602
	11	4	5	3	3	18	5	413
	5	4	5	4	3	14	6	489
	11	4	4	4	3	15	2	604
	7	8	4	3	3	16	2	373
	4	2	4	4	3	12	4	344
	5	7	5	3	4	19	4	427
	13	5	4	3	4	13	3	480
	10	6	5	7	4	15	3	215

ients named more than 1 material.

Suede, leather	Cotton- poly- ester	Wool- cotton	Other wool mixtures	All other	No pref- erence	Not ascer- tained	Cases
Percent	Percent	Percent	Percent	Percent	Percent	Percent	Number
9	6	2	3	14	11	2	1,466
5	5	3	2	13	13	3	379
9	6	1	3	13	12	2	398
10	6	2	3	15	10	1	413
12	7	4	4	13	11	2	276
12	6	2	2	11	12	2	450
7	5	2	4	14	13	1	602
8	7	3	2	15	11	2	413
9	3	2	5	14	16	2	489
7	7	2	2	13	12	2	604
13	7	3	2	14	6	2	373
7	2	2	3	11	12	3	344
8	3	3	3	16	11	2	427
11	11	2	2	13	11	2	480
8	7	2	5	14	13	2	215

129

Table 140.--Boys who had winter outer jackets or short coats and said they liked certain materials best: "Why do you prefer (material liked best) for outer jackets or short coats?"[1]

Reasons for preference	Material liked best for winter outer jackets or short coats[2]				
	Wool	Cotton	Nylon	Suede, leather	Cotton-polyester
	Percent	Percent	Percent	Percent	Percent
COMFORT AND WEIGHT------------------------	91	74	87	71	73
Warm-------------------------------------	82	30	15	44	22
Wind resistant---------------------------	6	2	17	16	4
Lightweight but warm---------------------	5	13	40	7	16
Doesn't irritate, scratch, itch----------	4	14	8	4	7
Doesn't cling, bind----------------------	2	5	6	2	5
Water repellent--------------------------	2	4	11	25	15
Weight just right------------------------	1	4	1	2	4
Not too warm; lightweight, airy----------	(*)	14	18	--	16
Miscellaneous----------------------------	1	4	5	3	6
APPEARANCE AND STYLING-------------------	30	31	29	47	33
Looks nice (general)---------------------	7	4	6	15	7
Variety of styles available-------------	6	9	4	7	5
Good colors, patterns available---------	5	6	4	2	4
Stylish, popular, fashionable-----------	4	5	8	6	4
Fits well-------------------------------	3	3	2	4	7
Dressier, more formal--------------------	3	2	1	3	2
Like texture (general)-------------------	2	3	3	3	1
Looks neat, clean, fresh-----------------	2	1	1	3	5
Versatile; can wear for any occasion-----	1	2	--	3	1
Goes well with other clothes-------------	1	1	--	4	--
Looks expensive--------------------------	1	(*)	1	2	--
Good for everyday, casual wear-----------	(*)	1	1	3	1
Miscellaneous----------------------------	2	1	2	2	1
PERFORMANCE AND DURABILITY---------------	27	25	27	45	37
Durable, wears well----------------------	10	8	6	16	11
Doesn't soil, stain easily--------------	9	5	11	24	9
Doesn't wrinkle-------------------------	5	6	8	5	14
Holds shape, doesn't shrink, stretch-----	5	3	1	2	6
Miscellaneous----------------------------	4	6	7	5	7
CARE AND LAUNDERING----------------------	3	20	19	10	26
Washable; no drycleaning required--------	(*)	11	4	4	8
Machine washable-------------------------	(*)	3	5	--	9
Little or no ironing required------------	(*)	(*)	3	1	6
Easy to wash and care for---------------	(*)	4	4	2	2
Dries quickly---------------------------	--	1	5	--	--
Miscellaneous----------------------------	3	5	4	5	6
OTHER:					
Inexpensive------------------------------	(*)	2	--	--	--
All other--------------------------------	(*)	2	--	1	1
Not ascertained-------------------------	--	1	7	--	--
Number of cases-------------------------	336	294	143	129	86

[1] Percentages add to more than their group totals and these add to more than 100 because some respondents gave more than 1 answer.
[2] Numbers preferring other materials too small for separate analysis.
*Less than 1 percent.

130

--Boys who had winter outer jackets or short coats and said they liked
n materials best: "Is there anything that you don't like so well about
ial liked best) for outer jackets or short coats?"[1]

Criticisms of ferred material	Material liked best for winter outer jackets or short coats[2]				
	Wool	Cotton	Nylon	Suede, leather	Cotton-polyester
	Percent	Percent	Percent	Percent	Percent
ND WEIGHT--------------	23	11	13	9	5
es, scratches, itches--	14	(*)	1	--	--
n, not cool enough-----	5	1	2	2	--
er repellent-----------	4	2	3	2	2
binds----------------	1	(*)	3	4	1
n enough---------------	--	7	4	2	2
aneous-----------------	2	1	1	1	--
CE AND DURABILITY------	11	18	31	33	19
stains easily----------	2	8	6	12	11
hold shape, shrinks, ches------------------	2	1	1	1	1
p, fuzzes, sheds-------	2	1	1	--	--
s lint-----------------	2	(*)	1	--	1
r when wet-------------	2	--	--	1	--
tears easily----------	1	3	15	10	4
able------------------	1	1	1	2	1
s easily---------------	--	4	4	2	2
aneous-----------------	2	2	5	8	1
LAUNDERING-------------	5	3	--	12	2
nable; has to be eaned------------------	4	2	--	8	1
care for, wash--------	--	(*)	--	4	--
aneous----------------	1	1	--	1	1
nce and styling--------	4	3	6	4	1
ve--------------------	1	(*)	--	3	--
er--------------------	--	--	3	1	--
ertained--------------	(*)	(*)	--	1	1
ISM OF MATERIAL--------	62	68	52	48	72
cases-----------------	336	294	143	129	86

ntages may add to more than their group totals and these may add to more
because some respondents gave more than 1 answer.
rs preferring other materials too small for separate analysis.
nan 1 percent.

Table 142.--Boys who had readymade summer sport shirts (not including knitted shirts or T-shirts). "What material are most of your summer sport shirts made of?" "What other materials are your summer sport shirts made of?" "What material do you like best for summer sport shirts?"[1]

Material	Materials in summer sport shirt wardrobe	Material most summer sport shirts made of	Material preferred for summer sport shirts
	Percent	Percent	Percent
Cotton---------------------	89	81	61
Cotton-polyester------------	17	5	8
Nylon----------------------	13	3	5
Rayon/acetate---------------	11	3	3
Polyester------------------	10	3	3
Acrylic--------------------	4	1	1
Silk-----------------------	4	(*)	1
Cotton-rayon/acetate-------	3	1	1
Cotton-nylon---------------	2	1	1
Other materials------------	4	1	1
Unspecified----------------	(*)	(*)	(*)
No preference--------------			11
Not ascertained------------	2	2	4
Number cases--------------	1,612	1,612	1,612

[1] Percentages may add to more than 100 because some respondents named more than 1 material.
* Less than 1 percent.

	Number
	1,612
	420
	439
	447
	306
	514
	655
	442
	550
	657
	405
	380
	461
	524
	247

dd to more than 100 because some respondents named more than 1 material.

Table 144.--Boys who had readymade summer sport shirts: Material preferred for summer sport shirts

round ristics	Cotton	Cotton-polyester	Nylon	Polyester	Rayon/acetate	All other	No perference	Not ascertained	Cases
	Percent	Percent	Percent	Percent	Percent	Percent	Percent	Percent	Number
al----------	61	8	5	3	3	5	11	4	1,612
------------	59	8	6	3	3	5	13	3	420
------------	65	6	5	3	3	4	10	4	439
------------	59	9	3	4	2	6	13	4	447
------------	59	11	4	4	4	4	11	3	306
up:									
------------	59	7	7	4	4	5	11	3	514
------------	61	8	4	4	3	4	12	4	655
------------	62	11	2	2	3	6	11	3	442
tan---------	55	8	5	4	2	6	16	4	550
olitan------	63	11	4	3	4	3	9	3	657
------------	64	5	5	4	3	7	9	3	405
------------	57	8	5	4	4	3	14	5	380
------------	63	6	5	3	2	6	11	4	461
------------	66	10	4	3	3	4	8	2	524
------------	53	9	5	3	4	9	15	2	247

Table 145.--Boys who had readymade summer sport shirts and said they liked certain materials best: "Why do you prefer (material liked best) for summer sport shirts?"[1]

Reasons for preference	Material liked best for summer sport shirts[2]		
	Cotton	Cotton-polyester	Nylon
	Percent	Percent	Percent
COMFORT AND WEIGHT------------------------------	81	77	90
Cool, lightweight, airy-----------------------	71	66	86
Doesn't cling, bind---------------------------	14	13	4
Doesn't irritate, scratch, itch--------------	13	10	10
Miscellaneous--------------------------------	6	2	3
CARE AND LAUNDERING-----------------------------	31	37	25
Easy to wash and care for--------------------	12	14	8
Easy to iron, press--------------------------	10	14	--
Machine washable-----------------------------	6	2	1
Little or no ironing required----------------	4	11	18
Doesn't need starch--------------------------	2	5	--
Good appearance after washing----------------	2	3	--
Washable; no drycleaning required------------	2	2	4
Easy to starch-------------------------------	2	--	--
Dries quickly--------------------------------	1	5	1
Miscellaneous--------------------------------	1	1	--
APPEARANCE AND STYLING--------------------------	27	22	21
Variety of styles available------------------	8	5	3
Good colors, prints, available---------------	8	8	4
Fits well------------------------------------	4	5	3
Stylish, popular, fashionable----------------	4	--	--
Looks nice (general)-------------------------	3	3	3
Looks neat, clean, fresh---------------------	3	2	--
Dressier; more formal------------------------	1	3	1
Miscellaneous--------------------------------	4	3	8
PERFORMANCE AND DURABILITY----------------------	22	50	32
Durable, wears well--------------------------	6	3	3
Doesn't wrinkle------------------------------	5	37	16
Holds colors; doesn't fade, run--------------	4	5	3
Holds shape; doesn't shrink, stretch---------	3	7	4
Doesn't soil, stain easily-------------------	3	6	8
Miscellaneous--------------------------------	4	3	3
OTHER:			
Inexpensive----------------------------------	4	2	--
All other------------------------------------	1	--	1
Not ascertained------------------------------	(*)	--	--
Number of cases------------------------------	980	133	73

[1] Percentages add to more than their group totals and these add to more than 100 because some respondents gave more than 1 answer.

[2] Numbers preferring other materials too small for separate analysis.

*Less than 1 percent.

134

Criticisms of preferred material	Material liked best for summer sport shirts[2]		
	Cotton	Cotton-polyester	Nylon
	Percent	Percent	Percent
) DURABILITY--------------------------------------	16	11	25
ly--	8	4	1
colors, fades, runs-------------------------	4	--	6
easily---------------------------------------	2	4	11
easily---------------------------------------	2	3	4
--	1	2	3
shape; shrinks, stretches--------------------	1	2	1
--	1	2	--
GHT---	4	8	12
gh---	3	2	3
--	1	1	7
--	1	5	3
RING---	3	2	3
STYLING--------------------------------------	2	5	8
ty of styles--------------------------------	1	1	3
gh---	(*)	1	3
--	1	3	3
--	(*)	2	--
--	(*)	--	--
ed--	(*)	--	--
MATERIAL--------------------------------------	76	75	56
--	980	133	73

may add to more than their group totals and these may add to more than 100 because some
e more than 1 answer.
ferring other materials too small for separate analysis.
. percent.

s who had readymade summer sport coats: "What material are most of your summer sport
of?" "What other materials are your summer sport coats made of?" "What material do you
or summer sport coats?"[1]

Material	Materials in summer sport coat wardrobe	Material most summer sport coats made of	Material preferred for summer sport coats
	Percent	Percent	Percent
--	38	34	32
r--	21	18	16
--	7	6	4
--	6	5	6
--	5	4	2
--	5	4	2
--	4	3	3
etate---------------------------------------	4	3	2
--	3	3	2
--	3	2	2
--	3	2	1
--	2	2	1
ures--	2	1	1
--	4	3	3
--	3	2	1
--	--	--	19
--	4	9	3
--	689	689	689

may add to more than 100 because some respondents named more than 1 material.

Table 148.--Boys who had readymade summer sport coats: Materials in summer sport coats[1]

Background characteristics	Cotton	Cotton-polyester	Rayon/acetate	Polyester	Linen	Wool	Wool mixtures[2]	Other cotton mixtures	All other	Not ascertained	Cases
	Percent	Percent	Percent	Percent	Percent	Percent	Percent	Percent	Percent	Percent	Number
United States total--------	38	21	7	6	5	5	6	7	14	4	689
Age:											
14 years-------------------	35	18	9	6	5	4	6	8	14	4	173
15 years-------------------	41	14	4	7	5	7	3	6	15	6	190
16 years-------------------	41	29	8	3	6	4	6	4	12	3	191
17 years-------------------	35	21	7	8	5	4	8	10	16	4	135
Family income group:											
Lower----------------------	38	17	8	7	10	5	4	9	17	4	184
Middle---------------------	36	22	8	4	4	5	7	8	14	4	277
Upper----------------------	42	22	6	7	3	4	5	4	12	5	228
Size of place:											
Urban metropolitan--------	42	20	8	8	3	6	8	5	13	5	260
Urban nonmetropolitan----	39	23	6	5	5	4	5	8	14	4	292
Town and farm-------------	30	19	7	4	9	3	4	8	17	5	137
Region:											
Northeast-----------------	49	17	7	8	2	5	4	6	10	5	195
North Central-------------	33	19	7	5	1	7	5	8	15	7	162
South---------------------	36	27	6	5	10	2	2	7	13	2	256
West----------------------	30	12	12	5	7	9	22	5	26	4	76

[1] Percentages add to more than 100 because some respondents named more than 1 material.
[2] Wool-cotton is included in "All other."

Table 149.--Boys who had readymade summer sport coats. Material preferred for summer sport coats

Background characteristics	Cotton	Cotton-polyester	Polyester	All other	No preference	Not ascertained	Cases
	Percent	Percent	Percent	Percent	Percent	Percent	Number
United States total-----------------------	32	16	6	24	19	3	689
Age:							
14 years-------------------------------	30	15	6	25	20	4	173
15 years-------------------------------	39	13	6	22	16	4	190
16 years-------------------------------	30	21	3	22	21	3	191
17 years-------------------------------	28	16	7	30	17	2	135
Family income group:							
Lower----------------------------------	33	13	5	30	16	3	184
Middle---------------------------------	30	18	4	25	20	3	277
Upper----------------------------------	35	17	8	18	18	4	228
Size of place:							
Urban metropolitan---------------------	29	15	8	20	23	5	260
Urban nonmetropolitan------------------	34	17	5	25	16	3	292
Town and farm--------------------------	34	17	1	31	15	2	137
Region:							
Northeast------------------------------	38	14	7	18	19	4	195
North Central--------------------------	24	14	5	32	21	4	162
South----------------------------------	35	22	5	22	14	2	256
West-----------------------------------	26	5	5	32	29	3	76

136

Table 150.--Boys who had readymade summer sport coats and said they liked certain materials best: "Why do you prefer (material liked best) for summer sport coats?"[1]

Reasons for preference	Material liked best for summer sport coats[2]	
	Cotton	Cotton-polyester
	Percent	Percent
COMFORT AND WEIGHT------------------------------------	81	85
Cool, lightweight, airy------------------------------	75	75
Doesn't irritate, scratch, itch----------------------	7	10
Doesn't cling, bind----------------------------------	7	9
Year-round weight------------------------------------	--	4
Miscellaneous--	3	3
APPEARANCE AND STYLING-------------------------------	31	34
Good colors, patterns available----------------------	11	8
Variety of styles available--------------------------	6	8
Fits, hangs well-------------------------------------	5	5
Stylish, popular, fashionable------------------------	5	4
Looks nice (general)---------------------------------	4	2
Dressier; more formal--------------------------------	2	8
Goes well with other clothes-------------------------	2	4
Looks neat, clean, fresh-----------------------------	2	1
Versatile, can wear for any occasion-----------------	1	2
Miscellaneous--	3	2
PERFORMANCE AND DURABILITY---------------------------	25	53
Doesn't wrinkle--------------------------------------	13	37
Doesn't soil, stain easily---------------------------	6	5
Holds shape; doesn't shrink, stretch-----------------	5	11
Durable, wears well----------------------------------	3	3
Holds colors; doesn't fade, run----------------------	1	4
Miscellaneous--	2	5
CARE AND LAUNDERING----------------------------------	14	14
Washable; no drycleaning required--------------------	5	6
Easy to wash and care for----------------------------	4	3
Easy to iron, press----------------------------------	3	2
Machine washable-------------------------------------	2	--
Little or no ironing required------------------------	--	5
Miscellaneous--	2	3
OTHER:		
Inexpensive--	3	1
All other--	1	--
Not ascertained-------------------------------------	--	--
Number of cases--------------------------------------	220	112

[1] Percentages add to more than their group totals and these add to more than 100 because some respondents gave more than 1 answer.

[2] Numbers preferring other materials too small for separate analysis.

Table 151.--Boys who had readymade summer sport coats and said they liked
certain materials best: "Is there anything that you don't like so well
about (material liked best) for summer sport coats?"[1]

| Criticisms of preferred material | Material liked best for summer coat coats[2] | |
	Cotton	Cotton-polyester
	Percent	Percent
PERFORMANCE AND DURABILITY----------------------	16	13
Wrinkles easily--------------------------------	10	5
Doesn't hold shape; shrinks, stretches--------	3	2
Soils, stains easily--------------------------	2	3
Snags, tears easily---------------------------	1	2
Doesn't hold crease, press--------------------	1	2
Miscellaneous---------------------------------	3	3
NOT COOL ENOUGH, TOO WARM----------------------	4	5
OTHER:		
Care and laundering--------------------------	1	2
Appearance and styling-----------------------	1	1
All other------------------------------------	1	3
Not ascertained------------------------------	3	--
NO CRITICISM OF MATERIAL-----------------------	74	79
Number of cases-------------------------------	220	112

[1] Percentages may add to more than their group totals and these may add to
more than 100 because some respondents gave more than 1 answer.
[2] Numbers preferring other materials too small for separate analysis.

Table 152.--Boys who had readymade summer pants: "Do you get some of your summer pants
for everyday wear and others for Sunday or special occasions, or do you get the same
kind for both everyday and dress-up wear?"

Background characteristics	Different pants for each	Same pants for both	Have only everyday pants	Have only dress-up pants	Cases
	Percent	Percent	Percent	Percent	Number
United States total-----------	69	26	3	2	1,612
Age:					
14 years---------------------	74	20	4	2	421
15 years---------------------	68	27	4	1	437
16 years---------------------	67	28	3	2	450
17 years---------------------	66	28	3	3	304
Family income group:					
Lower------------------------	67	27	4	2	525
Middle-----------------------	69	27	3	1	651
Upper------------------------	72	23	3	2	435
Size of place:					
Urban metropolitan-----------	62	32	4	2	549
Urban nonmetropolitan--------	69	25	4	2	656
Town and farm----------------	78	18	2	2	407
Region:					
Northeast--------------------	66	29	4	1	384
North Central----------------	70	25	4	1	459
South------------------------	71	24	2	3	531
West-------------------------	66	26	5	3	238

had dress-up summer pants: "What material are <u>most</u> of
er pants made of?" "What other materials are <u>your</u> dress-
ade of?" "What material do you like <u>best</u> for dress-up

	Materials in dress-up sum- mer pants wardrobe	Material most dress-up sum- mer pants made of	Material preferred for dress-up summer pants
	<u>Percent</u>	<u>Percent</u>	<u>Percent</u>
-----------	58	46	40
-----------	23	18	17
-----------	9	6	6
-----------	6	4	3
-----------	6	4	3
-----------	6	4	2
-----------	3	2	2
-----------	3	2	1
-----------	3	2	1
-----------	2	1	1
-----------	2	2	1
-----------	5	3	3
-----------	2	2	(*)
-----------	--		17
-----------	3	5	3
-----------			

add to more than 100 because some respondents named more

ent.

139

Table 154.--Boys who had dress-up summer pants: Materials in dress-up summer pants[1]

Background characteristics	Cotton	Cotton-poly-ester	Poly-ester	Rayon/acetate	Cotton-rayon/acetate	Wool	Wool-cotton	Other wool mixtures	All other	Not ascer-tained	Cases
	Percent	Percent	Percent	Percent	Percent	Percent	Percent	Percent	Percent	Percent	Number
United States total-------	58	23	9	6	6	6	3	5	12	3	1,142
Age:											
14 years----------------	61	20	7	8	6	4	2	4	10	3	319
15 years----------------	57	21	9	3	8	8	3	4	13	3	303
16 years----------------	57	26	8	6	5	5	2	8	13	3	310
17 years----------------	54	26	11	9	5	8	3	6	13	2	210
Family income group:											
Lower-------------------	64	21	7	8	7	4	3	4	11	2	365
Middle------------------	55	25	9	7	7	5	2	5	10	3	456
Upper-------------------	54	23	11	4	4	9	3	8	16	3	320
Size of place:											
Urban metropolitan------	60	19	8	6	5	7	3	7	14	3	354
Urban nonmetropolitan---	56	25	11	7	6	7	2	6	12	2	461
Town and farm----------	58	24	6	6	8	3	2	3	11	3	327
Region:											
Northeast---------------	60	21	8	6	6	5	4	5	11	2	258
North Central----------	58	17	7	7	6	7	3	6	13	3	323
South-------------------	55	31	11	6	6	3	1	4	12	2	397
West--------------------	59	19	8	7	5	13	3	9	13	4	164

[1] Percentages add to more than 100 because some respondents named more than 1 material.

Table 155.--Boys who had dress-up summer pants: Material preferred for dress-up summer pants

Background characteristics	Cotton	Cotton-polyester	Polyester	Wool	Wool mix	All other	No preference	Not ascer-tained	Cases
	Percent	Percent	Percent	Percent	Percent	Percent	Percent	Percent	Number
United States total-----	40	17	6	2	3	12	17	3	1,142
Age:									
14 years--------------	43	14	4	2	3	13	17	4	319
15 years--------------	40	17	9	2	2	12	15	3	303
16 years--------------	43	16	5	2	3	11	16	4	310
17 years--------------	33	22	7	3	2	14	17	2	210
Family income group:									
Lower-----------------	46	15	4	2	3	12	16	2	365
Middle----------------	38	18	6	1	3	13	17	4	456
Upper-----------------	38	18	9	3	2	11	16	3	320
Size of place:									
Urban metropolitan----	38	13	5	3	3	12	22	4	354
Urban nonmetropolitan-	38	20	9	2	2	14	12	3	461
Town and farm--------	45	17	4	1	2	13	15	3	327
Region:									
Northeast-------------	43	16	6	2	2	12	16	3	258
North Central--------	39	13	5	3	3	16	18	3	323
South-----------------	40	23	8	1	2	11	12	3	397
West------------------	39	11	4	4	4	9	24	5	164

dress-up summer pants and said they liked certain materials
refer (material liked best) for dress-up summer pants?"[1]

eference

	Cotton	Cotton-polyester	Polyester
		Percent	?nt
------------------		68	
y-----------------	64	59	69
tch, itch--------	11	9	9
------------------	10	3	7
------------------	2	2	3
------------------	1	3	1
------------------	28	21	14
for--------------	9	4	3
ing required------	8	6	4
------------------	8	4	7
------------------	5	1	3
required----------	2	8	1
------------------	3	3	3
ITY---------------	27	63	51
------------------	7	4	6
------------------	6	30	33
------------------	5	29	19
shrink, stretch---	5	7	9
asily-------------	4	8	3
fade, run--------	3	3	1
------------------	1	1	1
------------------	2	?	33
------------------	7	5	6
esh---------------	5	4	4
hionable----------	4	--	--
------------------	3	8	10
available--------	3	4	6
------------------	3	4	1
ilable------------	3	3	6
.) ----------------	1	4	4
clothes-----------	--	1	3
------------------	2	2	1
------------------	4	1	--
------------------	2	1	1
------------------	(*)	1	--

----

more than their group totals and these add to more than 100
:s gave more than 1 answer.
other materials too small for separate analysis.

141

Table 157.--Boys who had dress-up summer pants and said they liked certain materials best: "Is there anything that you don't like so well about (material liked best) for dress-up summer pants?"[1]

Criticisms of preferred material	Material liked best for dress-up summer pants[2]		
	Cotton	Cotton-polyester	Polyester
	Percent	Percent	Percent
PERFORMANCE AND DURABILITY-----------------------------	19	11	17
Wrinkles easily--------------------------------------	8	8	9
Doesn't hold shape; shrinks, stretches--------------------	2	2	3
Soils, stains easily-----------------------------------	2	2	--
Doesn't hold crease, press---------------------------	2	1	1
Doesn't hold colors, fades, runs-----------------------	2	1	--
Miscellaneous---------------------------------------	5	4	4
COMFORT AND WEIGHT-------------------------------	5	4	4
Not cool enough------------------------------------	3	1	--
Clings, binds---------------------------------------	1	2	1
Miscellaneous---------------------------------------	1	1	3
APPEARANCE AND STYLING---------------------------	2	2	6
CARE AND LAUNDERING-----------------------------	1	4	3
Hard to iron--	1	1	3
Not washable; has to be drycleaned-------------------	--	3	--
Miscellaneous---------------------------------------	(*)	1	--
OTHER:			
Expensive--	(*)	1	3
All other---	(*)	--	--
Not ascertained-------------------------------------	1	1	--
NO CRITICISM OF MATERIAL--------------------------	73	80	67
Number of cases-------------------------------------	460	192	70

[1] Percentages may add to more than their group totals and these may add to more than 100 because some respondents gave more than 1 answer.
[2] Numbers preferring other materials too small for separate analysis.
*Less than 1 percent.

Table 158.--Boys had everyday summer pants: "What material are most of your everyday summer pants made of?" "What other materials are your everyday summer pants made of?" "What material do you like best for everyday summer pants?"[1]

Material	Material in summer pants wardrobe	Material most summer pants made of	Material preferred for summer pants
	Percent	Percent	Percent
Cotton-------------------------	91	87	76
Cotton-polyester-----------------	10	5	6
Polyester----------------------	3	1	1
Rayon/acetate-------------------	3	1	1
Nylon--------------------------	2	(*)	(*)
Other cotton mixtures-------------	2	1	1
Other material-------------------	4	2	2
Unspecified---------------------	(*)	(*)	(*)
No preference-------------------	--	--	11
Not ascertained------------------	2	3	2
Number of cases-----------------	1,583	1,583	1,583

[1] Percentages may add to more than 100 because some respondents named more than 1 material.
*Less than 1 percent.

142

cs	Cotton	Cotton-polyester	Polyester	Rayon/acetate	All other	Not ascertained	Cases
	Percent	Percent	Percent	Percent	Percent	Percent	Number
1----	91	10	3	3	7	2	1,583
-----	93	9	2	3	4	1	412
-----	90	11	3	3	7	2	433
-----	92	10	3	3	8	2	443
-----	91	13	4	1	8	1	295
p:							
-----	92	8	1	3	7	2	512
-----	91	9	4	2	7	2	643
-----	91	15	4	3	5	3	427
an---	90	11	4	4	8	3	539
litan	92	12	3	2	6	2	644
-----	93	7	1	2	5	1	400
-----	90	12	4	4	7	3	380
-----	91	8	1	2	7	1	456
-----	92	11	3	2	6	1	516
-----	91	11	4	3	8	2	231

[1]d to more than 100 because some respondents named more than 1 material.

.--Boys who had everyday summer pants: Material preferred for everyday summer pants

ics	Cotton	Cotton-polyester	All other	No preference	Not ascertained	Cases
	Percent	Percent	Percent	Percent	Percent	Number
al----	76	6	5	11	2	1,583
------	77	4	5	13	1	412
------	75	7	6	10	2	433
------	76	6	5	11	2	443
------	78	6	6	9	1	295
up:						
------	81	4	5	9	1	512
------	73	6	6	13	2	643
------	77	7	5	9	2	427
tan---	70	4	6	17	3	539
olitan	77	7	7	8	1	644
------	83	6	4	6	1	400
------	71	5	5	16	3	380
------	81	5	.6	7	1	456
------	77	8	6	8	1	516
------	74	3	5	16	2	231

143

Table 161.--Boys who had everyday summer pants and said they liked certain materials best: "Why do you prefer (material liked best) for everyday summer pants?"[1]

| Reásons for preference | Material liked best for everyday summer pants[2] | |
| | Cotton | Cotton-polyester |
	Percent	Percent
COMFORT AND WEIGHT---	57	71
Cool, lightweight, airy---	46	63
Doesn't cling, bind--	7	12
Doesn't irritate, scratch, itch-------------------------------	7	9
Year-round weight--	2	1
Miscellaneous--	4	1
PERFORMANCE AND DURABILITY---	44	64
Durable, wears well--	26	21
Doesn't soil, stain easily-----------------------------------	7	10
Doesn't snag, tear easily------------------------------------	7	6
Doesn't wrinkle---	4	26
Holds crease, press---	4	14
Holds shape; doesn't shrink, stretch------------------------	3	7
Holds colors; doesn't fade, run----------------------------	2	3
Miscellaneous--	1	3
CARE AND LAUNDERING--	38	37
Machine washable---	13	9
Easy to wash and care for----------------------------------	12	8
Easy to iron, press--	8	6
Washable; no drycleaning required-------------------------	8	3
Little or no ironing required-----------------------------	6	10
Good appearance after washing-----------------------------	2	5
Dries quickly---	1	3
Miscellaneous--	2	2
APPEARANCE AND STYLING---	26	29
Stylish, popular, fashionable------------------------------	7	5
Fits well---	7	5
Variety of styles available--------------------------------	4	8
Good colors, patterns available----------------------------	4	6
Versatile; can wear for any occasion-----------------------	2	6
Looks nice (general)---------------------------------------	2	2
Good for everyday, casual wear-----------------------------	2	1
Dressier; more formal--------------------------------------	1	2
Miscellaneous--	3	2
OTHER:		
Inexpensive---	6	2
All other---	2	--
Not ascertained---	(*)	--
Number of cases--	1,202	89

[1] Percentages add to more than their group totals and these add to more than 100 because some respondents gave more than 1 answer.

[2] Numbers preferring other materials too small for separate analysis.

*Less than 1 percent.

144

io had everyday summer pants and said they liked certain materials best: "Is
that you don't like so well about (material liked best) for everyday summer

iticisms of preferred material	Material liked best for everyday summer pants[2]	
	Cotton	Cotton-polyester
	Percent	Percent
ABILITY------------------------------------	20	21
rs; fades, runs----------------------------	6	3
---	5	5
ily---	3	7
se, press-----------------------------------	3	3
e; shrinks, stretches-----------------------	3	2
ly--	2	5
---	2	1
---	1	3
---	8	7
---	5	3
---	2	3
---	1	1
yling---------------------------------------	2	1
ng--	2	1
---	(*)	1
---	1	2
'ERIAL--------------------------------------	70	67
---	1,202	89

· add to more than their group totals and these may add to more than 100 because
.ve more than 1 answer.
·ing other materials too small for separate analysis.
·cent.

io had readymade sweaters: "What material are most of your readymade sweaters
, other materials are your readymade sweaters made of?" "What material do you
sweaters?"[1]

Material	Materials in sweater wardrobe	Material most sweaters made of	Material preferred for sweaters
	Percent	Percent	Percent
------------------------------	70	56	39
------------------------------	24	14	14
------------------------------	17	10	8
------------------------------	11	5	5
------------------------------	7	4	4
------------------------------	7	3	4
------------------------------	6	2	2
------------------------------	4	2	2
------------------------------	3	1	1
------------------------------	2	(*)	1
------------------------------	8	3	5
------------------------------	--	--	13
------------------------------	2	3	2
------------------------------	1,403	1,403	1,403

· add to more than 100 because some respondents named more than 1 material.
·cent.

Table 164.--Boys who had readymade sweaters: Materials in sweaters[1]

Background characteristics	Wool	Acrylic	Cotton	Wool-acrylic	Wool-cotton	Nylon	Poly-ester	Wool-nylon	Rayon/acetate	All other	Not ascertained	Cases
	Percent	Percent	Percent	Percent	Percent	Percent	Percent	Percent	Percent	Percent	Percent	Number
United States total-------------	70	24	17	11	7	7	6	4	3	10	2	1,403
Age:												
14 years---------	69	24	19	10	7	8	5	4	4	5	2	362
15 years---------	71	23	17	11	4	8	5	4	4	9	2	380
16 years---------	71	25	17	10	7	4	7	5	3	11	3	397
17 years---------	70	24	13	11	10	9	6	2	2	14	2	264
Family income group:												
Lower------------	65	20	22	8	8	8	4	3	3	5	2	401
Middle-----------	72	27	17	11	7	8	6	5	4	9	2	583
Upper------------	73	23	12	13	5	5	6	4	2	15	3	418
Size of place:												
Urban metro-politan--------	72	25	15	11	6	6	6	4	4	12	2	489
Urban non-metropolitan---	71	24	17	11	7	7	7	5	3	10	2	587
Town and farm----	66	21	21	9	8	8	3	3	4	6	3	327
Region:												
Northeast--------	75	25	14	11	5	7	7	4	3	11	1	346
North Central----	70	28	15	8	5	6	5	2	2	10	3	416
South------------	67	19	20	11	8	9	3	5	3	8	2	426
West-------------	69	24	22	13	8	6	9	6	5	10	4	215

[1] Percentages add to more than 100 because some respondents named more than 1 material.

Table 165.--Boys who had readymade sweaters: Material preferred for sweaters

Background characteristics	Wool	Acrylic	Cotton	Wool-acrylic	Wool-cotton	Nylon	All other	No pref-erence	Not ascertained	Cases
	Percent	Percent	Percent	Percent	Percent	Percent	Percent	Percent	Percent	Number
United States total-----------	39	14	8	5	4	4	11	13	2	1,403
Age:										
14 years---------------------	35	16	12	6	3	4	9	12	3	362
15 years---------------------	41	14	9	5	3	6	10	10	2	380
16 years---------------------	40	12	6	5	4	2	12	17	2	397
17 years---------------------	41	13	6	6	6	3	11	12	2	264
Family income group:										
Lower------------------------	36	12	14	5	5	5	14	7	2	401
Middle-----------------------	38	16	7	6	3	4	12	12	2	583
Upper------------------------	44	12	5	5	3	2	5	21	3	418
Size of place:										
Urban metropolitan-----------	38	13	6	6	3	2	11	19	2	489
Urban nonmetropolitan--------	41	15	8	5	4	4	11	10	2	587
Town and farm----------------	37	13	13	6	5	5	8	10	3	327
Region:										
Northeast--------------------	43	13	6	5	3	3	12	13	2	346
North Central----------------	38	18	7	4	4	3	10	13	3	416
South------------------------	40	11	11	7	4	5	10	11	1	426
West-------------------------	33	13	10	6	4	1	9	20	4	215

166.--Boys who had readymade sweaters and said they liked certain materials best: "Why do you prefer (material liked best) for sweaters?"[1]

Reasons for preference	Material liked best for sweaters[2]			
	Wool	Acrylic	Cotton	Wool-acrylic
	Percent	Percent	Percent	Percent
AND WEIGHT	80	77	80	71
---	71	15	25	27
t irritate, scratch, itch	7	53	42	43
t cling, bind	4	5	9	5
eight but warm	3	5	3	5
o warm; lightweight, airy	2	13	18	11
just right	1	6	6	5
ound weight	1	1	3	--
laneous	2	--	2	--
CE AND STYLING	41	28	18	31
olors, patterns available	11	7	3	5
y of styles available	10	5	4	8
exture (general)	5	7	3	4
ell	5	4	4	5
nice (general)	5	2	1	7
h, popular, fashionable	4	--	2	3
er; more formal	2	3	--	1
neat, clean, fresh	2	2	1	--
ell with other clothes	2	1	2	3
expensive	2	1	--	--
or everyday, casual wear	2	1	--	--
laneous	2	--	1	1
ANCE AND DURABILITY	28	45	27	48
shape; doesn't shrink, stretch	15	31	16	31
le, wears well	7	4	3	4
't wrinkle	3	6	5	8
't soil, stain easily	3	4	1	7
't ball up, fuzz, shed	2	5	4	4
colors, doesn't fade, run	2	4	3	4
't snag, tear	1	2	--	1
laneous	1	2	1	--
) LAUNDERING	5	28	19	24
to wash and care for	2	10	7	11
le; no drycleaning required	1	9	4	4
e or no ironing required	1	3	3	1
appearance after washing	(*)	2	1	3
quickly	--	2	2	3
laneous	2	8	5	7
ensive	1	3	2	--
---	2	1	4	--
ther	(*)	1	--	--
scertained	(*)	1	--	--
of cases	551	194	118	75

centages add to more than their group totals and these add to more than 100 because some
ents gave more than 1 answer.
ers preferring other materials too small for separate analysis.
s than 1 percent.

Criticisms of preferred material	Material liked best for sweaters[2]			
	Wool	Acrylic	Cotton	Wool-acrylic
	Percent	Percent	Percent	Percent
COMFORT AND WEIGHT------------------	37	6	5	13
Irritates, scratches, itches------	28	3	1	5
Too warm, not cool enough---------	8	3	2	4
Clings, binds---------------------	2	1	--	3
Not warm enough-------------------	--	1	3	--
Miscellaneous --------------------	1	1	--	3
PERFORMANCE AND DURABILITY----------	20	23	21	17
Doesn't hold shape, shrinks, stretches-----------------------	10	5	14	8
Balls up, fuzzes, sheds-----------	4	10	3	7
Snags, tears easily---------------	4	6	1	3
Soils, stains easily-------------	2	2	2	--
Collects lint--------------------	2	2	1	--
Not colorfast; fades, runs--------	1	--	3	--
Miscellaneous --------------------	1	3	2	1
OTHER:				
Care and laundering---------------	5	2	2	3
Appearance and styling------------	1	3	2	1
All other-------------------------	(*)	2	--	1
Not ascertained-------------------	1	2	2	1
NO CRITICISM OF MATERIAL------------	44	66	70	64
Number of cases---------------------	551	194	118	75

[1] Percentages may add to more than their group totals and these may add to more than 100 because some respondents gave more than 1 answer.

[2] Numbers preferring other materials too small for separate analysis.

* Less than 1 percent.

Table 168.--Boys who had readymade sweaters (wool sweaters): "Do you think making wool sweaters that can be washed in a machine is a good idea or not such a good idea?"

Background characteristics	Owners of sweaters			
	Machine-washable wool sweaters are--		Not ascertained	Cases
	A good idea	Not a good idea		
	Percent	Percent	Percent	Number
United States total------------------------	89	10	1	1,403
Age:				
14 years--------------------------------	90	9	1	362
15 years--------------------------------	89	10	1	380
16 years--------------------------------	87	12	1	397
17 years--------------------------------	90	10	--	264
Family income group:				
Lower-----------------------------------	91	8	1	401
Middle----------------------------------	91	9	(*)	583
Upper-----------------------------------	86	13	1	418
Size of place:				
Urban metropolitan----------------------	89	10	1	489
Urban nonmetropolitan-------------------	88	11	1	587
Town and farm---------------------------	92	7	1	327
Region:				
Northeast-------------------------------	88	11	1	260
North Central---------------------------	89	10	1	290
South-----------------------------------	90	9	1	287
West------------------------------------	89	11	--	149

Background characteristics	Owners of wool-sweaters			
	Machine-washable wool sweaters are--		Not ascertained	Cases
	A good idea	Not a good idea		
	Percent	Percent	Percent	Number
United States total------------------------	91	9	(*)	986
Age:				
14 years--------------------------------	93	7	(*)	249
15 years--------------------------------	91	8	1	270
16 years--------------------------------	89	11	(*)	282
17 years--------------------------------	90	10	--	185
Family income group:				
Lower-----------------------------------	93	6	1	261
Middle----------------------------------	93	7	(*)	417
Upper-----------------------------------	86	14	--	307
Size of place:				
Urban metropolitan----------------------	90	9	1	352
Urban nonmetropolitan-------------------	89	11	--	417
Town and farm---------------------------	94	6	(*)	217
Region:				
Northeast-------------------------------	90	9	1	260
North Central---------------------------	91	9	(*)	290
South-----------------------------------	92	8	(*)	287
West------------------------------------	89	11	--	149

*Less than 1 percent.

Table 169.--Boys who had readymade sweaters (wool sweaters) and said they thought that machine-washable wool sweaters were a good idea: "Why do you say that?"[1]

Reasons for favorable opinion	Owners of sweaters	Owners of wool sweaters
	Percent	Percent
CARE AND LAUNDERING------------------------------	82	83
Saves time; easier to care for----------------	51	51
Saves money; less expensive to care for-------	39	40
No special care required----------------------	5	5
Would be cleaner if machine washed------------	2	2
Miscellaneous---------------------------------	2	2
PERFORMANCE AND DURABILITY----------------------	19	20
Retains shape after washing-------------------	10	10
Could wear sweaters more often----------------	7	8
Miscellaneous---------------------------------	3	4
OTHER:		
More convenient; do not have to take to cleaners--------------------------------------	10	10
Conditional; it depends-----------------------	5	5
Less expensive--------------------------------	2	3
Appearance------------------------------------	1	1
Comfort and weight----------------------------	1	1
All other-------------------------------------	4	3
Not ascertained-------------------------------	(*)	(*)
Number of cases-------------------------------	1,252	894

[1] Percentages add to more than their group totals and these add to more than 100 because some respondents gave more than 1 answer.
*Less than 1 percent.

ys who had readymade sweaters (wool sweaters) and said they
at machine-washable sweaters were not such a good idea: "Why do
at?"[1]

Reasons for unfavorable opinion	Owners of sweaters	Owners of wool sweaters
	Percent	Percent
D DURABILITY----------------------------------	48	56
ld lose shape, shrink, stretch------------	24	30
ng sweaters to drycleaners-----------------	10	15
ld not be durable-------------------------	6	9
t lint------------------------------------	6	5
up, fuzzes------------------------------	4	3
t--	4	6
s--	4	5
ERING--------------------------------------	25	25
ability not safe-------------------------	13	14
k good after washing---------------------	5	5
special care-----------------------------	4	3
ing wouldn't get sweater as clean as hand drycleaning-------------------------------	4	5
s--	1	--
wool---------------------------------------	20	8
rs more important-------------------------	4	3
e cares for sweaters----------------------	4	7
hability not important--------------------	3	3
sweaters----------------------------------	3	3
more---------------------------------------	3	3
---	1	1
ined---------------------------------------	1	1
es---	141	88

es add to more than their group totals and these add to more than
ome respondents gave more than 1 answer.

151

Table 171.--Boys who had readymade sweaters (wool sweaters): ". . . tell me if you think machine washability would be important to you or not in deciding whether to buy a particular new wool sweater?"

Background characteristics	Owners of sweaters gave rating of--						
	5 (most important)	4	3	2	1 (not important at all)	Not ascertained	Cases
	Percent	Percent	Percent	Percent	Percent	Percent	Number
United States total-----------	35	21	18	8	18	(*)	1,403
Age:							
14 years---------------------	42	18	17	5	18	(*)	362
15 years---------------------	35	19	19	9	17	1	380
16 years---------------------	32	21	20	8	19	(*)	397
17 years---------------------	28	29	15	9	19	--	264
Family income group:							
Lower------------------------	41	21	16	5	17	(*)	401
Middle-----------------------	36	21	18	7	18	(*)	583
Upper------------------------	27	21	20	11	21	(*)	418
Size of place:							
Urban metropolitan-----------	31	22	16	9	21	1	489
Urban nonmetropolitan--------	32	20	20	8	20	(*)	587
Town and farm----------------	45	22	16	5	12	--	327
Region:							
Northeast--------------------	34	19	18	7	22	(*)	346
North Central----------------	31	20	21	10	18	(*)	416
South------------------------	42	19	16	6	17	(*)	426
West-------------------------	31	30	16	7	15	1	215

Background characteristics	Owners of sweaters gave rating of--						
	5 (most important)	4	3	2	1 (not important at all)	Not ascertained	Cases
	Percent	Percent	Percent	Percent	Percent	Percent	Number
United States total-----------	38	20	18	8	16	(*)	986
Age:							
14 years---------------------	49	14	18	4	15	--	249
15 years---------------------	37	19	19	9	15	1	270
16 years---------------------	34	22	20	8	16	(*)	282
17 years---------------------	27	29	15	10	19	--	185
Family income group:							
Lower------------------------	46	23	14	4	13	(*)	261
Middle-----------------------	40	20	19	7	13	1	417
Upper------------------------	26	19	21	12	22	--	307
Size of place:							
Urban metropolitan-----------	34	22	17	9	17	1	352
Urban nonmetropolitan--------	34	19	21	8	18	--	417
Town and farm----------------	52	20	14	4	10	--	217
Region:							
Northeast--------------------	38	20	18	6	18	(*)	260
North Central----------------	32	19	23	10	16	(*)	290
South------------------------	45	18	15	7	15	--	287
West-------------------------	32	30	15	7	15	1	149

*Less than 1 percent.

152

Table 172.--Boys who had readymade sweaters and gave a rating as to the importance of machine washability in the decision to buy a wool sweater: "Why is that?"[1]

Reasons for rating of importance	5 (most impor- tant)	4	3	2	1 (not impor- tant at all)
	Percent	Percent	Percent	Percent	Percent
POSITIVE REASONS					
CARE AND LAUNDERING	76	53	17	7	3
Saves time, easier to care for	48	38	11	3	--
Less expensive to care for	36	21	6	4	2
No special care required	5	2	1	--	1
Would be cleaner if machine washed	3	2	(*)	1	--
Miscellaneous	2	2	--	1	1
PERFORMANCE AND DURABILITY	23	16	6	1	--
Could wear sweaters more often	11	11	3	--	--
Retains shape after washing	10	4	2	--	--
More durable	3	1	1	--	--
Miscellaneous	1	(*)	(*)	1	--
OTHER:					
Appearance	3	1	(*)	--	--
Comfort and weight	(*)	1	--	1	--
More convenient; do not have to take to cleaners	9	6	2	--	(*)
Conditional; it depends	2	2	2	1	--
Could have more sweaters	2	1	--	--	--
Less expensive	1	2	1	--	--
All other	4	4	2	--	--
NEGATIVE REASONS					
PERFORMANCE AND DURABILITY	1	2	1	9	19
Prefer to send to cleaners	--	--	4	2	12
Might/or would lose shape, shrink, stretches	1	1	2	5	4
Might/or would not be durable	--	(*)	--	5	2
Miscellaneous	(*)	1	1	1	3
CARE AND LAUNDERING	--	1	5	8	9
Machine washability not safe	--	(*)	2	6	5
Wool needs special care	--	--	2	1	2
Miscellaneous	--	1	1	2	2
OTHER FACTORS MORE IMPORTANT	1	25	43	45	20
Style	(*)	11	22	23	9
Color, prints, patterns	(*)	7	22	22	9
Looks	--	4	6	8	3
Price	1	3	6	6	1
Material	--	3	2	10	3
Fit	--	1	5	5	3
Miscellaneous	--	7	9	8	7
OTHER:					
Don't like wool	1	1	6	10	26
Someone else cares for clothes	--	1	8	11	10
Machine washability not important	--	1	6	8	7
Don't wear sweaters	--	1	4	5	4
Would cost more	(*)	1	1	3	1
All other	--	(*)	4	8	6
Not ascertained	1	2	2	--	2
Number of cases	488	293	251	107	257

[1] Percentages may add to more than their group totals and these add to more than 100 because some respondents gave more than 1 answer.
*Less than 1 percent.

Table 173.--All boys were asked: "Do you have a raincoat--one that's meant to be worn only in rainy weather?" "Do you have a coat that is meant to be worn in dry as well as rainy weather and is specially treated so that it is water repellent?"

Background characteristics	Only raincoats	Only multipurpose coats	Have both	Have neither	Cases
	Percent	Percent	Percent	Percent	Number
United States total----------------	16	40	12	32	1,648
Age:					
14 years------------------------	19	34	13	34	431
15 years------------------------	17	40	11	32	447
16 years------------------------	13	45	14	28	459
17 years------------------------	12	43	11	34	311
Family income group:					
Lower---------------------------	15	34	8	43	534
Middle--------------------------	16	43	13	28	664
Upper---------------------------	15	44	17	24	449
Size of place:					
Urban metropolitan--------------	17	46	12	25	564
Urban nonmetropolitan-----------	15	41	15	29	664
Town and farm-------------------	15	31	9	45	420
Region:					
Northeast-----------------------	15	51	12	22	388
North Central-------------------	9	48	12	31	467
South---------------------------	20	31	11	38	535
West----------------------------	19	32	14	35	258

Table 174.--Boys who had rainwear: "What material is this coat (meant to be worn only in rainy weather) made of?" "What material is this coat (meant to be worn in dry as well as rainy weather) made of?" "What material do you like best for rainwear?"

Material	Material rainwear made of		
	Raincoats	Multipurpose coats	Material preferred for rainwear
	Percent	Percent	Percent
Plastic-------------------------------	57	3	16
Cotton--------------------------------	7	36	20
Oilskin-------------------------------	6	(*)	1
Cotton-polyester----------------------	3	12	9
Nylon---------------------------------	3	7	6
Rayon/acetate-------------------------	3	6	4
Cotton-rayon/acetate------------------	1	7	4
Polyester-----------------------------	1	4	3
Wool----------------------------------	(*)	3	1
Other materials-----------------------	12	9	6
Unspecified---------------------------	(*)	1	(*)
No preference-------------------------	--	--	29
Not ascertained-----------------------	7	12	1
Number of cases-----------------------	459	870	1,127

*Less than 1 percent.

154

Background characteristics	Cotton	Cotton-poly-ester	Nylon	Cotton-rayon/acetate	Rayon/acetate	All othe
	Percent	Percent	Percent	Percent	Percent	Perce:
tal--------------------------	36	12	7	7	6	
--------------------------	33	11	9	8	5	
--------------------------	40	12	8	4	6	
--------------------------	33	15	4	7	5	
--------------------------	40	10	8	9	8	
up:						
--------------------------	35	10	8	4	7	
--------------------------	35	14	7	7	6	
--------------------------	39	12	6	8	5	
itan----------------------	38	10	6	8	6	
politan--------------------	37	16	6	6	6	
--------------------------	31	10	11	6	4	
--------------------------	37	12	6	9	7	
--------------------------	43	10	4	8	5	
--------------------------	35	17	7	6	5	
--------------------------	19	8	17	4	9	

le table on materials owned in raincoats (ones meant only to be worn in rainy weat:
there were too few owners of raincoats to be significant.

istics	Cotton	Plastic	Cotton-poly-ester	Nylon	Cotton-rayon/acetate	Rayon/acetate	All other	No pref erenc
	Percent	Percent	Percent	Percent	Percent	Percent	Percent	Perce:
tal--------	20	16	9	6	4	4	11	
-----------	17	17	8	7	3	3	15	29
-----------	24	18	9	6	5	4	9	25
-----------	18	14	10	5	4	3	12	33
-----------	22	15	8	6	4	4	8	32
oup:								
-----------	18	21	7	7	2	3	13	28
-----------	20	15	9	6	4	4	9	33
-----------	22	12	10	6	5	3	13	28
itan-------	17	11	8	5	5	4	11	38
politan----	21	16	10	6	3	4	11	29
-----------	23	24	7	8	4	2	14	17
-----------	20	8	9	5	5	6	8	38
-----------	28	12	7	5	7	2	10	28
-----------	18	25	11	7	3	3	11	22
-----------	10	18	5	10	2	3	20	32

percent

Table 177.--Boys who had rainwear and said they liked certain materials best: "Why do you prefer (material liked best) for rainwear?"[1]

Reasons for preference

APPEARANCE AND STYLING--
  Versatile; can wear for more than one purpose or occasion--
  Like appearance (general)-----------------------------------
  Variety of styles available---------------------------------
  Stylish, popular, fashionable-------------------------------
  Dressier, more adult-looking--------------------------------
  Fits well---
  Good colors available---------------------------------------
  Like texture (general)--------------------------------------
  Looks neat (general)--
  Miscellaneous---

COMFORT AND WEIGHT--
  Not too warm, cool--
  Lightweight---
  Warm--
  Doesn't cling---
  Not bulky, can be worn over other coat----------------------
  Year-round weight---
  Lightweight but warm--
  Doesn't irritate, scratch, itch-----------------------------
  Comfortable (general)---------------------------------------
  Miscellaneous---

PERFORMANCE AND DURABILITY------------------------------------
  Water repellent, sheds water well---------------------------
  Doesn't wrinkle easily when wet-----------------------------
  More durable--
  Doesn't soil, stain easily----------------------------------
  Dries quickly---
  Holds shape; doesn't sag, shrink----------------------------
  Doesn't tear, rip, snag-------------------------------------
  Doesn't crack, peel---
  Wind breaker--
  Doesn't fade--
  Miscellaneous---

CARE AND LAUNDERING--
  Washable, no drycleaning required---------------------------
  Easy to care for, cleans easily-----------------------------
  Little or no ironing required-------------------------------
  Miscellaneous---

OTHER:
  Inexpensive---
  All other---
  Not ascertained---

Number of cases--

[1] Percentages add to more than their group totals and these add to more than 100 because some respondents gave more than 1 answer.
[2] Numbers preferring other materials too small for separate analysis.
*Less than 1 percent.

156

Table 178.--Boys who had rainwear and said they liked certain materials best: "Is there anything that you don't like so well about (material liked best) for rainwear?"[1]

Criticisms of preferred material	Material liked best for rainwear[2]			
	Cotton	Plastic	Cotton-polyester	Nylon
	Percent	Percent	Percent	Percent
PERFORMANCE AND DURABILITY----------	26	41	19	17
Soils, stains easily--------------	8	--	2	3
Wrinkles easily when wet----------	7	2	4	4
Not water repellent--------------	7	1	6	3
Water repellency wears off--------	3	--	5	1
Tears, rips easily----------------	(*)	29	1	7
Becomes stiff, hard--------------	(*)	3	--	--
Burns, melts---------------------	--	5	--	--
Cracks, peels--------------------	--	3	--	--
Miscellaneous--------------------	2	5	3	--
MUST BE DRY CLEANED, HARD TO CARE FOR-------------------------------	5	2	1	--
COMFORT AND WEIGHT-----------------	3	20	2	7
Too hot--------------------------	2	12	2	6
Too cool-------------------------	1	2	--	--
Clings---------------------------	(*)	4	--	--
Miscellaneous--------------------	(*)	3	--	1
OTHER:				
Appearance and styling------------	1	7	--	1
All other-----------------------	1	1	--	3
Not ascertained-----------------	2	2	1	6
NO CRITICISM OF MATERIAL------------	64	36	77	70
Number of cases---------------------	227	178	98	69

[1] Percentages may add to more than their group totals and these may add to more than 100 because some respondents gave more than 1 answer.
[2] Numbers preferring other materials too small for separate analysis.
*Less than 1 percent.

157

Table 179.--Boys who had readymade winter sport shirts (winter sport coats, winter dress-up pants, winter everyday pants, summer sport shirts, summer sport coats, summer dress-up pants, summer everyday pants, sweaters): "Would you say that most of yours are washed at home by hand, by machine, or taken to the drycleaners, or just what?"

Owners, by material predominating in wardrobe	Commercial cleaner	Machine washed	Hand washed	All other	Not ascertained	Cases
	Percent	Percent	Percent	Percent	Percent	Number
Winter sport shirt owners---------------------	10	82	7	1	(*)	1,613
Mostly cotton---------------------------------	6	86	7	1	(*)	1,197
Mostly wool-----------------------------------	24	62	13	1	--	217
Winter sport coat owners----------------------	93	--	--	5	2	1,073
Mostly wool-----------------------------------	97	--	--	2	1	539
Mostly cotton---------------------------------	84	--	--	14	2	136
Mostly wool-polyester-------------------------	93	--	--	6	1	79
Winter dress-up pants owners------------------	82	12	4	2	(*)	1,283
Mostly wool-----------------------------------	90	4	3	3	--	462
Mostly cotton---------------------------------	66	28	4	2	(*)	283
Mostly wool-polyester-------------------------	85	4	8	3	--	121
Mostly cotton-polyester-----------------------	79	16	4	--	1	96
Winter everyday pants owners------------------	12	83	4	1	(*)	1,631
Mostly cotton---------------------------------	5	90	4	1	(*)	1,237
Mostly wool-----------------------------------	64	30	3	3	--	118
Mostly cotton-polyester-----------------------	9	89	1	--	1	78
Summer sport shirt owners---------------------	4	88	7	1	(*)	1,612
Mostly cotton---------------------------------	3	90	6	1	(*)	1,299
Mostly cotton-polyester-----------------------	2	85	11	2	--	83
Summer sport coat owners----------------------	88	8	--	4	(*)	689
Mostly cotton---------------------------------	84	10	--	5	1	238
Mostly cotton-polyester-----------------------	91	7	--	2	--	125
Summer dress-up pants owners------------------	63	30	5	2	(*)	1,142
Mostly cotton---------------------------------	53	41	5	1	(*)	525
Mostly cotton-polyester-----------------------	71	22	6	1	--	208
Summer everyday pants owners------------------	7	88	4	1	(*)	1,583
Mostly cotton---------------------------------	5	90	4	1	(*)	1,373
Mostly cotton-polyester-----------------------	19	72	7	2	--	85
Sweater owners--------------------------------	37	18	43	2	(*)	1,403
Mostly wool-----------------------------------	43	11	44	1	1	784
Mostly acrylic--------------------------------	25	24	47	4	(*)	198
Mostly cotton---------------------------------	22	43	35	--	--	135

* Less than 1 percent.

Table 180.--Boys owning winter (summer) clothes that were hand washed: "Who would you say generally does most of the hand washing of your winter (summer) clothes?"

Person doing most hand washing	United States total	Person doing most hand washing	United States total
	Percent		Percent
Winter clothes:		Summer clothes:	
Mother---------------------	83	Mother---------------------	79
Other----------------------	12	Other----------------------	15
Not ascertained------------	5	Not ascertained------------	6
Number of cases-------------	186	Number of cases-------------	171

weaters that were hand washed: "Who would you say generally does
most of the hand washing of sweaters?"

ics	Person doing most hand washing of sweaters			
	Mother	Other	Not ascer-tained	Cases
	Percent	Percent	Percent	Number
-------------------	87	10	3	607
-------------------	89	8	3	151
-------------------	86	12	2	183
-------------------	86	12	2	161
-------------------	85	9	6	112

dymade winter sport shirts (winter sport coats, dress-up winter pants,
ummer sport shirts, summer sport coats, dress-up summer pants, every-
ade sweaters) that were cared for by a method other than by commercial
hem usually pressed or not?"

dominating	Pressed	Not pressed	Not ascertained	Cases
	Percent	Percent	Percent	Number
-------------------	98	2	(*)	1,459
-------------------	99	1	(*)	1,124
-------------------	98	2	--	165
-------------------	59	15	26	70
-------------------	97	2	1	235
-------------------	90	9	1	1,432
-------------------	97	3	(*)	1,552
-------------------	98	2	(*)	1,257
-------------------	93	7	--	81
-------------------	88	7	5	84
-------------------	97	2	1	416
-------------------	98	2	--	248
-------------------	85	13	2	1,478
-------------------	69	27	4	886
-------------------	68	27	5	444
-------------------	70	28	2	149
-------------------	60	38	2	105

159

Table 183.--Boys owning winter clothes (summer clothes) that were pressed other than by commercial
cleaner: "Who would you say generally does most of the pressing of your winter clothes
(summer clothes)?"[1]

| Background characteristics | Person doing most pressing of winter clothes | | | | | Cases |
	Mother	Respondent	Maid	Other	Not ascertained	
	Percent	Percent	Percent	Percent	Percent	Number
United States total------	81	7	6	5	1	1,543
Age:						
14 years---------------	82	6	7	5	(*)	408
15 years---------------	81	7	6	5	1	428
16 years---------------	85	7	4	3	1	425
17 years---------------	75	10	8	7	(*)	282

| Background characteristics | Person doing most pressing of summer clothes | | | | | Cases |
	Mother	Respondent	Maid	Other	Not ascertained	
	Percent	Percent	Percent	Percent	Percent	Number
United States total------	81	8	6	5	1	1,576
Age:						
14 years---------------	83	5	6	6	1	414
15 years---------------	79	10	5	5	1	427
16 years---------------	84	7	4	4	2	440
17 years---------------	77	8	8	8	(*)	295

[1] Percentages may add to more than 100 because some respondents named more than 1 person.
*Less than 1 percent.

Table 184.--Boys owning sweaters that were pressed: "Who would you say
generally does most of the pressing of your sweaters?"[1]

| Background characteristics | Person doing most pressing of sweaters | | | Cases |
	Mother	Other	Not ascertained	
	Percent	Percent	Percent	Number
United States total-------	87	9	4	242
Age:				
14 years---------------	85	12	3	78
15 years---------------	92	4	4	75
16 or 17 years----------	86	9	5	89

[1] Does not include sweaters that are pressed by a commercial cleaner.

ere asked: "Which <u>one</u> of the six materials listed on this card would you say: Is the
't weather? Is the best to wear in cold weather? Lasts the longest? Keeps its shape
o care for? Is least likely to wrinkle? Is the best value for the money?"

wered	Cotton	Rayon	Nylon	Acrylic (Orlon)	Polyester (Dacron)	Wool	Not ascertained	Cases
	Percent	Percent	Percent	Percent	Percent	Percent	Percent	Number
ather?------	66	6	11	3	11	(*)	3	1,648
eather?-----	20	(*)	1	3	2	72	2	1,648
-----------	29	4	15	4	11	27	10	1,648
-----------	36	6	9	6	16	17	10	1,648
-----------	61	4	8	5	9	6	7	1,648
e?---------	17	6	14	9	18	24	12	1,648
ey?--------	48	3	7	4	9	17	12	1,648

ere asked: "Which <u>one</u> of the six materials listed on this card would you say is the
best to wear in hot weather?"

d tics	Cotton	Poly-ester (Dacron)	Nylon	Rayon	Acrylic (Orlon)	Wool	Not ascertained	Cases
	Percent	Percent	Percent	Percent	Percent	Percent	Percent	Number
-----------	66	11	11	6	3	(*)	3	1,648
-----------	64	8	11	9	4	(*)	4	431
-----------	63	12	13	6	4	(*)	2	447
-----------	65	13	11	4	3	(*)	4	459
-----------	71	9	10	5	2	(*)	3	311
-----------	63	9	16	7	2	(*)	3	534
-----------	65	12	10	6	4	(*)	3	664
-----------	69	11	9	5	3	(*)	3	449
-----------	66	11	10	4	4	(*)	5	564
n----------	67	12	11	5	3	(*)	2	664
-----------	65	8	14	9	2	(*)	2	420
-----------	69	12	7	4	3	(*)	5	388
-----------	65	10	13	6	2	(*)	4	467
-----------	68	11	12	5	3	(*)	1	535
-----------	57	9	14	10	6	1	3	258

Table 187.--All boys were asked: "Which one of the six materials listed on this card would you say is the best to wear in cold weather?"

Background characteristics	Wool	Cotton	Acrylic (Orlon)	Polyester (Dacron)	Nylon	Rayon	Not ascertained	Cases
	Percent	Percent	Percent	Percent	Percent	Percent	Percent	Number
United States total------	72	20	3	2	1	(*)	2	1,648
Age:								
14 years---------------	68	21	4	3	1	1	2	431
15 years---------------	72	21	3	2	1	(*)	1	447
16 years---------------	72	20	3	2	1	--	2	459
17 years---------------	74	18	1	3	1	1	2	311
Family income group:								
Lower------------------	68	22	3	3	1	1	2	534
Middle-----------------	74	18	3	2	1	1	1	664
Upper------------------	72	19	3	3	1	--	2	449
Size of place:								
Urban metropolitan-----	77	16	2	2	1	(*)	2	564
Urban nonmetropolitan--	70	21	4	2	1	1	1	664
Town and farm----------	69	23	2	3	1	(*)	2	420
Region:								
Northeast--------------	81	12	3	2	1	--	1	388
North Central----------	71	20	3	3	1	1.	1	467
South------------------	67	24	2	3	1	1	2	535
West-------------------	68	22	5	1	2	(*)	2	258

*Less than 1 percent.

Table 188.--All boys were asked: "Which one of the six materials listed on this card would you say lasts the longest?"

Background characteristics	Cotton	Wool	Nylon	Polyester (Dacron)	Acrylic (Orlon)	Rayon	Not ascertained	Cases
	Percent	Percent	Percent	Percent	Percent	Percent	Percent	
United States total------	29	27	15	11	4	4	10	1,648
Age:								
14 years---------------	29	29	14	10	4	4	10	
15 years---------------	32	24	15	12	4	2	11	
16 years---------------	26	25	17	11	4	5	12	
17 years---------------	27	29	14	11	4	5	10	
Family income group:								
Lower------------------	35	26	13	9	3	4	10	
Middle-----------------	25	29	15	11	4	5	11	
Upper------------------	27	24	16	13	5	3	12	
Size of place:								
Urban metropolitan-----	23	34	13	8	5	3	14	
Urban nonmetropolitan--	33	24	14	13	3	4	9	
Town and farm----------	31	22	18	11	4	5	9	
Region:								
Northeast--------------	22	35	14	9	4	5	11	
North Central----------	27	28	15	10	4	4	12	
South------------------	37	20	13	14	2	4	10	
West-------------------	29	25	19	9	7	2	9	

Table 189.--All boys were asked: "Which one of the six materials listed on this card would you say keeps its shape best?"

Background characteristics	Cotton	Wool	Polyester (Dacron)	Nylon	Acrylic (Orlon)	Rayon	Not ascertained	Cases
	Percent	Percent	Percent	Percent	Percent	Percent	Percent	Number
United States total------	36	17	16	9	6	6	10	1,648
Age:								
14 years---------------	35	17	13	9	8	7	11	431
15 years---------------	35	17	16	9	6	8	9	447
16 years---------------	34	17	17	9	7	5	11	459
17 years---------------	37	18	18	9	3	5	10	311
Family income group:								
Lower-----------------	40	16	12	9	5	8	10	534
Middle----------------	34	18	17	8	7	6	10	664
Upper-----------------	32	17	19	10	6	5	11	449
Size of place:								
Urban metropolitan-----	30	22	15	9	5	7	12	564
Urban nonmetropolitan--	35	16	17	9	8	6	9	664
Town and farm---------	42	13·	15	9	5	6	10	420
Region:								
Northeast-------------	26	23	17	9	6	6	13	388
North Central---------	36	16	15	9	5	7	12	467
South-----------------	43	13	17	8	4	6	9	535
West------------------	37	18	12	9	11	6	7	258

Table 190.--All boys were asked: "Which one of the six materials listed on this card would you say is easiest to care for?"

Background characteristics	Cotton	Polyester (Dacron)	Nylon	Wool	Acrylic (Orlon)	Rayon	Not ascertained	Cases
	Percent	Percent	Percent	Percent	Percent	Percent	Percent	Number
United States total------	61	9	8	6	5	4	7	1,648
Age:								
14 years---------------	60	9	8	3	6	5	9	431
15 years---------------	63	10	8	8	4	3	4	447
16 years---------------	61	9	7	7	5	3	8	459
17 years---------------	63	11	9	5	4	3	5	311
Family income group:								
Lower-----------------	62	8	9	6	4	5	6	534
Middle----------------	62	10	6	6	6	3	7	664
Upper-----------------	61	10	8	6	5	3	7	449
Size of place:								
Urban metropolitan-----	56	9	8	8	4	4	11	564
Urban nonmetropolitan--	64	12	7	5	5	3	4	664
Town and farm---------	66	8	8	4	5	4	5	420
Region:								
Northeast-------------	53	11	7	8	5	4	12	388
North Central---------	62	9	8	6	6	3	6	467
South-----------------	67	11	7	4	3	3	5	535
West------------------	59	7	10	6	6	7	5	258

Table 191.--All boys were asked: "Which <u>one</u> of the six materials listed on this card would you say is least likely to wrinkle?"

Background characteristics	Wool	Poly-ester (Dacron)	Cotton	Nylon	Acrylic (Orlon)	Rayon	Not ascertained	Cases
	Percent	Percent	Percent	Percent	Percent	Percent	Percent	Number
United States total------	24	18	17	14	9	6	12	1,648
Age:								
14 years---------------	22	16	20	14	10	8	10	431
15 years---------------	26	15	16	17	10	5	11	447
16 years---------------	24	20	16	14	8	5	13	459
17 years---------------	26	22	15	13	6	5	13	311
Family income group:								
Lower------------------	21	14	21	16	10	6	12	534
Middle-----------------	25	19	16	13	9	6	12	664
Upper------------------	28	21	13	15	7	5	11	449
Size of place:								
Urban metropolitan-----	26	18	15	13	8	6	14	564
Urban nonmetropolitan--	25	19	16	14	10	6	10	664
Town and farm---------	22	15	19	17	9	7	11	420
Region:								
Northeast--------------	25	18	15	13	9	7	13	388
North Central----------	30	16	14	14	9	6	11	467
South------------------	21	22	18	15	7	6	11	535
West-------------------	24	12	21	18	11	4	10	258

Table 192.--All boys were asked: "Which <u>one</u> of the six materials listed on this card would you say is the best value for the money?"

Background characteristics	Cotton	Wool	Polyester (Dacron)	Nylon	Acrylic (Orlon)	Rayon	Not ascertained	Cases
	Percent	Percent	Percent	Percent	Percent	Percent	Percent	Number
United States total------	48	17	9	7	4	3	12	1,648
Age:								
14 years---------------	50	16	8	6	4	3	13	431
15 years---------------	53	16	8	6	3	3	11	447
16 years---------------	44	17	10	8	4	3	14	459
17 years---------------	46	22	10	6	3	2	11	311
Family income group:								
Lower------------------	50	17	8	7	4	4	10	534
Middle-----------------	48	17	10	7	3	2	13	664
Upper------------------	47	18	8	6	4	3	14	449
Size of place:								
Urban metropolitan-----	40	21	8	5	4	3	19	564
Urban nonmetropolitan--	54	15	10	7	4	2	8	664
Town and farm---------	52	17	9	7	2	3	10	420
Region:								
Northeast--------------	37	22	7	8	5	4	17	388
North Central----------	47	18	9	6	3	2	15	467
South------------------	59	12	11	5	2	2	9	535
West-------------------	48	22	7	7	6	3	7	258

	Very interested	Fairly interested	Not very interested	Cases
	Percent	Percent	Percent	Number
---------	52	38	10	1,648
---------	45	44	11	431
---------	52	39	9	447
---------	54	36	10	459
---------	59	32	9	311
---------	48	38	14	534
---------	52	40	8	664
---------	55	37	8	449
---------	53	38	9	564
---------	54	37	9	664
---------	45	41	14	420
---------	51	40	9	388
---------	47	42	11	467
---------	58	32	10	535
---------	47	42	11	258

	Very interested	Fairly interested	Not very interested	Cases
	Percent	Percent	Percent	Number
---------	66	25	9	1,648
---------	56	32	12	431
---------	68	23	9	447
---------	69	23	8	459
---------	76	18	6	311
---------	62	27	11	534
---------	67	25	8	664
---------	72	22	6	449
---------	70	22	8	564
---------	70	23	7	664
---------	58	30	12	420
---------	64	26	10	388
---------	65	27	8	467
---------	70	22	8	535
---------	68	23	9	258

165

Table 195.--Boys who said they were very interested, fairly interested, or not very interested in selecting the clothes they wear: "Why is that?"[1]

Reasons for degree of interest	Degree of interest		
	Very interested	Fairly interested	Not very interested
	Percent	Percent	Percent
Positive reasons:			
Particular, fussy, prefer own taste----	27	10	--
Want to be stylish; want to wear what other teenagers wear-----------------	21	11	--
Clothes and appearance are important---	20	14	--
Want to select color, patterns---------	17	12	--
Want to select style-------------------	17	10	--
Want to be certain of fit, size--------	16	11	--
Want good value, quality---------------	5	2	--
People judge you by your clothes, clothes affect personality, character	5	1	--
Want to select fabrics-----------------	4	2	--
On clothes budget and want to be satisfied---------------------------	3	1	--
All other-----------------------------	5	6	--
Not ascertained-----------------------	1	--	--
Negative reasons:			
Mother does a good job-----------------	--	20	35
Don't care about clothes---------------	--	7	27
No choice; mother does it--------------	--	6	17
Don't like to shop--------------------	--	4	15
Don't have time-----------------------	--	4	8
Clothes mostly gifts, hand-me-downs----	--	(*)	2
All other-----------------------------	--	3	5
Not ascertained-----------------------	--	3	4
Number of cases-----------------------	1,098	405	145

[1] Percentages add to more than 100 because some respondents gave more than 1 answer.
*Less than 1 percent.

166

Table 196.--All boys were asked: "Where do you pick up ideas about what clothes you'd like to get?"[1]

Sources of ideas	U.S. total	Age of boys				Family income group			Size of place			Region			
		14 years	15 years	16 years	17 years	Lower	Middle	Upper	Urban metro-politan	Urban non-metro-politan	Town and farm	North-east	North Central	South	West
	Percent	Percent	Percent	Percent	Percent	Percent	Percent	Percent	Percent	Percent	Percent	Percent	Percent	Percent	Percent
FRIENDS AND RELATIVES------	87	86	87	87	91	83	89	91	87	90	83	87	90	86	85
Friends------	74	71	75	74	76	69	76	77	76	77	67	74	77	73	71
Parents------	17	23	15	15	14	16	19	15	19	14	19	25	14	14	16
Brothers or sisters------	7	9	6	7	4	5	7	9	7	6	6	7	6	5	10
Other relatives------	(*)	1	1	(*)	--	(*)	1	(*)	1	(*)	1	(*)	(*)	1	(*)
STORES AND SHOPPING------	50	43	49	50	62	53	49	49	48	52	50	55	44	53	47
Looking in stores------	38	32	36	39	49	40	36	39	34	41	39	39	35	40	38
Window shopping------	24	20	23	24	30	26	24	21	27	23	21	33	18	25	20
FORMAL MEDIA------	38	35	35	38	46	40	36	40	32	36	48	36	42	39	33
Magazines------	17	10	16	18	24	15	15	22	15	17	17	17	17	17	13
Catalogs------	14	14	13	13	15	19	12	11	6	12	28	6	17	17	13
Television------	13	11	13	14	13	13	12	14	12	12	15	11	14	13	13
Newspapers------	11	8	9	14	15	9	11	12	13	9	9	14	10	10	8
Movies------	3	1	2	4	4	2	3	2	3	3	2	3	3	2	3
OTHER PEOPLE------	4	3	4	4	4	5	3	4	4	4	3	4	4	3	5
ALL OTHER------	2	1	2	4	3	3	2	3	1	2	4	1	3	3	2
NOT ASCERTAINED------	1	1	--	1	(*)	1	(*)	(*)	(*)	(*)	1	(*)	--	1	1
Number of cases------	1,648	431	447	459	311	534	664	449	564	664	420	388	467	535	258

[1] Percentages add to more than their group totals and these add to more than 100 because some respondents gave more than 1 answer.
*Less than 1 percent.

167

Table 197.--All boys were asked: "Which one of these (sources of ideas) do you think is most helpful?"

Sources of ideas	U.S. total	Age of boys				Family income group			Size of place			Region			
	Percent	14 years	15 years	16 years	17 years	Lower	Middle	Upper	Urban metropolitan	Urban non-metropolitan	Town and farm	North-east	North Central	South	West
		Percent	Percent	Percent	Percent	Percent	Percent	Percent	Percent	Percent	Percent	Percent	Percent	Percent	Percent
FRIENDS AND RELATIVES----	61	66	63	60	54	53	67	64	62	64	56	61	65	59	58
Friends-----------	50	49	50	51	47	42	54	53	52	53	41	50	53	49	45
Parents-----------	9	14	9	8	5	9	11	8	8	8	13	10	9	8	11
Brothers and sisters----	2	3	3	1	2	2	2	3	2	3	2	1	3	2	2
Other relatives------	(*)	-	1	(*)	-	(*)	(*)	(*)	(*)	(*)	(*)	(*)	(*)	(*)	(*)
STORES AND SHOPPING------	23	18	23	23	31	28	19	23	24	23	22	27	19	25	23
Looking in stores------	17	12	17	17	23	20	14	18	16	18	18	17	15	18	19
Window shopping------	6	6	6	6	8	8	5	5	8	5	4	10	4	7	4
FORMAL MEDIA----------	11	13	11	9	10	13	11	8	9	9	16	9	12	12	9
Catalogs----------	5	6	5	3	5	7	4	2	2	3	10	3	6	6	3
Magazines---------	3	3	3	3	4	3	4	2	3	3	3	3	3	3	3
Television--------	2	3	2	2	1	2	2	2	3	2	2	2	2	2	2
Other media-------	1	1	1	1	(*)	1	1	2	1	1	1	1	1	1	1
ALL OTHER----------	2	1	2	4	2	3	2	3	2	2	3	2	2	2	4
NO PARTICULAR SOURCE-----	2	1	1	3	3	2	1	2	2	2	2	1	2	1	5
NOT ASCERTAINED-------	1	1	(*)	1	(*)	1	(*)	(*)	1	(*)	1	(*)	(*)	1	1
Number of cases-------	1,648	431	447	459	311	534	664	449	564	664	420	388	467	535	258

*Less than 1 percent.

Table 198.--All boys were asked: "Are you usually the one who suggests that you need an outer jacket or sport coat, or does someone else suggest it first?" "How about other clothing items such as shirts and sweaters--are you usually the one who suggests that you need things like this, or does someone else suggest it first?"[1]

Clothing items	Re-spondent	Mother	Father	All others	Not ascer-tained	Cases
	Percent	Percent	Percent	Percent	Percent	Number
Outer jackets or sport coats						
Total--------------	60	37	6	1	(*)	1,648
14 years----------	49	48	8	1	(*)	431
15 years----------	58	38	5	1	(*)	447
16 years----------	64	36	4	(*)	(*)	459
17 years----------	74	24	5	1	1	311
Shirts and sweaters						
Total--------------	69	32	2	(*)	--	1,648
14 years----------	55	45	3	1	--	431
15 years----------	69	32	2	(*)	--	447
16 years----------	72	28	3	--	--	459
17 years----------	83	18	2	--	--	311

[1] Percentages may add to more than 100 because some respondents named more than 1 person.
*Less than 1 percent.

Table 199.--All boys were asked: "Who has the most to say about whether or not you might get an outer jacket or sport coat?...such articles as shirts and sweaters?"

Clothing items	Mother	Father	Re-spondent	All others	Not ascer-tained	Cases
	Percent	Percent	Percent	Percent	Percent	Number
Outer jackets or sport coats						
Total--------------	59	25	15	1	(*)	1,648
14 years----------	69	27	3	1	--	431
15 years----------	61	25	12	1	1	447
16 years----------	56	27	15	1	1	459
17 years----------	44	21	33	2	(*)	311
Shirts and sweaters						
Total--------------	63	13	23	1	(*)	1,648
14 years----------	75	16	8	1	(*)	431
15 years----------	67	11	20	1	1	447
16 years----------	60	14	25	1	(*)	459
17 years----------	43	11	45	1	--	311

*Less than 1 percent.

Table 200.--All boys were asked: "Who usually shops for your sport shirts?...
your sport coats?... your everyday pants?... your dress-up pants?... your
sweaters?... your outer jackets or short coats?"

Clothing items	Boys shopping alone	Mothers shopping alone	Mothers and sons both shopping	Other	Not ascer- tained	Cases
	Percent	Percent	Percent	Percent	Percent	Number
Sport shirts						
Total------------	44	33	19	4	(*)	1,641
14 years--------	23	46	26	4	1	428
15 years--------	38	34	21	7	(*)	445
16 years--------	52	28	17	3	--	459
17 years--------	68	18	10	3	1	309
Sport coats						
Total------------	32	22	26	18	2	1,214
14 years--------	16	33	30	20	1	316
15 years--------	23	23	30	22	2	337
16 years--------	40	18	24	15	3	331
17 years--------	57	12	16	11	4	230
Everyday pants						
Total------------	47	34	15	4	(*)	1,645
14 years--------	25	47	21	6	1	431
15 years--------	42	36	16	6	(*)	447
16 years--------	53	30	12	5	(*)	457
17 years--------	74	18	7	1	(*)	310
Dress-up pants						
Total------------	33	30	25	12	(*)	1,398
14 years--------	15	43	30	11	1	390
15 years--------	27	30	26	17	--	372
16 years--------	40	25	24	10	1	379
17 years--------	58	16	16	9	1	257
Sweaters						
Total------------	46	30	17	7	(*)	1,403
14 years--------	26	43	24	7	(*)	362
15 years--------	43	32	15	10	--	380
16 years--------	49	28	16	7	--	397
17 years--------	76	13	8	2	1	264
Outer jackets or short coats						
Total------------	37	25	24	13	1	1,466
14 years--------	17	36	31	15	1	379
15 years--------	27	27	27	18	1	398
16 years--------	45	20	23	11	1	413
17 years--------	65	13	14	6	2	276

* Less than 1 percent.

s were asked: "Who usually has the most to say about the
t is finally selected? ...the sport coat? ...the everyday
iress-up pants? ...your sweater? ...the outer jacket or

s	Boys	Mothers	Fathers	All others	Not ascertained	Cases
	Percent	Percent	Percent	Percent	Percent	Number
.---	64	32	3	1	1	1,641
.---	48	46	5	--	1	428
.---	61	35	3	1	1	445
.---	72	25	3	(*)	1	459
.---	79	18	1	1	2	309
.---	57	32	10	1	2	1,214
.---	42	44	15	1	1	316
.---	52	35	12	1	1	337
.---	64	26	7	1	2	331
.---	73	20	3	1	4	230
.---	66	31	3	(*)	1	1,645
.---	52	44	4	(*)	1	431
.---	63	34	3	--	1	447
.---	71	27	3	--	1	457
.---	81	17	1	(*)	1	310
---	57	37	8	(*)	1	1,398
---	39	52	10	(*)	1	390
.---	50	41	10	(*)	2	372
---	67	30	6	1	(*)	379
---	78	18	3	(*)	1	257
---	64	31	3	3	1	1,403
---	48	46	4	3	(*)	362
---	61	32	4	3	1	380
---	70	26	3	3	1	397
---	80	17	(*)	2	1	264
rt						
---	59	33	9	(*)	1	1,466
---	45	47	11	(*)	1	379
---	52	37	11	1	1	398
---	65	25	9	(*)	1	413
---	79	18	1	1	1	276

to more than 100 because some respondents gave more than

nt.

171

Table 202.--All boys were asked: "Generally speaking, at what age do you think a boy is old enough to go shopping and pick out his own clothing by himself?"

Suggested age at which boy is old enough to shop	U.S. total	Age of boys			
		14 years	15 years	16 years	17 years
	Percent	Percent	Percent	Percent	Percent
Under 14 years--------------------------------	15	16	15	15	10
14 years--------------------------------------	25	31	29	21	16
15 years--------------------------------------	22	17	23	24	26
16 years--------------------------------------	25	24	19	28	30
17 years--------------------------------------	7	7	9	4	10
18 years--------------------------------------	4	2	3	6	6
19 years or over------------------------------	2	3	1	2	2
Not ascertained-------------------------------	(*)	--	1	(*)	(*)
Median age named (years)----------------------	15.4	15.2	15.3	15.6	15.9
Number of cases-------------------------------	1,648	431	447	459	311

*Less than 1 percent.

Table 203.--All boys were asked: "Are you still enrolled in school?" "What grade are you in now?" "What was the last grade of school you completed?"

Not enrolled--------------------------------
  Last grade completed:
    Under first year high school-------------
    First year high school-------------------
    Second year high school------------------
    Third year high school-------------------
    Fourth year high school------------------
    Other------------------------------------

Enrolled------------------------------------
    Under first year high school-------------
    First year high school-------------------
    Second year high school------------------
    Third year high school-------------------
    Fourth year high school------------------
    College freshman-------------------------
    Other------------------------------------
    Not ascertained--------------------------

Number of cases-----------------------------

*Less than 1 percent.

--All boys were asked: "Have you done any kind of work at all for
the past 12 months?" "Do you have a regular job that you go to
week?"

Work status	U.S. total	Age of boys			
		14 years	15 years	16 years	17 years
	Percent	Percent	Percent	Percent	Percent
rked in past year---	24	32	24	24	13
i in past year-------	76	68	76	76	87
ilar job-------------	21	10	20	22	40
ave regular job------	33	31	31	33	34
ilar and nonregular					
-------------------	22	27	25	21	13
rtained-------------	(*)	(*)	(*)	(*)	(*)
cases---------------	1,648	431	447	459	311

han 1 percent.

5.--Boys who worked in the past year: "About how much money did
you earn in the past year from working?"

it of money earned	U.S. total	Age of boys			
		14 years	15 years	16 years	17 years
	Percent	Percent	Percent	Percent	Percent
$25------------------	16	32	19	11	2
-------------------	32	45	37	27	16
.99------------------	17	11	17	22	18
;99------------------	11	5	10	13	14
;99------------------	6	3	6	8	9
.99------------------	5	2	4	6	7
;99------------------	3	1	3	3	7
>re------------------	9	1	3	10	26
ained---------------	1	(*)	1	(*)	1
cases---------------	1,255	295	339	350	271

han 1 percent.

173

Table 206.--Boys who worked in the past year and earned $25 or more: Uses of money earned[1]

Uses of money earned	U.S. total	Age of boys			
		14 years	15 years	16 years	17 years
	Percent	Percent	Percent	Percent	Percent
Recreation and amusement---	66	64	68	65	61
Clothing-------------------	62	49	62	65	70
School supplies------------	19	18	21	18	20
Dates----------------------	18	4	10	22	33
Gifts, presents------------	17	17	15	16	20
Luxuries-------------------	9	12	9	9	6
Board, family expenses-----	7	6	5	6	11
Car, car maintenance-------	7	1	2	9	16
Trip, vacation, camp-------	6	4	5	7	7
Miscellaneous--------------	5	6	4	6	5
Saved it-------------------	51	55	56	49	44
Education----------------	21	24	21	19	20
Car---------------------	11	7	13	11	11
Clothes-----------------	2	3	3	3	1
Trip, vacation, camp-----	2	3	4	2	1
Sports equipment---------	2	5	2	3	--
Emergency-rainy day------	2	1	2	2	2
Motorcycle, boat---------	2	3	2	1	--
Miscellaneous-----------	5	4	5	5	6
No special reason--------	7	9	8	5	8
Not ascertained------------	1	1	1	2	1
Number of cases -----------	1,048	200	272	312	264

[1] Percentages add to more than 100 (or more than the subtotal shown) because some respondents named more than 1 use of money earned.

ed in the past year and earned $25 or more: "What
with <u>most</u> of the money you earned?"[1]

U.S. total	Age of boys			
	14 years	15 years	16 years	17 years
<u>Percent</u>	<u>Percent</u>	<u>Percent</u>	<u>Percent</u>	<u>Percent</u>
31	26	32	29	36
21	21	21	22	19
5	8	5	5	3
5	--	2	5	12
4	4	5	4	3
4	3	4	4	6
3	1	1	4	6
3	3	2	2	3
2	2	2	1	3
32	39	35	32	22
14	17	15	13	12
7	6	9	8	5
2	3	2	1	--
1	2	1	2	--
1	2	1	1	--
1	2	1	1	--
3	5	2	3	2
3	5	5	4	3
3	4	2	2	2
1,048	200	272	312	264

than 100 (or more than the subtotal shown) because
than 1 use of money earned.

175

Uses of money earned	U.S. total	Age of boys			
		14 years	15 years	16 years	17 years
	Percent	Percent	Percent	Percent	Percent
Recreation and amusement--	46	43	49	43	47
Clothing------------------	32	24	30	36	35
Dates---------------------	15	3	9	19	27
School supplies-----------	15	14	16	14	17
Gifts, presents-----------	15	15	13	14	16
Trip, vacation, camp------	4	3	3	6	4
Luxuries------------------	4	5	4	5	3
Board, family expenses----	3	4	2	2	6
Car, car maintenance------	3	1	--	5	5
Miscellaneous-------------	3	4	3	3	2
Saved it------------------	20	17	21	17	23
Education---------------	7	7	7	6	9
Car--------------------	4	2	3	3	6
Clothes----------------	1	--	2	1	1
Trip-------------------	1	1	2	(*)	1
Sports equipment--------	1	2	2	1	--
Emergency-rainy day-----	1	--	2	2	1
Motorcycle, boat--------	1	2	1	(*)	--
Gifts, presents---------	(*)	--	1	(*)	1
Musical instruments, radio, phono----------	(*)	--	1	(*)	--
Miscellaneous-----------	3	1	1	1	3
No special reason-------	4	5	4	3	6
Not ascertained-----------	4	5	4	3	4
Number of cases-----------	1,048	200	272	312	264

[1] Percentages add to more than 100 (or more than the subtotal shown) because some respondents named more than 1 use of money earned.
  *Less than 1 percent.

Table 209.--Interviewers' report on whether or not
present during the boys' interviews besides the respo

Person present
o other person present------------------------------
ther person present--------------------------------
Mother---
Sister---
Father---
Brother--
Male friend--
All other--
lot ascertained------------------------------------
Jumber of cases------------------------------------

[1] Subtotals add to more than total because interview
:han 1 person was present during interview.

Table 210.--Interviewers' impressions about whether th
persons seemed to have a great influence, some inf
on boy respondents' answers

Amount of influence
lreat influence------------------------------------
3ome influence-------------------------------------
No influence---------------------------------------
Not ascertained------------------------------------
Number of cases------------------------------------

*Less than 1 percent.

Table 211.--Background characteristics of boys

Background characteristics	Background characteristics						
	Age				Family income group		
	14 years	15 years	16 years	17 years	Lower	Middle	Upper
	Percent	Percent	Percent	Percent	Percent	Percent	Percent
Age:							
14 years----------------	100	--	--	--	26	29	22
15 years----------------	--	100	--	--	27	27	28
16 years----------------	--	--	100	--	26	30	28
17 years----------------	--	--	--	100	21	14	22
Family income group:							
Lower-------------------	33	32	30	36	100	--	--
Middle------------------	44	40	43	31	--	100	--
Upper-------------------	23	28	27	33	--	--	100
Size of place:							
Urban metropolitan------	32	32	36	38	19	40	44
Urban nonmetropolitan---	39	43	39	39	38	41	42
Town and farm----------	29	25	25	23	43	19	14
Region:							
Northeast---------------	23	25	24	22	20	25	25
North Central-----------	28	29	28	28	21	34	29
South-------------------	32	34	30	34	49	24	26
West--------------------	17	12	18	16	10	17	20

Background characteristics	Background characteristics						
	Size of place			Region			
	Urban metro-politan	Urban non-metro-politan	Town and farm	North-east	North Central	South	West
	Percent	Percent	Percent	Percent	Percent	Percent	Percent
Age:							
14 years----------------	24	26	30	25	26	26	29
15 years----------------	26	29	26	28	28	29	21
16 years----------------	29	27	27	29	28	25	31
17 years----------------	21	18	17	18	18	20	19
Family income group:							
Lower-------------------	18	31	55	27	24	49	21
Middle------------------	47	41	31	44	48	30	44
Upper-------------------	35	28	14	29	28	21	35
Size of place:							
Urban metropolitan------	100	--	--	58	36	10	42
Urban nonmetropolitan---	--	100	--	31	38	51	38
Town and farm----------	--	--	100	11	26	39	20
Region:							
Northeast---------------	41	18	10	100	--	--	--
North Central-----------	30	26	28	--	100	--	--
South-------------------	10	41	50	--	--	100	--
West--------------------	19	15	12	--	--	--	100

Budget Bureau No. 40-6214.1
Expiration Date: December 31, 1963

With the exception of check-box material, some instructions to interviewers, office-record information, and free-answer space, the questionnaires used for this study are reproduced below in entirety. Instructions to interviewers are in upper case letters enclosed in parentheses; optional questions or phrases are in lower case letters enclosed in parentheses.

Girls' Form

Part 1

Introduction: I'd like to ask you a few questions about your ready-made clothes. Ready-made means clothes which were bought from a store. We are not interested in clothes which were made at home.

Winter Clothes

1. Are most of your ready-made winter clothes dresses, or skirt and blouse or sweater combinations?

(IF "ONLY DRESSES" IS CHECKED, PROBE TO BE SURE RESPONDENT DOES NOT HAVE READY-MADE WINTER SKIRTS OR BLOUSES, CONTINUE WITH NEXT PARAGRAPH, THEN SKIP TO 20)

As you know, clothes are made of many materials these days. By material we mean either the fiber or the blends and mixtures of two or three fibers that are in the clothes. We are going to ask you what materials your clothes are made of and what you think of these materials. There aren't any right or wrong answers to most of these questions. We are interested in hearing your opinions.

A. Winter Skirts

2. First let's take winter skirts. What material are most of your ready-made winter skirts made of? (IF "DON'T OWN," SKIP TO 14)

3. What other materials are your ready-made winter skirts made of?

4. What material do you like best for winter skirts? (IF "NO PREFERENCE," SKIP TO 7)

5. Why do you prefer (NAME ANSWER TO 4) for winter skirts? Anything else?

6. Is there anything that you don't like so well about (NAME ANSWER TO 4) for winter skirts? Anything else?

7a. Let's talk about permanently pleated wool skirts for a minute--that is, wool skirts which have been processed or treated so that the pleats stay in without pressing, even when the skirt is washed or cleaned. Do you think that permanent pleating in wool skirts is a good idea or not such a good idea?

7b. Why do you say that? Anything else?

8a. Now, using this scale card (HAND RESPONDENT CARD I), tell me how you would feel about permanent pleating in deciding whether to buy a pleated wool skirt. You can give a rating anywhere from "Most important" which is number 5 to "Not important at all" which is number 1. Which block number best tells how important permanent pleating would be to you in deciding whether or not to buy a particular pleated skirt made of wool?

CARD 1

5	MOST IMPORTANT
4	
3	
2	
1	NOT IMPORTANT AT ALL

179

8b. Why is that? Anything else?

9. Do you have any pleated winter skirts? (IF "NO," SKIP TO 14)

10. Are any of your pleated winter skirts specially processed or treated so that the pleats stay in? (IF "NO," SKIP TO 12)

11. What materials are your permanently pleated skirts made of?

12. Do you have any other pleated winter skirts, that is, ones that are not processed or treated to hold the pleats? (IF "NO," SKIP TO 14)

13. What materials are your other pleated winter skirts made of?

B. Winter Blouses

14. Now let's turn to your blouses that you wear mainly during the wintertime. What material are most of them made of? (IF "DON'T OWN," SKIP TO 19)

15. What other materials are your winter blouses made of?

16. What material do you like best for winter blouses? (IF "NO PREFERENCE," SKIP TO 19)

17. Why do you prefer (NAME ANSWER TO 16) for winter blouses? Anything else?

18. Is there anything that you don't like so well about (NAME ANSWER TO 16) for winter blouses? Anything else?

C. Winter Dresses

19. Do you have any ready-made winter dresses? (IF "NO," SKIP TO 26)

20. Do you get some of your winter dresses for everyday wear and others for Sunday or special occasion or do you get the same kind for both everyday and dress-up wear?

Different dresses for each	☐ (ASK 21. PREFACE QUESTION BY SAYING: "Let's talk about just your everyday winter dresses.")
Same dresses for both	☐ (ASK 21 - OMIT WORD "EVERYDAY")
Only everyday dresses	☐ (ASK 21 AS PRINTED)
Only dress-up dresses	☐ (SKIP TO 26)

21. Now, can you tell me what material most of your everyday winter dresses are made of?

22. What other materials are your everyday winter dresses made of?

23. What material do you like best for everyday winter dresses? (IF "NO PREFERENCE," SKIP TO 26)

24. Why do you prefer (NAME ANSWER TO 23) for everyday winter dresses? Anything else?

25. Is there anything that you don't like so well about (NAME ANSWER TO 23) for everyday winter dresses? Anything else?

D. Outer Jackets or Short Coats for Winter

26. Do you have any outer jackets or short coats, that is, ones which are meant to be worn outdoors ir wintertime? (IF "NO," SKIP TO 31)

27. What materials are your outer jackets or short coats made of? (EXCLUDE THE LINING)

28. What material do you like best for outer jackets or short coats? (EXCLUDE THE LINING) (IF "NO PREFERENCE," SKIP TO 31)

29. Why do you prefer (NAME ANSWER TO 28) for outer jackets or short coats? Anything else?

30. Is there anything that you don't like so well about (NAME ANSWER TO 28) for outer jackets or short coats? Anything else?

Winter Garment Care

31a. Now we'd like to know how these ready-made clothes are usually taken care of. Let's take winter skirts first. Would you say that most of your winter skirts are washed at home by hand, by machine, o. taken to the dry cleaners, or just what? (IF 'DON't OWN" or "COMMERCIAL CLEANER," SKIP TO 32a)

31b. Are most of them usually pressed or not?

32a. How are most of your winter blouses taken care of? (Would you say that most of your winter blouses are washed at home by hand, by machine, or taken to the dry cleaners, or what?) (IF "DON'T OWI or 'COMMERCIAL CLEANER," SKIP TO 33a)

st of them usually pressed or not?

out your everyday winter dresses? (Would you say that most of them are washed at home by
hine, taken to the dry cleaners, or what?) (IF "DON'T OWN" or "COMMERCIAL CLEANER,"

st of them usually pressed or not?

AND WASHED" CHECKED IN ANY OF THE ABOVE, ASK:) Who would you say generally does most of the
g of your winter clothes?

RESSED" CHECKED IN ANY OF THE ABOVE, ASK:) Who would you say generally does most of the
your winter clothes?

es

t's change the season a bit and talk about summer clothes. Are most of your ready-made
es dresses, or blouse and skirt combinations? (IF "ONLY DRESSES" CHECKED, PROBE TO BE
DENT DOES NOT HAVE READY-MADE SUMMER SKIRTS OR BLOUSES, THEN SKIP TO 48)

Skirts

let's take summer skirts. What material are most of your ready-made summer skirts made of?
OWN," SKIP TO 42)

ther materials are your ready-made summer skirts made of?

aterial do you like best for summer skirts? (IF "NO PREFERENCE," SKIP TO 42)

you prefer (NAME ANSWER TO 39) for summer skirts? Anything else?

re anything that you don't like so well about (NAME ANSWER TO 39) for summer skirts?
se?

Blouses

aterial are most of your summer blouses made of? (IF "DON'T OWN," SKIP TO 47)

ther materials are your summer blouses made of?

aterial do you like best for summer blouses? (IF "NO PREFERENCE," SKIP TO 47)

you prefer (NAME ANSWER TO 44) for summer blouses? Anything else?

re anything that you don't like so well about (NAME ANSWER TO 44) for summer blouses?
se?

Dresses

have any ready-made summer dresses? (IF "NO," SKIP TO 54)

get some of your summer dresses for everyday wear and others for Sunday or special
or do you get the same kind for both everyday and dress-up wear?

Different dresses for each	☐	(ASK 49. PREFACE QUESTION BY SAYING: "Let's talk about just your everyday summer dresses")
Same dresses for both	☐	(ASK 49 - OMIT WORD "EVERYDAY")
Only everyday dresses	☐	(ASK 49 AS PRINTED)
Only dress-up dresses	☐	(SKIP TO 54)

can you tell me what material most of your everyday summer dresses are made of?

ther materials are your everyday summer dresses made of?

aterial do you like best for everyday summer dresses? (IF "NO PREFERENCE," SKIP TO 54)

you prefer (NAME ANSWER TO 51) for everyday summer dresses? Anything else?

re anything that you don't like so well about (NAME ANSWER TO 51) for everyday summer
nything else?

ment Care

e'd like to know how these ready-made summer clothes are usually taken care of. Let's take
rts first. Would you say that most of your summer skirts are washed at home by hand, by
taken to the dry cleaners, or just what? (IF "DON'T OWN" or "COMMERCIAL CLEANER,"

54b. Are most of them usually pressed or not?

55a. How are most of your summer blouses taken care of? (Would you say that most of your summer blouses are washed at home by hand, by machine, or taken to the dry cleaners, or what?) (IF "DON'T OWN" or "COMMERCIAL CLEANER," SKIP TO 56)

55b. Are most of them usually pressed or not?

56a. How about your everyday summer dresses? (Would you say that most of them are washed at home by hand, by machine, taken to the dry cleaners, or what?) (IF "DON'T OWN" or "COMMERCIAL CLEANER," SKIP TO 57)

56b. Are most of them usually pressed or not?

57. (IF "HAND WASHED" CHECKED IN ANY OF THE ABOVE, ASK:) Who would you say generally does most of the hand washing of your summer clothes?

58. (IF "PRESSED" CHECKED IN ANY OF THE ABOVE, ASK:) Who would you say generally does most of the pressing of your summer clothes?

H. Sweaters

59. Now let's talk about sweaters. This would include all types of sweaters but not Polo shirts or T-shirts. Do you have any ready-made sweaters that you've worn during the past twelve months?

60. What material are most of your ready-made sweaters made of?

61. What other materials are your ready-made sweaters made of?

62. What material do you like best for sweaters? (IF "NO PREFERENCE," SKIP TO 65)

63. Why do you prefer (NAME ANSWER TO 62) for sweaters? Anything else?

64. Is there anything that you don't like so well about (NAME ANSWER TO 62) for sweaters? Anything else?

65a. How are most of your sweaters usually taken care of? (Would you say that most of them are washed at home by hand, by machine, or taken to a dry cleaner, or what?) (IF "COMMERCIAL CLEANER," SKIP TO 66)

65b. Are most of them usually pressed or not?

65c. (IF "HAND WASHED" CHECKED ABOVE, ASK:) Who would you say generally does most of the hand washing of your sweaters?

65d. (IF "PRESSED" CHECKED ABOVE, ASK:) Who would you say generally does most of the pressing of your sweaters?

66a. Let's talk a minute about a new kind of wool sweater. These new wool sweaters have been treated so that it is perfectly safe to wash them in a machine without special care. Do you think making wool sweaters that can be washed in a machine is a good idea or not such a good idea?

66b. Why do you say that? Anything else?

67a. Here is the scale card again. (HAND RESPONDENT CARD I) [SEE 8a OF QUESTIONNAIRE]. Tell me if you think machine washability would be important to you or not in deciding whether to buy a particular new wool sweater.

67b. Why is that? Anything else?

I. Slips

68a. Do you have any half slips? (IF "NO," SKIP TO 69)

68b. What material are most of them made of?

68c. What other materials are your half slips made of?

69a. Do you have any regular (full-length) slips? (IF "NO")-- Then let's talk about half slips. (SKIP TO 71)

69b. What material are most of them made of?

69c. What other materials are your regular full-length slips made of?

70. (IF "NO" TO EITHER 68a OR 69a, ASK 71 NEXT) (IF "YES" TO BOTH 68a AND 69a, ASK:) Which would you say you wear most often: half slips or regular (full-length) slips?

71. What material do you like best for them? (IF "NO PREFERENCE," SKIP TO 74)

72. Why do you prefer (NAME ANSWER TO 71) for slips? Anything else?

73. Is there anything you don't like so well about (NAME ANSWER TO 71) for slips? Anything else?

ips washed at home by hand, or by machine, or what?

ually pressed or not?

HECKED ABOVE, ASK:) Who would you say generally does <u>most</u> of the hand washing

ED ABOVE, ASK:) Who would you say generally does <u>most</u> of the pressing of

at--one that's meant to be worn only in rainy weather? (IF "NO," SKIP TO 77)

s coat made of?

hat is meant to be worn in dry as well as rainy weather and is specially
er repellent? (IF "NO," SKIP TO 79)

s coat made of?

AND 77, SKIP TO 82 NEXT) (IF "YES" TO EITHER 75 OR 77, ASK:) What material
wear? (IF "NO PREFERENCE," ASK 82)

AME ANSWER TO 79) for rainwear? Anything else?

at you don't like so well about (NAME ANSWER TO 79) for rainwear?

Part II

her all your ideas about materials. (HAND RESPONDENT CARD II). Which <u>one</u> of
on this card would you say:

o wear in hot weather?   CARD II

o wear in cold weather?
                                                Cotton
gest?   Rayon
                                                Nylon
pe best?   Orlon
                                                Dacron
care for?   Wool

ly to wrinkle?

alue for the money?

Part III

ites about your interest in clothes.

ou are very interested, fairly interested, or not very interested in what kinds

choosing the clothes--are you very interested, fairly interested, or not very
he clothes you wear?

ing else?

ip ideas about what clothes you'd like to get? (IF <u>MORE THAN ONE</u> SOURCE

do you think is most helpful? In your family, how does the decision to buy an
-such as a dress or a coat--come about?

ou usually the one who suggests that you need a dress or coat, or does someone

rs usually decide whether or not you might get an important clothing item such
IF MORE THAN ONE MENTIONED, ASK:)

say about whether or not you might get a dress or a coat?

thing items such as blouses and skirts--are you usually the one who suggests
this, or does someone else suggest it first?

89a. Which family members usually decide whether or not you might get articles such as blouses or skirts? (IF MORE THAN ONE MENTIONED, ASK:)

89b. Who has the most to say about whether or not you might get such articles as blouses or skirts?

Now let's talk about shopping for clothes.

90. Who usually shops for...

90a. Your skirts?

90b. How about your blouses? (Who usually shops for them?)

90c. Your everyday dresses?

90d. Your sweaters?

90e. Your outer jackets or short coats?

91a. Who usually has the most to say about the skirt that is finally selected?

91b. The blouse (that's finally selected?)

91c. The everyday dress?

91d. The sweater?

91e. The outer jacket or short coat?

92. Generally speaking, at what age do you think a girl is old enough to go shopping and pick out her own clothing by herself?

CLASSIFICATION INFORMATION

Just a few more questions and we'll be finished.

93a. Are you still enrolled in school? (Were you enrolled in school last month?) (IF "YES," ASK 93b, c, and d) (IF "NO," ASK 93e)

93b. What grade are you in now? (were you in last month?)

93c. What grades are there in the school you go to now? (went to?)

93d. Is (was) your school an all girls' school? (SKIP TO 94)

93e. What was the last grade of school you completed?

94. Have you done any kind of work at all for pay in the past 12 months? (IF "NO," SKIP TO 99)

95a. Do you have a regular job that you go to every week? (IF "NO," SKIP TO 96a)

95b. What kind of work do you do?

95c. How many hours a week do you usually work?

96a. During the past year, have you done any other kind of work for pay--such as baby sitting or working in a store? (IF "NO," SKIP TO 97)

96b. What kind of work have you done?

96c. What time of year was this?

97. About how much money did you earn in the past year from working? (HAND RESPONDENT CARD III) (IF "LESS THAN $25," SKIP TO 99)

98a. What did you do with most of the money you earned? (IF "SAVED IT," ASK:)

CARD III

98b. What are (were) you saving for?

Less than $25
$25 - $99

98c. What did you do with the rest of the money you earned? (IF "SAVED IT," ASK:)

$100 - $199
$200 - $299

98d. What are (were) you saving for?

$300 - $399
$400 - $499

99. What kind of work does your father (or head-of-household) do?

$500 - $599
$600 or more

That covers all my questions for you.

RACE)

other person present during the interview? (IF NO, SKIP TO 102)

presence of this other person seem to have a great influence, some influence, or no
respondent's answers?

hager married?

Boys' Form

Part 1

I'd like to ask you a few questions about your ready-made clothes. Ready-made means
were bought from a store. We are <u>not</u> interested in clothes which were made at home.

clothes are made of many materials these days. By material we mean either the fiber or
d mixtures of two or three fibers that are in the clothes. We are going to ask you what
r clothes are made of and what you think of these materials. There aren't any right or
 to most of these questions. We are interested in hearing your opinions.

ort Shirts

's talk about ready-made winter sport shirts, ones that are usually worn without a tie,
nitted shirts or T-shirts. What material are <u>most</u> of your winter sport shirts made of?
N," SKIP TO 6)

r materials are your winter sport shirts made of?

rial do you like <u>best</u> for winter sport shirts? (IF "NO PREFERENCE," SKIP TO 6)

u prefer (NAME ANSWER TO 3) for winter sport shirts? Anything else?

anything that you don't like so well about (NAME ANSWER TO 3) for winter sport shirts?
?

ort Coats

few questions are about winter sport coats - the suit-type jackets which are bought
o be worn with slacks or pants that do not necessarily match. Do you have any winter
 (IF "NO," SKIP TO 12)

rial are most of your winter sport coats made of?

r materials are your winter sport coats made of?

rial do you like <u>best</u> for winter sport coats? (IF "NO PREFERENCE," SKIP TO 12)

u prefer (NAME ANSWER TO 9) for winter sport coats? Anything else?

anything that you don't like so well about (NAME ANSWER TO 9) for winter sport coats?

. talk about winter slacks or trousers. Do you get some of your winter pants for everyday
s for Sunday or special occasions, or do you get the same kind for both everyday and

Different pants for each	☐ (ASK SECTIONS "C" & "D")
Same pants for both	☐ (SKIP TO SECTION "D" - OMIT WORD "EVERYDAY")
Only everyday pants	☐ (SKIP TO SECTION "D")
Only dress-up pants	☐ (ASK SECTION "C," THEN SKIP TO 23a)

inter Pants

rial are <u>most</u> of your dress-up winter pants made of? (IF "DON'T OWN," SKIP TO 18)

r materials are your dress-up winter pants made of?

rial do you like <u>best</u> for dress-up winter pants? (IF "NO PREFERENCE," SKIP TO 18)

u prefer (NAME ANSWER TO 15) for dress-up winter pants? Anything else?

185

17. Is there anything that you don't like so well about (NAME ANSWER TO 15) for dress-up winter pants? Anything else?

D. Everyday Winter Pants

18. What about (everyday) winter pants? What material are most of your (everyday) winter pants made of? (IF "DON'T OWN," SKIP TO 23)

19. What other materials are your (everyday) winter pants made of?

20. What material do you like best for (everyday) winter pants? (IF "NO PREFERENCE," SKIP TO 23)

21. Why do you prefer (NAME ANSWER TO 20) for (everyday) winter pants? Anything else?

22. Is there anything that you don't like so well about (NAME ANSWER TO 20) for (everyday) winter pants? Anything else?

23a. Let's talk about permanently creased wool pants for a minute - that is, wool pants which have been processed or treated so that the creases stay in without pressing, even when the pants are washed or cleaned.

Do you think that permanent creasing in wool pants is a good idea or not such a good idea?

23b. Why do you say that? Anything else?

24a. Now, using this scale card (HAND RESPONDENT CARD I), [SEE QUESTION 8a, GIRLS' FORM OF QUESTIONNAIRE] tell me how you would feel about permanent creases in deciding whether to buy a pair of wool pants. You can give a rating anywhere from "Most important" which is number 5 to "Not important at all" which is number 1. Which block number best tells how important permanent creases would be to you in deciding whether or not to buy a particular pair of pants made of wool?

24b Why is that? Anything else?

25a. Are any of your winter pants specially treated so that the creases stay in? (IF "NO," SKIP TO 26)

25b. What materials are your permanently creased pants made of?

E. Outer Jackets or Short Coats for Winter

26. Do you have any outer jackets or short coats, that is, ones which are meant to be worn outdoors in wintertime? (IF "NO," SKIP TO 31)

27. What materials are your outer jackets or short coats made of? (EXCLUDE THE LINING)

28 What material do you like best for outer jackets or short coats? (EXCLUDE THE LINING) (IF "NO PREFERENCE," SKIP TO 31)

29 Why do you prefer (NAME ANSWER TO 28) for outer jackets or short coats? Anything else?

30. Is there anything that you don't like so well about (NAME ANSWER TO 28) for outer jackets or short coats? Anything else?

Winter Garment Care

31a. Now, we'd like to know how these ready-made winter clothes are usually taken care of. Let's take winter sport shirts first. Would you say that most of your winter sport shirts are washed at home by hand, by machine, or taken to the dry cleaners, or just what? (IF "DON'T OWN" OR "COMMERCIAL CLEANER," SKIP TO 32a)

31b. Are most of them usually pressed or not?

32a. How are most of your winter sport coats taken care of? (Would you say that most of your winter sport coats are washed at home by hand, by machine, or taken to the dry cleaners, or what?) (IF "DON'T OWN" OR "COMMERCIAL CLEANER," SKIP TO 33a)

32b Are most of them usually pressed or not?

33a. How are your dress-up winter pants usually taken care of? (Would you say that most of them are washed at home by hand, by machine, or taken to the dry cleaners, or what?) (IF "DON'T OWN" OR "COMMERCIAL CLEANER," SKIP TO 34a)

33b. Are most of them usually pressed or not?

34a. How about everyday winter pants? (Would you say that most of them are washed at home by hand, by machine, or taken to the dry cleaners, or what?) (IF "DON'T OWN" OR "COMMERCIAL CLEANER," SKIP TO 35)

34b. Are most of them usually pressed or not?

35. (IF "HAND WASHED" CHECKED IN ANY OF THE ABOVE, ASK:) Who would you say generally does most of the hand washing of your winter clothes?

SED" CHECKED IN ANY OF THE ABOVE, ASK:) Who would you say generally does most of the
ur winter clothes?

rt Shirts

change the season a bit and talk about ready-made summer sport shirts. You recall that
s I mean ones that are usually worn without a tie but are not knitted shirts or T-shirts.
are most of your summer sport shirts made of? (IF "DON'T OWN," SKIP TO 42)

r materials are your summer sport shirts made of?

rial do you like best for summer sport shirts? (IF "NO PREFERENCE,"SKIP TO 42)

u prefer (NAME ANSWER TO 39) for summer sport shirts? Anything else?

anything that you don't like so well about (NAME ANSWER TO 39) for summer sport shirts?

rt Coats

t few questions are about summer sport coats. That is, a suit-type jacket which is bought
be worn with slacks or pants that do not necessarily match. Do you have any summer sport
0," SKIP TO 48)

rial are most of your summer sport coats made of?

r materials are your summer sport coats made of?

rial do you like best for summer sport coats? (IF "NO PREFERENCE," SKIP TO 48)

u prefer (NAME ANSWER TO 45) for summer sport coats? Anything else?

anything that you don't like so well about (NAME ANSWER TO 45) for summer sport coats?

the slacks or trousers you wear in the summer. Do you get some of your summer pants for
and others for Sunday or special occasions, or do you get the same kind for both everyday
ear?

Different pants for each	☐ (ASK SECTIONS "H" & "I")
Same pants for both	☐ (SKIP TO SECTION "I" - OMIT WORD "EVERYDAY")
Only everyday pants	☐ (SKIP TO SECTION "I")
Only dress-up pants	☐ (ASK SECTION "H," THEN SKIP TO 59a)

Summer Pants

erial are most of your dress-up summer pants made of? (IF "DON'T OWN," SKIP TO 54)

er materials are your dress-up summer pants made of?

erial do you like best for dress-up summer pants? (IF "NO PREFERENCE," SKIP TO 54)

ou prefer (NAME ANSWER TO 51) for dress-up summer pants? Anything else?

anything that you don't like so well about (NAME ANSWER TO 51) for dress-up summer pants?
?

Summer Pants

erial are most of your (everyday) summer pants made of? (IF "DON'T OWN," SKIP TO 59)

er materials are your (everyday) summer pants made of?

erial do you like best for (everyday) summer pants? (IF "NO PREFERENCE," SKIP TO 59)

ou prefer (NAME ANSWER TO 56) for (everyday) summer pants? Anything else?

anything that you don't like so well about (NAME ANSWER TO 56) for (everyday) summer
ing else?

t Care

d like to know how these ready-made summer clothes are usually taken care of. Let's take
shirts first. Would you say that most of your summer sport shirts are washed at home by
ine, or taken to the dry cleaners, or just what? (IF "DON'T OWN" OR "COMMERCIAL CLEANER,"

187

59b. Are most of them usually pressed or not?

60a. How are most of your summer sport coats taken care of? (Would you say that most of your summer sport coats are washed at home by hand, by machine, or taken to the dry cleaners, or just what?) (IF "DON'T OWN" OR "COMMERCIAL CLEANER," SKIP TO 61a)

60b. Are most of them usually pressed or not?

61a. How are your dress-up summer pants usually taken care of? (Would you say that most of them are washed at home by hand, by machine, or taken to the dry cleaners, or just what?) (IF "DON'T OWN" OR "COMMERCIAL CLEANER," SKIP TO 62a)

61b. Are most of them usually pressed or not?

62a. How about your everyday summer pants? Would you say that most of them are washed at home by hand, by machine, or taken to the dry cleaners, or what? (IF "DON'T OWN" OR "COMMERCIAL CLEANER," SKIP TO 63)

62b. Are most of them usually pressed or not?

63. (IF "HAND WASHED" CHECKED IN ANY OF THE ABOVE, ASK:) Who would you say generally does most of the hand washing of your summer clothes?

64. (IF "PRESSED" CHECKED IN ANY OF THE ABOVE, ASK:) Who would you say generally does most of the pressing of your summer clothes?

J. Sweaters

65. Now let's talk about sweaters. This would include all types of sweaters but not Polo shirts or T-shirts. Do you have any ready-made sweaters that you've worn during the past twelve months? (IF "NO," SKIP TO 74)

66. What material are most of your ready-made sweaters made of?

67. What other materials are your ready-made sweaters made of?

68. What material do you like best for sweaters? (IF "NO PREFERENCE," SKIP TO 71a)

69. Why do you prefer (NAME ANSWER TO 68) for sweaters? Anything else?

70. Is there anything you don't like so well about (NAME ANSWER TO 68) for sweaters? Anything else?

71a. How are most of your sweaters usually taken care of? (Would you say that most of them are washed at home by hand, by machine, or taken to a dry cleaners, or what?) (IF "COMMERCIAL CLEANER," SKIP TO 72a)

71b. Are most of them usually pressed or not?

71c. (IF "HAND WASHED" CHECKED ABOVE, ASK:) Who would you say generally does most of the hand washing of your sweaters?

71d. (IF "PRESSED" CHECKED ABOVE, ASK:) Who would you say generally does most of the pressing of your sweaters?

72a. Let's talk a minute about a new kind of wool sweater. These new wool sweaters have been treated so that it is perfectly safe to wash them in a machine without special care. Do you think making wool sweaters that can be washed in a machine is a good idea or not such a good idea?

72b. Why do you say that? Anything else?

73a. Here is the scale card again. (HAND RESPONDENT CARD I) [SEE QUESTION 8a, GIRLS' FORM OF QUESTIONNAIRE] Tell me if you think machine washability would be important to you or not in deciding whether to buy a particular new wool sweater.

73b. Why is that? Anything else?

K. Raincoats

74. Do you have a raincoat - one that's meant to be worn only in rainy weather? (IF "NO," SKIP TO 76)

75. What material is this coat made of?

76. Do you have a coat that is meant to be worn in dry as well as rainy weather and is specially treated so that it is water repellent? (IF "NO," SKIP TO 78)

77. What material is this coat made of?

78. (IF "NO" TO BOTH 74 AND 76 SKIP TO 81) (IF "YES" TO EITHER 74 OR 76, ASK:) What material do you like best for rainwear? (IF "NO PREFERENCE," SKIP TO 81)

79. Why do you prefer (NAME ANSWER TO 78) for rainwear? Anything else?

80. Is there anything that you don't like so well about (NAME ANSWER TO 78) for rainwear? Anything else?

cr all your ideas about materials. (HAND RESPONDENT CARD II) [SEE QUESTION 82, RE] Which one of the six materials listed on this card would you say:

e best to wear in hot weather?

e best to wear in cold weather?

the longest?

its shape best?

siest to care for?

ast likely to wrinkle?

e best value for the money?

PART III

tes about your interest in clothes.

ou are very interested, fairly interested, or not very interested in what kinds

choosing the clothes--are you very interested, fairly interested, or not very he clothes you wear?

ing else?

p ideas about what clothes you'd like to get?
CHECKED, ASK:)

do you think is most helpful?

the decision to buy an important clothing item--such as an outer jacket or

u usually the one who suggests that you need an outer jacket or sport coat, or it first?

s usually decide whether or not you might get an important clothing item such rt coat?
ED, ASK:)

say about whether or not you might get an outer jacket or sport coat?

hing items such as shirts and sweaters--are you usually the one who suggests this, or does someone else suggest it first?

s usually decide whether or not you might get articles such as shirts and

ED, ASK:)

say about whether or not you might get such articles as shirts and sweaters?

ping for clothes.

t coats? (Who usually shops for them?)
?

or short coats?

most to say about the sport shirt that is finally selected?

90b. The sport coat (that's finally selected?)

90c. The everyday pants?

90d. Your dress-up pants?

90e. Your sweater?

90f. The outer jacket or short coat?

91. Generally speaking, at what age do you think a boy is old enough to go shopping and pick out his own clothing by himself?

CLASSIFICATION INFORMATION

Just a few more questions and we'll be finished.

92a. Are you still enrolled in school? (Were you enrolled in school last month?)

(IF "YES," ASK 92b, c,and d) (IF "NO," ASK 92e)

92b. What grade are you in now? (were you in last month?)

92c. What grades are there in the school you go to now? (went to?)

92d. Is (was) your school an all boys' school?

92e. What was the last grade of school you completed?

93. Have you done any kind of work at all for pay in the past 12 months?

(IF "NO," SKIP TO 98)

94a Do you have a regular job that you go to every week? (IF "NO," SKIP TO 95a)

94b What kind of work do you do?

94c. How many hours a week do you usually work?

95a. During the past year, have you done any other kind of work for pay--such as baby sitting or working in a store? (IF "NO," SKIP TO 96)

95b. What kind of work have you done?

95c. What time of year was this?

96 About how much money did you earn in the past year from working? (HAND RESPONDENT CARD III) [SEE QUESTION 97, GIRLS'FORM OF QUESTIONNAIRE] (IF "LESS THAN $25," SKIP TO 98)

97a. What did you do with _most_ of the money you earned?

(IF "SAVED IT," ASK:)

97b. What are (were) you saving for?

97c. What did you do with the _rest_ of the money you earned?

(IF "SAVED IT," ASK:)

97d. What are (were) you saving for?

98. What kind of work does your father (or head-of-household) do?

That covers all my questions for you.

(INTERVIEWER: BE SURE TO FILL IN THE FOLLOWING QUESTIONS _AFTER_ COMPLETING THE INTERVIEW.)

99. (CHECK RACE)

100a. Was any other person present during the interview? (IF "NO," SKIP TO 101)

100b Who?

100c. Did the presence of this other person seem to have a great influence, some influence, or no influence on respondent's answers?

101. Was teen-ager married?

☆ U. S GOVERNMENT PRINTING OFFICE 1966 O - 222-911

CPSIA information can be obtained
at www.ICGtesting.com
Printed in the USA
BVHW040856180219
540528BV00005B/93/P